C000256557

THE TREE OF
AND THE HOLY

To Jennifer &
Vic
with much
love from
Sylvia Francke.

THE TREE OF LIFE AND THE HOLY GRAIL

Sylvia Francke
and Thomas Cawthorne

TEMPLE LODGE
London

Dedication

For Helen
(Pipy)

Temple Lodge Publishing
51 Queen Caroline Street
London W6 9QL

Published by Temple Lodge 1996

© Sylvia Francke and Thomas Cawthorne 1996

The moral rights of the authors have been asserted under the Copyright, Designs and Patents Act, 1988

All rights reserved. No part of this publication may be reproduced, stored in a retrieval system, or transmitted, in any form or by any means, electronic, mechanical, photocopying, recording or otherwise, without the prior permission of the publishers

A catalogue record for this book is available from the British Library

ISBN 0 904693 79 1

Cover by S. Gulbekian

Typeset by Imprint, Crawley Down, Sussex
Printed and bound in Great Britain by Cromwell Press Limited, Broughton Gifford, Wiltshire

Contents

Illustration credits: 1, 6, 7, 9, 12, 13, 14, 16, from the collection of David Wood. 2, Verlag am Goetheanum. 3, 5, Rudolf Steiner House Library, London.

Preface and Acknowledgements

The Tree of Life and the Holy Grail is the result of 13 years of intensive research. It explores the interrelated themes of Rennes-le-Château, etheric science and the quest for the Grail, and it aims at a re-synthesis of the Grail material utilizing neglected research from the early part of this century. While both authors were equally involved in the production of this work, it is written from the perspective of one of them, Sylvia Francke, as Chapter 1, and the short commentaries that introduce each chapter, will make clear.

As this book serves as an introduction to a vast area of neglected writings we have interwoven quotes from this literature throughout the text. However, the real source of this work has been the living inspiration of a modern day Grail family, a vast 'Company' of people spread across the world, whom we cannot mention here individually, but to whom we are deeply grateful. Needless to say none of these individuals, or those mentioned by name below, can be held responsible for the use we have made of their inspiration.

We are deeply indebted to Margaret Jonas for her unstinting enthusiasm and invaluable practical support, for allowing us to quote from some of her ground-breaking but as yet unpublished writings, and for taking time out of a busy schedule to read through an earlier version of the manuscript. We have also been greatly aided by Nelson Willby of the Wellspring Bookshop, London, by his encouragement and practical assistance.

Of the few friends we can mention by name our thanks go to the following: Stanley Messenger for his friendship and inspiration, Jehanne and Rob Mehta for their musical, poetic and spiritual encouragement, and David Wood for his kind hospitality and invaluable practical assistance.

And for compiling the index and allowing us to use his poem our thanks go to Richard Carlyon. Richard, the next move is yours!

Sylvia Francke and Thomas Cawthorne
Surrey, March 1996

Prologue

He sought the source,
He found the power,
He used the light of the bridal bower.
And terrible he found that place;
And crossed with fear now is his face.

Richard Carlyon

1
Taking up the Challenge

Upon a deep green archmardi she bore the perfection of Paradise, both root and branch. That was a thing called the Grail, which surpasses all earthly perfection.

Wolfram von Eschenbach, *Parzival*, Book V

In the autumn of 1983 my husband came into the house with some new paperbacks. He took one of them from the pile and threw it to me saying, 'This isn't my subject. It looks historical, so perhaps you should read it.' I turned the book over, recognizing the title immediately: *The Holy Blood and the Holy Grail*, by Michael Baigent, Richard Leigh and Henry Lincoln.[1] I began to read and from that moment on became one of the many thousands of people captivated by the complex historical, spiritual and geographic mysteries surrounding the enigmatic village of Rennes-le-Château in Southern France. However, my own involvement in this mystery was not to be confined to reading the seemingly endless stream of books and articles that flowed in the wake of the book. Almost as soon as I had decided to research the mystery for myself, information began to find its way into my hands.

The publication of *The Holy Blood and the Holy Grail* in hardback had released shock waves of controversy and debate of a kind unseen for many years. It began as an exploration into the possible sources of incredible wealth bestowed upon the obscure and relatively unimportant priest of Rennes-le-Château, Berenger Saunière (1872–1917). It ended, having followed a convoluted path through a historical thicket involving Cathars, Templars and Freemasonry, with a sweeping challenge levelled at the historical basis of orthodox Christianity. The authors claimed that at the heart of the Rennes-le-Château mystery lay forbidden knowledge concerning Christ's survival of the Crucifixion and his marriage to Mary Magdalene. They also claimed that from this union flowed the blood-line that eventually bore the Merovingian kings of France, and later many of the royal houses of Europe.

A friend of mine was in W. H. Smith's shortly after publication of *The Holy Blood and the Holy Grail* when a man came up to him and pointed to a copy saying, 'I was a Christian before I read that, now I don't believe in anything.' My personal reaction to the book was more positive. My certainty of Christ's presence in the world had been born of a process that took place within me independently of established Christian tradition. While the more 'orthodox' forms of Christianity had little to offer me, based as they were on dogma rather than direct and personal experience, I found inspiration in the works of Rudolf Steiner (1861–1925), the great Austrian scientist and educator. Steiner's science of the spirit, known as Anthroposophy (human oriented wisdom), was based on an understanding that the advance of modern civilization demands that all of the phenomena available to human experience be explained from a scientific and rational point of view. Calls to simple faith and passive belief are no longer apt for a humanity that has come of age. This does not mean, however, that we are driven to accept a purely *materialistic* or *reductionist* ethos. One of the central aims of Rudolf Steiner's Anthroposophy or spiritual science is the enhancement of the powers of human cognition, on the basis that it is *here* that the spiritual reality of our world is first discovered.

As I began to read *The Holy Blood and the Holy Grail* I found that I was able to combine knowledge I had gained through studying Anthroposophy with original ideas of my own, in order to shed new light upon the mysteries of Rennes-le-Château. I felt that the three authors of this book had in fact come close to the truth but, lacking the wider historical and spiritual perspective found in the original knowledge of *esoteric* Christianity, they had been diverted down false paths. These ideas came to fruition partly through my own research, and partly as a result of the meetings which brought me into relationship with a growing company of people. As my research unfolded, 'Cathars' and 'Templars' began to appear on train and aeroplane journeys and through chance meetings that brought ever more vital facts to my notice. I found the motifs of the Grail quest manifesting in my daily life through a web of synchronicities. These intensified the closer I drew to the centre of the mystery.

The mysteries of Rennes-le-Château seem to affect people in much the same way as the gentlemen in the familiar nursery rhyme:

> There were three jovial Welchmen,
> As I have heard them say,
> And they would go a-hunting
> Upon St David's day.
>
> All the day they hunted,
> And nothing could they find,
> But a ship a-sailing,
> A-sailing with the wind.
>
> One said it was a ship,
> The other he said, Nay:
> The third said it was a house,
> With the chimney blown away.
>
> And all the night they hunted
> And nothing could they find
> But the moon a-gliding,
> A-gliding with the wind.
>
> One said it was the moon,
> The other he said Nay;
> The third said it was a cheese,
> An half o't cut away.
>
> (*Anon.*)

Rennes-le-Château is like a 'magic mirror' in which we can see our own subjective wishes or ideals reflected back to us. An exploration into its mystery becomes a process of self-exploration. This is due to the area's unique relationship with certain types of 'energy', as we will see later. Resting firmly on a base of

The village of Rennes-le-Château in southern France

Cretaceous limestone, this area in Southern France is alive with Gnostic overtones. Nestling closely together are such landmarks as the 'Black Castle' and the 'Village of Light'. Elsewhere the 'Priest's Canyon' and the 'Devil's Ramparts' continue the theme of dualistic powers in perpetual war.

When the writer Henry Lincoln acquired a copy of *Le Trésor Maudit* by Gérard de Sède while on holiday in France in 1969, the mystery expounded there captivated his attention. De Sède's book gave a basic outline of the central mystery. Saunière had been made priest of the village of Rennes-le-Château in 1885. He had served in this capacity for several years, living a frugal life until apparently uncovering some encoded manuscripts while restoring the church. Shortly after this discovery Saunière became the recipient of an enormous amount of wealth. He spent this on his church, lavish entertainments, and upon extravagant new building projects. He died under seemingly mysterious circumstances, the body subjected to a bizarre daytime ritual with Gnostic overtones. Lincoln was fascinated by all this, and by speculation as to the role of a mysterious organization, the Prieuré de

Sion, which appeared to be connected to the mystery.

Lincoln teamed up with Baigent and Leigh and the result was a trilogy of televised *Chronicle* documentaries and the best-selling book *The Holy Blood and the Holy Grail*. In 1986 the same authors brought out a sequel, *The Messianic Legacy*, which portrayed Jesus and his followers as a gang of Zionist guerrillas, and which also levelled not undue criticisms at many of the extremes of organized religion. A third strand in *The Messianic Legacy* is curiously involved in a search for 'meaning' in contemporary life. This culminates in the handing of a joint first prize to the writings of Jung, and to royal weddings as a source of solace for a spiritually bankrupt society. The Epilogue rounds the whole thing off by intimating that the Prieuré de Sion considers that it would be a grand thing for a modern king, descended from Jesus, to be crowned in Jerusalem.

Further books followed from the three authors, writing together or individually. These investigated the Scottish Templar source of Freemasonry in *The Temple and the Lodge*, and the motives of the *Dead Sea Scrolls Deception*.

In his fascinating book *Genisis*, published in 1985, David Wood, an experienced surveyor and cartographer, referred for the first time in print to significant relationships to be found in the landscape around Rennes-le-Château. Seemingly in answer to Wood's research Henry Lincoln then returned to the theme of the 'Pentagram' in a further book, *The Holy Place*. The notion of such significant geomantic relationships had been explored in the last of the original three BBC *Chronicle* programmes but was curiously missing when *The Holy Blood and the Holy Grail* was published.

The work of these authors was the start of an ever-expanding quest, one that has succeeded in keeping successive 'Jolly Huntsmen' in full cry ever since. Could all this public attention have been fanned into a plethora of conflicting answers by 'someone' who meant to hide some fact or encroaching event of great importance? Or is it because, as hinted before, Rennes-le-Château lies in a geographical setting which by its very nature confuses subjective and objective experiences. Certainly the main effect of this process has been to provide very effective fodder for a systematic programme aimed at eroding traditional religious belief, which has intensified considerably in the last few years. Whether this is a good or bad thing must be left to the individual to decide. The premature removal of a prop may cause an entire building to collapse; on the other hand, the cutting of dead branches from a tree can encourage new and vigorous growth.

It was in David Wood's ground-breaking discovery of the complex pentagonal geometry of which the village of Rennes-le-Château is a part, as described in his book *Genisis*, that I found a major clue. For reasons that will become clear as this book unfolds, the pentagram has a deep connection both with the universal 'life force' and with the individual 'ego-nature' of the human being—two aspects of the Grail. This together with other shapes which emerged from David's geometry made me now feel that I had the *central* key to solving the whole mystery. I felt that in presenting my solution to the mysteries of Rennes-le-Château I could, in the process, demonstrate in as clear a way as possible the spiritual and historical *reality* of the Grail tradition.

Balancing a busy family life with periods of intense research, I began to write. A hectic and very exciting decade passed and it was at this time that a version of the manuscript fell into the hands of Thomas Cawthorne, a young journalist who had specialized knowledge in exactly the areas where my own research or understanding had been lacking. For the next two years the book became a joint effort, writing and rewriting the manuscript, slowly crafting it into a coherent work, and filling out the gaps until an organic whole was formed.

Thomas Cawthorne's understanding of the Parzival legend—as written down in its most complete form by the German poet Wolfram von Eschenbach—and his comprehensive grasp of Rudolf Steiner's etheric science allowed us to knit together the many diverse themes of this book into a coherent picture of the spiritual and historical reality of the quest for the Grail.

Many readers familiar with the Grail material, or who have read any of the many books following on from *The Holy Blood and the Holy Grail*, may be unfamiliar with the ideas of Rudolf Steiner. Steiner is perhaps most famous for the schools, hospitals, farms and artistic activities that he founded or pioneered. The motif of the Holy Grail was central to Steiner's entire life and work, and he can be seen as one of the chief spokesmen of the Grail tradition in modern times. While Steiner's ideas are not always easy to grasp we have tried to present his Grail cosmology in as clear and concise a manner as possible, so that this book can also form the basis for an introduction to Steiner's ideas for those who have had no previous encounter with him.

Other readers already familiar with Rudolf Steiner's Anthroposophy will also find much new material here that may interest them. While we must take full responsibility for the use we have made of Steiner's spiritual research, we believe that this book demonstrates the living power inherent in Steiner's thinking when it is not just accepted passively but is put to work. Steiner's 'etheric science' led me to new interpretations of the central Rennes mysteries. Steiner's delineation of the motif of the Tree of Life, provided me with a way to tie together Cathars, Templars, royal blood-lines, the personage of Christ, and the quest for the Holy Grail in a new synthesis that also shed light upon the enigma of Rennes-le-Château.

Rennes-le-Château can be seen as a sacred centre where the earth's life process is enhanced and can be tapped. The name Rennes-le-Château announces the presence of 'the goddess', the Queen of the House, as David Wood mentions in his pioneering research. He found this area of southern France saturated with references to 'the goddess', particularly Isis. If 'the goddess' can be taken as symbolic of the living, formative 'life body' of the earth, then it can be seen that Rennes-le-Château is an *etheric powerhouse* whose rise to prominence in the modern world is by no means accidental.

2
Investigations into a New Science of Life

> On the one hand the study of lifeless nature has resulted in the formulation of the 'laws' according to which things relate to one another on and around the earth: the stone rolls down the mountainside, the pendulum swings to and fro, the apple falls to the ground. But how, indeed, does the apple get to the top of the tree in the first place? Is not the fact that it falls a secondary rather than a primal phenomena in the household of nature?
>
> George Adams and Olive Whicher,
> *The Plant Between Sun and Earth*

The Grail has been described as a source of inexhaustible energy, fulfilling humanity's needs and bringing healing to the earth. It was a chance conversation with Stanley Messenger, co-founder of the Gatekeeper Trust, *that first alerted me to the possible existence of earth-energy at Rennes-le-Château. My attention was then directed to the typescript of a lecture given by Colin Bloy at the Research Into Lost Knowledge Organization (RILKO) that meets on a regular basis in South Kensington. The lecture was entitled 'Dowsing Ley Lines and the Search for the Grail'. I had already been lent a copy of Guenther Wachsmuth's long out of print* Etheric Formative Forces in Cosmos, Earth and Man *by a fellow anthroposophist. By putting all three components of information together I was able to begin to comprehend the 'etheric' significance of Rennes-le-Château.*

As I delved ever deeper into the strange world of the etheric I discovered scientists and mathematicians whose work is neglected or ignored by the dominant scientific establishment. Some of these individuals I was to meet in person, often through convoluted chains of synchronicity.

My thesis in this book is that the life energies discovered and described by this 'alternative' tradition within science can be seen as an aspect of the Grail. Here I give a broad outline of my discoveries and lay an essential foundation for understanding what follows.

We are living at a time when a great turning-point is taking place in human consciousness. At the eleventh hour a new reverence for life has prompted increasing numbers of people to turn to holistic medicines and therapies. The desire to find alternatives to the materialistic medicine and science of our age has been driven by the widespread pollution and degradation of our living environment. At the same time the scientists are pulling back the familiar boundaries of reality and the ground is almost literally being whipped away from beneath our feet. As a result of these transformations in consciousness scientists are now standing on the edge of a threshold which they are not equipped to cross. In both medicine and other branches of science the experts are unprepared to cope with the next frontier. The enigma ahead of them is the mystery of life itself.

Awareness of what could be described as a living ocean of energy that moulds, informs and sustains the material and biological worlds has been commonplace in history. While it is a knowledge that was forced 'underground' by the rise of materialistic science, it has never really been lost. In fact it was only towards the middle of the last century that the mechanistic view took over completely in science and medicine. In 1905, Rudolf Steiner made the following comments:

> Physical, chemical and mineral laws hold sway in man's physical body. Yet even as far as his spiritual nature is concerned he belongs to the mineral kingdom since he understands through his intellect only what is mineral. Life, as such, he is only gradually learning to comprehend. Precisely for this reason, official science disowns life, being still at the stage of development in which it can only grasp the dead, the mineral. It is in the process of trying to understand this in very intricate detail. Hence it understands the human body only in so far as it is a dead, mineral thing. It treats the human body basically as something dead with which one works, as if with substances in a chemical

> laboratory. Other substances are poured into [the body], in the same way that substances are poured into a retort. Even when the doctor, who nowadays is brought up entirely on mineral science, sets about working on the human body, it is as though the latter were only an artificial product.[2]

The reason why it has been so difficult to understand the working of life in matter during the last two hundred years or more is connected with the fact that—as Rudolf Steiner has made clear—

> Life is not to be understood here on earth. Occultism alone can give knowledge of life; external science can never fathom it. It would be the wildest fantasy to believe that one could ever penetrate the laws of life as one can physical or chemical laws. To do so remains an ideal; it can never be reached. On the physical plane there is never any possibility of giving knowledge of life. This knowledge of life must remain the preserve of supersensible knowledge.[3]

The ancients knew this but it has been forgotten as the march of scientific progress has taken human curiosity into realms of intensifying materialism where the infinitesimal is investigated and the unity of creation is separated into ever-multiplying isolated subdivisions.

The realm from which the life-force streams can be thought of as a vast cosmic ocean that stretches beyond the limits of the zodiac. It controls and qualifies the planetary movements while also imbuing the tiniest living creatures with life and motion. Eric Bailey, reviewing *The Arrow of Time* by Roger Highfield and Dr Peter Coveney (1990) in the *Weekend Telegraph*, states that the book offers 'a view of science which suggests that a change in direction and attitude is imminent, drawing away from the obsessive delving into atoms and molecules of the last 40 years, and adopting a broader perspective'.[4] Later on in the review Bailey, referring to the second law of thermodynamics and entropy, asks: 'If the universe amounts to a progressive cosmic degradation, how do we explain the formation of life, which represents a formidable process of organization, evolution and improvement?' Elsewhere Bailey describes how, while the authors were 'studying the behaviour of chemicals mixed together', they 'found that the molecules formed transient symmetrical patterns. The patterns were apparently spontaneous and disappeared as the chemicals moved towards the complete mix—its state of equilibrium and maximum entropy. The patterns suggest that the molecules "knew" where to go and create the brief semblance of order. Could it be that the beginnings of life were self-organization in the primeval soup?'

Robert Anton Wilson in his book *The New Inquisition* suggests that there is an inquisitorial attitude within the domain of establishment science, one which manifests as aggressive intimidation and active repression of scientists and others whose work violates the principles of reductionist materialism. Wilson documents several famous cases in his book, but many more remain unknown to the general public.[5]

If there is a simple notion that links the diversity of unorthodox research it is perhaps the idea that as well as the laws of material nature, there is a *complementary* life force or principle, which is as real, if not more so, than the realm of pure matter.[6] Those who have become champions of this idea have arrived at it from many different directions, often after long and rigorous scientific journeys.

The process of renewal began among the poets and artists of the Romantic revival. William Blake (1757–1827) explicitly attacked Newton's atomic theory, which he felt dissolved the world into an abstract and indefinite system with little place for humanity and its evolutionary aspirations. In its place Blake asserted his poetic model of the world as an organic, *self-sustaining*, internally diverse system that was continuous with the being of man.

Wolfgang von Goethe (1749–1832) took the step beyond purely poetic models and into the realm of concrete scientific research. Goethe's scientific contribution was for a long time either ignored or derided, due to its strictly empiricist and phenomenological methodology, and its non-materialistic conclusions. Recent years have seen an increasing interest in Goethe's researches and a more positive reassessment of them.[7] This has been largely prompted by the return to a more holistic epistemology in daily life and an increased awareness of the deep errors in materialistic theory.

Goethe wished to remain steadfastly true to his actual experience of the world. He began with the rational assumption that, if attentively studied through time, phenomena would reveal their secrets to human consciousness. Close and intensive study of the development of plant and animal morphology led him to a basic yet revolutionary conception. He realized that the organic and biological form unfolded according to *laws of metamorphosis* in which the later development was a transformation of the earlier form. From this phenomenological approach evolved a non-reductionist scientific theory and evolutionary biology.

In his classic work on plant morphology[8] Goethe describes how the individual plant unfolds its being according to a rhythmical principle of expansion and contraction, through a modulated interweaving between polarities. Goethe discovered the workings of life in the plant.

Organic forms unfold, according to Goethe's observations, through a formative process involving metamorphosis and polarity. These ideas were phenomenologically derived through disciplined observation of organic forms and their development. While Goethe's work has been derided as 'pseudo-science' by the establishment, the mathematical underpinnings to support his views were already in existence.

The unity between Goethe's scientific world-conception and the new forms of *projective geometry* was explored in depth by George Adams (1894–1963). Adams was educated at Cambridge where he was inspired by the works of A. N. Whitehead and gained valuable help in his mathematical pursuits from such notables as Bertrand Russell and G. H. Hardy.

Adams became fascinated by the ideas of projective geometry. In his scientific research he wished to bring together a factual account of outer reality with the deep poetry of an intensely lived subjective experience. Modern science with its material monism did not seem to him to be true to the world it was attempting to describe.

In contrast to the rigid geometry of Euclid, with its description of fixed and static forms, the thought forms of projective geometry were mobile and living. Adams saw this geometry as the bridge to an understanding of a type of *counter-space* that underlies the space of the physical material world. Projective geometry describes the process of space-in-creation, the creation of form out of living formative processes. Goethe had described these laws of polarity and metamorphosis, and now Adams was explicating the mathematical underpinnings. Like his great predecessor Adams turned to the study of plant life.

In his book *The Plant Between Sun and Earth* (co-authored with Olive Whicher) Adams states: 'The new geometry has a close relationship to the quality of thinking of the great artist-scientist Goethe. It cultivates a qualitative, picture-forming aspect of mathematics, which approaches closely the Goethean experience of nature...Not only in the method but in the content of the new geometry we find significant possibilities of bridging the gulf between Goethe's qualitative and completely phenomenological way of approach to nature and the natural science of our time, permeated as it is with so much mathematical thought.'[9]

The prime, indivisible entity of projective geometry is not (as in Euclidean geometry) the point, but the *plane*. The plane is the *fundamental etheric unit*, and flows in from the *periphery* of the universe. Whereas material forces are 'point-centred', radiating out from fixed points, the formative forces, or 'counter-space', are 'planar'. These 'planes' are organic and holistic. Between the celestial plane and the material point weaves the rich tapestry of phenomenal existence. The term 'etheric' or 'ethereal' is used to denote these planar forces.

Adams continues: 'The ethereal forces...are the peripheral cosmic forces...With the ideas of projective geometry we have transcended the one-sidedly centric approach to form and are capable of becoming spiritually perceptive toward the signature of the peripheral forces and the planar space-formation of natural phenomena. The concept of ethereal space enables the earth-planet as a whole to be regarded as a living entity—not in a vaguely philosophic sense, but in a way that lends itself to detailed investigation.'[10]

As an example of how this works we can consider the *potentization* process utilized in the production of many homoeopathic and Weleda medicines. Potentization requires that some original substance (say a medicinal plant) be radically diluted in some pure medium (water or milk for instance). The dilutions continue to the point where any trace of the original substance has completely vanished. The process of dilution is dynamic, involving a rhythmic shaking process. According to Theodor Schwenk in his book *The Basis of Potentization Research*:

> Obviously the measurable sense-perceptible remedial substance disappears to an ever greater extent as potentization proceeds. This means that observation focused exclusively on matter sees only a stepwise dilution in progress, one which permeates all of nature: every natural happening is accompanied by a complementing visible or invisible process. For example, a *diluting* of earthly substances (comparable to a withdrawal from the terrestrial) is balanced by a *condensation* process of etheric universal forces running parallel to it (in other words, the inflowing of a cosmic element).[11]

When a material substance is *rhythmically diluted*, the loosening and dissipation of the material substance allows its corresponding etheric forces to stream more forcefully into the medium in which the material is being diluted. The etheric forces work into matter by taking up material substance. The process of dilution and hence potentization takes place constantly within the human body and also throughout nature. Schwenk continues: 'The forces inhering in plants, minerals and so on ray into a potentizing medium such as water and bind themselves to it.'[12]

Theodore Schwenk is most famous for his popular book *Sensitive Chaos*, in which he outlines a phenomenological reading of the nature of water. He describes how, as it flows through inter-crossing rivers, or as currents inter-cross deep within the oceans, subtle inner organs are created within the body of water. In the potentization process, planar surfaces are created between streams of fluid slipping past one another at varying speeds. The etheric forces have a natural affinity for plane surfaces in material nature. They work into nature more powerfully the more they encounter extended plane-surfaces. The large inner surfaces generated by rhythmic movements of fluids are ideal. As the material substance is liberated, the etheric forces ray into the dynamic medium with ever greater potency. Schwenk comments that: 'They [the inflowing planar forces] imprint themselves on these surfaces like a seal impressing its form into a mass of softened sealing wax. The usual view of this is of atoms being transferred from the remedial substance to the medium. But considering all that has been said above, there is no need to attribute the imprinting of the medium to material transference of elements of the remedy, as point-orientated atomistic thinking has the habit of doing. Indeed the fewer the atoms or molecules in the imprinting by the seal, the purer is the resulting picture.'[13]

Much of this material to do with the inner nature of water was discovered (or more aptly rediscovered) by the naturalist Viktor Schauberger (1885–1958). Schauberger was an ardent and gifted naturalist who was employed in about 1918 by Prince Adolf Schaumberg-Lippe to look after 21,000 hectares of almost untouched forest land in Bernerau, Steyerling. In this environment, where human intervention had not begun to destroy the natural patterns and activities of the forest, Schauberger was able to observe a wide variety of natural phenomena that had been unobserved by the scientists and naturalists of his day. Water was Schauberger's passion and his close, day by day study of its rich phenomena alerted him to natural laws that had slipped past the attention of others.[14] Often these observations of how nature behaved contradicted the supposed laws discovered by modern science. Schauberger derived workable and superior technology from these observations, and this earned him the hatred of many in the scientific community. It was Schauberger who discovered, for instance, that cool water carries loads better than warm water. Even the smallest change in temperature would dramatically affect the log-carrying capacity of a river. Schauberger applied this insight to the building of logging flumes, much to the contempt and derision of the local experts. The flumes Schauberger designed also followed the course of rivers and imitated their meandering flow. Special mixing stations replaced warm with cool water. Schauberger first proposed this design as part of a competition. His idea was instantly rejected as moronic and out of step with the development of modern knowledge. Schauberger's ability to solve insoluble problems with his self-gained and 'forbidden' knowledge was demonstrated for the first time when the flume was built, becoming the first of many.[15]

The Virbela Flowforms are among the most popular applications of etheric ideas in the realm of practical technology. These sculpted forms, developed by John Wilkes, allow water to flow through them in a pulsing figure-of-eight movement. The problem they were designed to solve was the reversal of water pollution via a process of water purification. The lemniscatory movement pursued by the water allows etheric forces to work powerfully into the medium. The Flowforms are also of great aesthetic and therapeutic value and are used as much for the purposes of landscape enhancement as they are for scientific purposes. However, within the realms of etheric science and technology, these are not functions that can be separated. The Flowforms combine visual and musical aesthetics with scientific methods to create a device that heals both the human and natural world at the same time.

If we visualize a sphere we can see that it exists between the two polar distances of point and plane. Shrink the sphere down to its smallest imaginable size and it vanishes into a point. Now inflate it again, but take it to the other extreme. Inflate the sphere out to infinity and eventually it becomes a plane, a plane at infinity. We experience this plane at infinity as an encompassing sphere, the sphere of the starry heavens.

Within this cosmology the planets and fixed stars are

recognized as much more than material realities. They have an etheric dimension too and it is these potencies, flowing down to the earth from the zodiac, the constellations and the planets, carried by the planar forces, that gives life its varied and complex characteristics. Not only the forms of all living things but also the colours and scents are differentiated and qualified by these 'formative forces'.

The formative forces come down to us from the spiritual regions of the planets and zodiacal stars. This has been verified through years of experimental research by individual researchers and on the biodynamic farms established under the guidance of Rudolf Steiner. In a lecture given at the 1984 Conference of the Anthroposophical Society at Michael Hall School in Sussex, Lawrence Edwards described how he had taken thousands of photographs of the leaf buds of beech trees, which are formed in September and hang on the branches until they open in the spring. Lawrence's photographs show that the buds were delicately changing all through the winter, turning in accordance with the great celestial movements of the moon and Saturn. Whenever the moon drew into a straight line with Saturn the sleeping bud gave a little 'wave' as if to acknowledge Saturn as the ruling planet of the tree. Edwards suggested that the buds of all trees ruled by Saturn could be measured for related movements.[16]

Rudolf Steiner clarifies the workings of the etheric further in distinguishing the four aspects of the etheric realm as being those of the 'warmth', 'light', 'chemical', and 'life' ethers.* These celestial, universal forces ray in from the periphery: 'From all sides they work, these forces, as if striving towards the central point of the earth. They would tear asunder the

* Scientific research into the functioning of the four ethers and their relationship with the formative forces has continued apace since the time of Steiner and Wachsmuth. As the present book is not intended to be a technical treatise on the etheric we have often relied on formulations, particularly from Wachsmuth, that are now considered by some researchers to be somewhat dated or imprecise. Newcomers to these ideas should be aware that etheric science is a genuine science and as such is in a process of evolution. A historical study of the development of these ideas remains a task for a future book.

material nature of the earthly realm, dissolve it into complete formlessness, were it not for the heavenly bodies beyond earth which mingle their influences in the field of these forces and modify the dissolving process.'[17]

There is a close relationship between the etheric forces as defined in this chapter and the form of the pentagram. The presence of one, if not several, immense pentagrams encoded into the landscape surrounding Rennes-le-Château can then be taken as an indication of the particularly strong connection of this area of southern France with the forces of the cosmos. As this book progresses this connection, between the pentagram and the life force, will be made clear.

3
Rudolf Steiner and the Foundation of a New Etheric Science

In nothing is Rudolf Steiner more outstanding than in his understanding of the nature of thinking and of its evolution in the history of mankind.

A. P. Shepherd, *Rudolf Steiner—Scientist of the Invisible*

Rudolf Steiner's contribution to an understanding of the 'life force' cannot be over-estimated. Many years of study of Steiner's world view had convinced me that his claim to be able to explore many varied subjects using higher states of consciousness was fully justifiable. Steiner not only conducted his own 'spiritual research' in this manner but also left detailed instructions for anybody who wished to be able to learn to do the same. In the last chapter we mentioned several individuals, such as George Adams, who were personal students of Steiner and applied his methodologies in their own research. In the chapters that follow we will take a journey through Steiner's Grail cosmology. But first we need to take a closer look at Steiner himself. A short description of the man, his philosophy, and the light he sheds on this new etheric science now follows.

'My preoccupation with the concepts of natural science had led me finally to a position in which I saw the activity of the human ego* as the only possible point from which to advance towards true knowledge.' So wrote the Austrian philosopher and educationalist Rudolf Steiner in his autobiography, *The Story of My Life.*[18] He continues, 'I put it to myself that when the ego is in action and contemplates its own activity, then a spiritual entity is directly present in the consciousness.'

* In Steiner's terminology the 'ego' refers to the reflective self-consciousness of the human individual and is to be taken in a thoroughly *positive* sense.

Steiner was born in 1861, on the borders of eastern and western Europe.[19] As a child he was able to experience not only the mountains and forests of Lower Austria, but penetrated beneath the surfaces of things to a direct experience of the mighty cosmic etheric forces that shaped and moulded the world from out of the cosmic periphery. He thus would have noted the changing patterns and flows of the formative forces through the turning of the seasons.

At university (technical high school) Steiner discovered the scientific works of Goethe, and at the recommendation of his teacher, Karl Julius Schröer, later went to work at the Goethe and Schiller Archives in Weimar. Here he had the task of editing Goethe's copious scientific papers.

It was during this period, one of an ever-deepening involvement with Goethe's thought, that Steiner wrote his first major works. These were: *Goethe's World View; A Theory of Knowledge Implicit in Goethe's World Conception*; and, most important of all, *The Philosophy of Freedom*, which was published in 1894.

Attempting a *descriptive* account of human cognition, Steiner finds that the act of intuitive thinking is central to any understanding of the human being:

> In thinking we take hold of a corner of the world process where we must be present if anything is to come about...it is just because we ourselves bring [thinking] forth that we can know the characteristic features of its course. What in all other spheres of observation can only be discovered indirectly is, in the case of thinking, known to us quite directly.[20]

The *reductionist* theory of human cognition states that all human brain activity is the result of other, invisible, unknowable forces (atoms, chemical forces, the unconscious). Steiner's main point is that, while this could be the case with some phenomena, it cannot be the case with thinking as defined above. It is self-generated, self-sustained, and has to be taken as the starting-point of all our knowledge about ourselves and the world. Without this self-sustaining activity we could know nothing about the world. All our knowing begins with the elaboration of thoughts about our perceptions. Steiner continues:

> The transparency in regard to the process of thinking is quite independent of any knowledge of the physiological basis of thinking. How one physical process in my brain causes or influences another while I carry out a line of thought is quite irrelevant. Observation of thinking shows that in connecting one thought with another I am not guided by material processes in the brain, but solely by the content of my thoughts. In a less materialistic age this remark would be entirely superfluous. For someone who has the ability to observe thinking...he has found the secure point from which one can set out with well-founded hope to seek explanations for the rest of the world's phenomena.[21]

According to Steiner, where thinking occurs the material aspects of the brain withdraw, they make room for the activity of thinking and allow that activity to be impressed upon the material substance. Thinking produces activity in the material substance of the brain. In the last chapter we discussed how, in the process of potentization, the withdrawal or dilution of the material substance makes room for an intensified inflowing of the etheric force. Steiner points out that the nervous system (the basis of human cognition) is composed of hardened matter—matter that is less alive than that of the tissues or the blood. This is because the etheric force working into the structures of the nervous system has been liberated to form the substance of cognition.

The developing foetus and the new-born baby are fully imbued with etheric life, the soft body utilizing all the etheric forces available to it for the purposes of physical growth. The faculties of memory and thought are absent. As the child grows the body hardens as portions of the etheric force are withdrawn from their formative activity to become the basis of memory and higher cognition. At the present time in evolution death is the price we pay for self-consciousness. In fact, thinking is a death force, reducing the living, flowing

Dr Rudolf Steiner, the founder of a new etheric science

phenomena of existence down to a set of inner mental representations or pictures. Jesaiah Ben-Aharon expresses this with superb concision and accuracy: 'Taking our start from...the empty picture nature of...thinking...man achieves individuation, experiencing himself as a separated, divided self over against a non-living, non-animate and non-human world.'[22]

In order to overcome this process, Steiner outlined a path of spiritual development that aimed to reintegrate the thinking process back into the living world. Awakening the inner potentialities of human cognition, the individual finds higher states of consciousness already present in a seed form within his or her daily consciousness. As humans evolve and perfect their moral and cognitive faculties, the realities of the etheric realm are made more directly available to them. Access to the etheric realms provides humanity with an energy source that is alive, formative and non-entropic.

Having acquired a thorough knowledge of the etheric, Steiner was able to guide prominent students such as George

Adams, Lily Kolisko, Ehrenfried Pffeiffer and Guenther Wachsmuth into new theoretical and practical research, utilizing the new etheric knowledge as the basis for new forms of education, medicine, agriculture, art and science. He backed up this experimental work with thousands of lectures and many written works detailing the results of his personal research into higher states of consciousness.

When he died in 1925 Steiner left behind him a rich legacy of schools, farms, hospitals and curative establishments, whose activities implemented his discoveries concerning the relationship between the etheric world and the physical. Steiner's teachings covered vast spans of cosmic evolution, and found their central focus in the work of the Christ Being in human evolution. The following chapters will explore this cosmology in outline, providing a foundation for the interweaving of the theme of the etheric with the Grail motif in the chapters on the four Mystery streams.

4
The Four Ethers

> Courteous reader, observe the meaning right; we understand not by this description a beginning of the Deity, but we shew you the manifestation of the Deity through nature; for God is without beginning, and has an eternal beginning, and an eternal end, which he is himself, and the nature of the inward world is in the like essence from eternity.
>
> Jacob Boehme, *Signatura Rerum*

As I delved further into 'etheric science' I began to feel that it was of vital importance to link it with what I already knew of the anthroposophical explanation of the creation of the universe. To be able to really understand the 'energy' of Rennes-le-Château and the beings connected with it necessitated going back to the origins of the ethers in cosmic evolution. While Steiner's cosmological ideas have often been regarded as outlandish or terribly difficult to understand I had always found them a revelation, fitting as they ultimately do with our actual experience of the world as alive and imbued with intelligence. Steiner never intended the results of his spiritual research to be taken on in the form of dogmas or as some sort of 'absolute truth'. The most he asked was that people approach the material objectively and come to their own conclusions on the basis of the expanded vision of reality he hoped to provide. Certainly these evolutionary ideas are very different from the 'normative' views of the dominant type of science, but we have already seen how Steiner's notion of the etheric has been confirmed by much recent research. While some of the content of the following chapter may seem to take us a long way from the mysteries of Rennes-le-Château, it is essential to a total comprehension, and later chapters will tie the concepts developed here into a profound understanding of the nature of the Grail.

Throughout the ages, saints and mystics have described an experience of attunement with nature, a fusing together of the individual consciousness with the full richness of the non-sense perceptible content of life itself. When we walk through a wood or in open countryside, even if we are not able to say that we share the vision of the great seers and initiates we can still dimly sense a connection with the life force and at the same time feel 'recharged' and uplifted when surrounded by all that is constantly coming into being, growing, and then passing out of existence again.

The etheric realm, as described in the previous chapter, is very much connected with rhythm and with all that lives in time.[23] If the same walk is taken every day throughout the year, awareness of the working of the etheric in nature becomes evident. One is then able to observe each bud and blade of grass as living in time rather than space.

The physical body is also constantly growing, developing and decaying, following a similar cycle to the other rhythms of nature around us. If left to itself, it would follow purely chemical and mineral laws. It is the etheric body or organism which maintains the principle of life within the physical body.

In his book *Occult Science—An Outline*, Rudolf Steiner explores the origins of the warmth, light, chemical, and life ethers in the process of evolutionary metamorphosis. He describes there how our world has gone through three previous stages of planetary transformation. Adopting the names of the planets to designate these evolutionary phases, he describes them in order as being Ancient Saturn, Ancient Sun, and Ancient Moon. The process of evolution is effected not through chance but through the continuous work of spiritual beings known within Grail traditions as the spiritual Hierarchies.

During Ancient Saturn, an all-permeating *warmth* became the basis for a future physical world. Steiner asks us to imagine this warmth as a *qualitative* substance, not reducible to the quantitative and hypothetical activity of atomic particles but, in the full Goethean sense, as a living reality. This 'state of warmth' was home to certain beings much as the earth is the home to human beings, animals and plants now. Some of these beings were going through their 'human' or 'ego' stage of evolution. Steiner called these particular beings 'Archai' or 'Spirits of Personality'. They 'caused their own being to be rayed back to them from the Saturn bodies, and this very process bestows upon the Saturn bodies the fine substantiality that we described above as "warmth".'[24]

This development takes place towards the middle of the Saturn evolutionary period. At this time the warmth-ether, relating to the element of fire, becomes active. Within evolution its function is to bring about at the upper border of physical nature the chaos which allows the material to be 'opened up' to the life forces. We see this in the fertilization of the egg in conception. The sperm introduces chaos into the previously quiescent egg, and the etheric forces flow into the material form, enlivening it and unfolding its latent potential.

Commenting on Saturn evolution in the series of lectures published under the title *Man as Symphony of the Creative Word*, Rudolf Steiner states that: 'This Saturn-condition must be thought of as already containing within itself everything belonging to our planetary system. The separate planets of our planetary system, from Saturn onwards to the moon, were at that time still within Old Saturn—which as you know consisted only of warmth ether, as undifferentiated world-bodies. Saturn which had not even attained to the density of air, merely warmth ether, contained in an undifferentiated etheric condition everything which later took on independent form, becoming individualized in the separate planets.'[25]

The temperature of human blood was first established on Ancient Saturn; the blood which during this present Earth evolution becomes the mediator between the highest principle in man—the ego—and the physical body was emerging as a *pattern of warmth* on Ancient Saturn. Steiner mentioned this in a lecture given in Stuttgart in 1907:

> It will be interesting to mention here a parallelism about which ordinary science has little to say. What does the man of today have in him of Saturn's warmth? His blood heat. What at that time was distributed over the whole of Saturn has in a measure freed itself and today forms the warm

> blood of man and animal. When you investigate the temperature of a beehive, you find it to be about the same temperature as that of human blood because, in accordance with the nature of its being, it goes back to the same source as does the human blood.[26]

Having reached this degree of evolutionary unfolding, it happened that not all the members of the Archai were able to progress to the next planetary incarnation. During Saturn evolution warmth came into being, but there was no light. Those Archai who were unable to progress to the next stage of evolution remained behind as beings who had only progressed to a state where there was no light. They remained beings of darkness. These beings are described by Steiner as still having a vital role to play in evolution:

> Those Spirits of Personality who reveal themselves not through light but through darkness are made use of in order to evoke the laws of earthly development, they are allotted their proper place, so that they can make their contribution to the orderly development of our existence... The Saturnian operation on our bodies had to be a constructive one. The destructive process takes place in the daytime under the influence of light, but on Saturn there was no light. Therefore the Saturn activity on our physical bodies was an up-building one and had to be maintained through Saturn beings remaining behind to care for it. [To this day the Saturn Archai are] active in us during sleep, when they work upon our physical and etheric bodies, building them up.[27]

At the end of this first stage of creation the whole of Saturn evolution enters a state of 'cosmic sleep' which gives way to the next planetary epoch which Steiner called Ancient or Old Sun. Light and space come into being now, and the light ether begins to operate. Air is the element that comes into existence for the first time on Old Sun. Space is that which creates an interval between things and thus a connection can be formed with light, which separates and forms around each object a

Guenther Wachsmuth

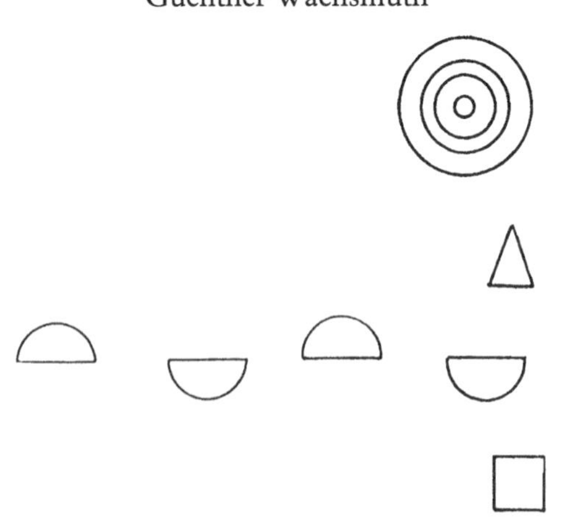

In his works Guenther Wachsmuth demonstrated a correlation between the four ethers and certain geometrical shapes which occur naturally where the relevant ether predominates in nature. We see here circle (warmth ether), triangle (light ether), crescent (chemical ether), and square (life ether).

coloured border. Light separates objects by making them distinguishable from each other.

The germs of the human physical body and of the future mineral kingdom were laid down on Old Saturn along with the activity of the warmth ether. On Old Sun, with the appearance of the light ether, comes the germ of mankind's etheric organism and of the future plant kingdom. Old Sun is also the realm where those beings known to us as the Archangels go through their human, ego-conscious stage.

When this Sun Epoch comes to an end, it emerges again, after a period of cosmic rest, as the Ancient Moon epoch. To the germs of the physical and etheric organisms, which have undergone further evolution by this time, are added the astral body, the bearer of sentience and desire. To the mineral and plant kingdoms the animal kingdom is added on Old Moon, and the element of water. The chemical or *tone* ether emerges and becomes active.

The activity of the chemical ether can be observed in the phenomenon of the 'sound figures' discovered by the German physicist Chladni in 1785: 'They are produced with the aid of a round or square plate of glass or brass, fixed at the centre so that it can vibrate freely at its edges. It is evenly, not too thickly, covered with lycopodium powder and then caused to vibrate acoustically by the repeated drawing of a violin bow with some pressure across the edge of the plate until a steady note becomes audible. Through the vibrations thus caused within the plate the particles of sand or powder are set in movement and caused to collect in certain stationary parts of the plate, thereby creating figures of very regular and often surprising form.'[28]

We have seen that the astral body is added to the twofold man on Ancient Moon. The astral brings form to the physical through the medium of the etheric body. Through the astral organism the feeling and desire nature of the individual arises, both in the animal and the human kingdoms. Through the variation of 'tone' the human being can convey a multitude of subtle or dramatic differentiations of feeling in music or in the human voice. In the animal world this is at a rudimentary stage where, for example, the tones of a dog's bark indicates whether the animal is feeling desperate or showing defiance.

In the visual arts the tones of colour and relationships between the objects represented in the picture convey feelings between artist and observer. In sculpture and architecture an experience of mood is conveyed by the relationships of heights, proportions and surfaces. All that has to do with differentiation and relationship between separate parts is created by the influence of the chemical ether. The present moon still fulfils this formative activity each time a new physical creation enters into being.

Also during the Moon phase of cosmogenesis, the planetary body separates into two members for the first time, namely, a sun (which is neither Ancient Sun nor our present sun) and a moon. Steiner explains this as follows: 'Along with the sun the higher beings and finer substances withdrew from the whole stellar mass, while the coarser substances and lower beings remained with the moon. So during the evolution of the Old Moon we have two heavenly bodies instead of one; [one] harbouring higher beings, and a moon body, the dwelling place of the lower beings.' The reason for this separation is described by Rudolf Steiner as follows: 'Had the whole remained united, with no separation occurring, certain beings could not have kept pace with the sun beings; they were not sufficiently mature and therefore had to segregate out the coarser substance and build themselves a sphere of action apart. Nor could the higher beings have remained united with these coarser substances for it would have obstructed their more rapid progress. They too required a special field for their development and that was the sun...the beings of the sun were of a more developed spirituality; those on the moon lagged behind at a coarser stage of development.'[29]

Those beings known to Christian esotericism as the Angels experienced their human stage of evolution upon Ancient Moon. It was here that they received into themselves from higher powers the self-conscious ego.

After a duration in which the substance and experiences of this transformative evolutionary epoch are absorbed back into the spiritual world, the evolutionary process begins anew. The present evolutionary epoch commences as the one in which the future Spirits of Freedom experience their human phase, that is, our current Earth phase. To the warmth, light, and chemical ethers is added the life ether. The life ether is connected both with the highest spiritual powers and with the lowest of the elements, earth. The life ether's activity can be found before the coming into being of matter and at its dissolution. If the life ether is to do with the coming into being of matter, it can also just as well be described as 'the coming into matter of being'.

To the threefold human organism that has been passed over to the Earth phase from the three previous epochs is added, in this fourth evolutionary period, the individual human ego. The ego, like the life ether, has the task of working down into and transforming matter. While all the evolving spiritual beings have had an ego phase, the conditions in which this phase has occurred has never been as dense, dangerous and difficult as the Earth phase. For the present-day human being the greatest possibilities and the most profound dangers open up. While those beings who experienced their ego-development on Ancient Saturn, Sun and Moon have developed self-conscious ego-awareness, the environment in which that awareness was gained presented them with less challenge than the present state does to modern man. Therefore the heights to which the ego could be evolved, the capacity for free will and total self-independence were not available to the degree they are now. The price paid for this is the all too obvious depths to which humanity can and often does sink.

With the Earth epoch the sun and moon again depart, leaving the earth to densify into its present condition. The individual human ego enters into the process of reincarnation. The ego incarnates into an organism built up of three 'sheaths'—the astral, etheric and physical bodies—and has the task of permeating and transforming them. The great task, laid as a seed within the human soul, is the attainment of free will and independence. A microcosm of this ultimately macrocosmic process can be seen when a human being creates a work of art—especially in the case of sculpture and architecture, where the most solid matter is taken hold of and impressed with forms which have been created in the high realms of spirit:

> Art is likewise the means of pouring spirit into lifeless matter. Try for a moment to picture in your mind how the wisdom in art gradually overcomes and masters lifeless nature and you will see how what is there without man's participation is reshaped piece by piece by man himself. Visualize the effect of the whole earth becoming a work of art, full of wisdom and radiating beauty, built by man's hand, conceived by wisdom![30]

However, with the event known as the Fall, other elements enter into human evolution—those workings of evil and temptation that in our present time threaten humanity with the abyss.

5
The Fall

> And the Elohim said, 'Behold, the man is become as one of us, to know good and evil: and now lest he put forth his hand and take also of the Tree of Life, and eat, and live forever...' Therefore the Elohim sent him forth from the garden of Eden...
>
> Genesis

A central theme in the Grail legends has to do with the overcoming of the forces of evil. In its most direct form this is embodied in the notion of brave knights riding off to fight fierce dragons or, in a more complex way, in the experiences of the knight Gawain in Klingsor's deadly Castle of Wonders as described by Wolfram von Eschenbach. Again and again in my personal thoughts and in my researches into the Grail Mysteries I came up against the question of the origin and nature of evil. The Gnostics taught that our world was not created by God but was an inferior material creation, the work of Lucifer, the Demiurge, and there were strong Gnostic elements incorporated into the Grail legends. It seemed, at first sight, hard to accept such a negative view of creation, but the orthodox Christian notion of the 'Fall' seemed worse. The idea that every child is born into a state of sin and damnation takes all the dignity from human life, and leaves us helplessly dependent upon a wrathful deity. I was convinced of the total dignity of human existence, yet the workings of evil in the world also seemed inescapable. One needed only to consider such recent historical events as the dropping of the atomic bombs on Nagasaki and Hiroshima to see the depths to which humanity could sink. Along with the positive life energies that were so deeply linked with the Grail, one could also see in the world such destructive energies as those unleashed by the atomic bomb. To make matters more complicated, the Grail legends often hinted at an extraordinary possibility: that evil was an integral part of the universe and that it was possible for evil to be made good (in Christian terms to be 'redeemed'). As I looked into Rudolf Steiner's teachings on the event known in Christian tradition as the 'Fall'—the origins of evil in the world—I began to come across some fundamental concepts that furnished me with a way to understand the relationship between the positive and negative energies in creation and in man. I was also to resolve the Gnostic's enigma of dualism—the creation of the earth by the Demiurge. In later chapters we will see how these forces are linked with the stream in human history that opposes the Grail.

At the beginning of the present planetary phase of evolution, sun, moon and earth interpenetrated one another as a single body and the four ethers worked together in balance. Humanity existed in a condition of paradisaical innocence, a cosmic new-born who bore the totality of future archetypes within himself. Adam was the sum of creation, the harmonious reflection of the Godhead. The gentle descent into ever-denser material conditions was intended to bring about the inward ripening of the spirit.

We saw in the previous chapter that certain beings can lag behind the normal course of evolution. In his book *Man or Matter*, Ernst Lehrs points out that:

> Essential to the picture of the abnormal hierarchies transmitted to us by Rudolf Steiner is the fact that the dropping out from the normal course of evolution rests originally upon a sacrificial renunciation by the beings concerned. They have brought this offering in order that man may through them experience those forms of opposition which he needs in order to gain the forces without which he could not reach the goal of his evolution. By the same token, every step man makes towards this goal becomes at the same time a step towards the redemption of those beings.[31]

Elsewhere Rudolf Steiner describes the luciferic rebellion against the progressive stream of evolution that resulted in the 'Fall':

> An impulse arose in a number of the Third Hierarchy to develop an inner life of their own. Everything else was

> simply the result, the consequence of this impulse. What then was this result? It was in fact a terrible one, namely, the betrayal of their own nature; untruth, falsehood...You should understand that the spirits of the Third Hierarchy, which had this impulse, did not do what they did for the sake of lying, but in order to develop an independent life of their own; but in so doing they had to take the consequence, they had to become Spirits of Untruth—spirits which betrayed their own being—in other words, Spirits of Lies. It is as though someone were to take a journey on foot and he meets with a wet day; he must of necessity make the best of it and put up with getting wet, which he did not at all intend. In the same way the spirits of which we are speaking had no intention of doing something in order to sink into untruth. Their action arose from their wish to develop an inner life, an inner activity, but the result, the consequence, was that they at the same time became Spirits of Untruth. Now all the spiritual beings which in this way, through betraying their own nature, arose as a second category besides the spirits of the Third Hierarchy are called in occultism luciferic spirits. These beings whom we may call the rebels of the Third Hierarchy had brought about nothing less than the actual independence of man—making it possible for him to develop an independent life of his own, which does not merely manifest externally, but can be independent of external manifestation.[32]

Wachsmuth deepens the discussion of these events in the following way:

> [At the time of the Fall] light ether permeated the organism of man to excess. This led to a cleavage in the use of the formative forces in man's organism, thereby differentiating male and female physically as well as spiritually...this process was connected with an enlightenment of the consciousness in relation to its environment. The permeation of warmth and life ether, the luciferic forces into the earth-sphere, signified for the human organism acceptance of the forces of the 'Tree of Knowledge' ...This event, shown in the Old

> Testament as the 'Temptation', the eating of the fruit of the 'Tree of Knowledge', indicates that man has accepted the forces surging in upon him which he was unable to resist...
>
> Man could not remain as he was after he had taken the luciferic influences into himself; he must be protected from the luciferic influences in his astral body. This was achieved by making the man of that time incapable of using the whole of his etheric body; part of the etheric body was withdrawn from man's jurisdiction. If this beneficial action had not taken place—if he had retained power over the whole of his etheric body—he would never have been able to find his way rightly through Earth evolution. Certain parts of the etheric body would have had to be taken away then, and reserved for later times...of these four ether forms only the two lower ones, warmth ether and light ether, were, in the Lemurian age, left at man's free disposal. The two higher ether forms were withdrawn from him. That is the inner meaning of the teaching that when man had attained the distinction between good and evil through luciferic influences—figuratively expressed by his having eaten of the 'Tree of Knowledge'—then partaking of the 'Tree of Life' was also withdrawn from him. That is to say, man retained absolute power over the forces of warmth and light ether only; power over the formative forces of sound and life ether were withdrawn from him.[33]

As a direct result of this loss of the Tree of Life, man's physical body—which had hitherto been composed of warmth, light and air—contracted, condensed and formed a body that was first of all fluid and later solid:

> It is not at all a figure of speech, but literally describes the situation when I say that through the contraction of the human body brought about by the luciferic influence man became heavier, sank down out of the periphery to the surface of the earth. That was how at the expulsion from Paradise man acquired for the first time the force of gravity. It was the luciferic influence which brought him down to earth, whereas he had hitherto dwelt in its periphery.[34]

As the condensation and solidification of the earth intensified the beings concerned with the forces of the life ether, the *six sun Elohim* could no longer endure matter which had condensed as far as the watery state:

> Out of the whole earth-mass they separate the substances which alone are suited to their use, and take their departure to make themselves a new dwelling-place in the sun. Henceforth they work upon the earth from without, from the sun. Man, on the other hand, needs for his further evolution a scene of action where matter will condense still more.[35] Six of the Elohim made the sun their dwelling place and what streams down to us in the physical light of the sun contains within it the spiritual force of love from these six spirits of light...One separated from the others and took a different path for the salvation of humanity. He did not choose the sun but the moon for his abode. And this spirit of light who voluntarily renounced life upon the sun and chose the moon instead is none other than the one whom the Old Testament calls 'Yahveh' or 'Jehovah'.[36]

A major proportion of the life ether was thus removed from the earth to the sun. Subsequently, in the same way, the chemical ether was removed to the moon. The forces of the Tree of Life were thus mainly removed from the earth-sphere at the time of the Fall.

After the Fall, the sun's rays channelled the life ether, which is experienced during the daytime when it effects the earth from a *vertical* direction. The effect of the chemical ether is received by night when the moon works upon the earth from a *horizontal* position. Together with the light ether Rudolf Steiner describes the chemical and life ethers as having a fallen residue that was left within the earth when the finer etheric substance was taken out into the cosmos. In this way fallen light ether relates to electricity, fallen chemical ether to magnetism, and the fallen life ether to the mysterious 'Third Force' whose incomparably destructive forces have yet to be tapped by mankind.

The Manichaeans and Gnostics taught that the earth was

a 'secondary' and not the original creation. In the light of Rudolf Steiner's description of the Fall the activity of the Demiurge in creation becomes understandable. The *original creation* proceeded from the Godhead. The *creation in matter*, as we have just seen, is a direct result of the Fall which was instigated by Lucifer. Later in this book we will consider the Gnostic wisdom of the Cathars, Templars and Rosicrucians. It is important to present a modern picture of the creation in some detail, not only to clarify the Gnostic claim but also in order to understand the mission of the earth and the grand task of humanity—which is not just to reverse the effects of the Fall, but to take cosmic evolution to previously undreamed of heights.

6
The Significance of the Incarnation

> Where there is an understanding of Jesus only, the Christian Sacrament perishes, and with it both Christian knowledge and Christian life. Then all that is left is only human thought, human words, human morality. Only when a new understanding of Christ is achieved, can sacrament, word and life be again filled with higher forces.
>
> Emil Bock, *The Childhood and Youth of Jesus*

Written down long before the social, religious, and political revolutions that would proclaim the dignity and spiritual autonomy of the individual human being, Wolfram von Eschenbach's epic poem Parzival *reads to me like a very early version of the Declaration of Independence. For the first time in human history it told the very personal story of a young man who had to find his own path from innocence to knowledge and self-fulfilment. Written down in an age of ecclesiastical power,* Parzival *ignores the priesthood almost totally, and never quotes the authority of the Church. At the same time the spiritual dimensions of the story are profoundly Christian, but in a deeper sense than that allowed by the dogmas of orthodoxy.*

The Grail legends had their origins in the pagan religions. The etheric energies were known and revered by the pagan peoples, as we will explore in depth in later chapters. These Mysteries were taken up and renewed in Christian times, and writers such as Wolfram von Eschenbach had much to say about the personage of Christ that clearly linked Him with the eternally life-giving energies of the Grail. Guenther Wachsmuth's work on the formative forces brought the Incarnation of Christ home to me in a way that nothing else ever had. Here was the closest meeting of religion and science that I had ever encountered. I found in Wachsmuth's work a system full of insight that fused the pagan and Christian streams together in perfect harmony. It also threw much light on 'New Age' interpretations of earth energy. Wachsmuth's work was based upon the cosmological research of Rudolf Steiner, and in Steiner's writings on the nature of the Incarnation I found answers to many of the criticisms of the Christian tradition raised by Lincoln, Baigent and Leigh in their book The Holy Blood and the Holy Grail. *They particularly note the discrepancy between the Matthew and Luke accounts of the Nativity, which seem to be describing two separate events, so profound are the contradictions between them. As the major aim of this book is to show the spiritual reality of the Grail quest, this will also need to involve demonstrating the existence of an original stream of esoteric Christianity flowing directly from Christ and His earliest followers, which reached one of its highest flowerings in the Parzival myth. By the time of Constantine this esoteric stream had been forced underground and Christianity was transformed into a tool of political power. We will begin to explore the inner relationships between Parzival and the Christian/pagan Grail tradition when we come onto the subject of the Mystery streams. But first we must continue our cosmological journey and outline Steiner's and Wachsmuth's perspectives on the Incarnation.*

In our essence as unique individuals we are derived from the same source as the Divinity. At the beginning of Earth evolution this individual 'I' was still contained as a latent potential within the substance of the Godhead. The spiritual world was waiting for the time when this Ego-substance could be poured out upon humanity as a Pentecostal gift:

> When the day of Pentecost came they were all together in one place. Suddenly a sound like the blowing of a mighty wind came from heaven and filled the whole house in which they were sitting. They saw what seemed to be tongues of fire that separated and came to rest on each of them. All of them were filled with the Holy Spirit and began to speak in tongues as the Spirit enabled them.[37]

Jesus Christ had pointed towards this historical moment and the capacity for free will that it would provide:

The wind
Blows where it wills
And you hear the sound it makes
But you do not know
Where it comes from
Or where it is going
It is the same with everyone
Born out of the spirit.[38]

It was as the living ambassador of this higher self of each man and woman that Christ came to the earth. But this raises the question: from *where* did this Being come? The Gospel of John identifies Christ with the cosmic Logos, the mighty Word, source of all creation. Dealing with the question of the origins of the Christ, Wachsmuth says:

> He came from those very regions which had been closed to man by the temptation of Lucifer, from the region of the Music of the Spheres, from the region of the cosmic life...With his soul man really belongs to the region of the living cosmic ether. But he was driven out from it. And so it is to be given to him again, so that by degrees he may once more be able to imbue himself with that which he had forfeited.[39]

Following the entry of Lucifer into the human evolutionary stream, as described in the previous chapter, came that being whom Rudolf Steiner referred to as Ahriman, god of darkness. Ahriman is described by Rudolf Steiner as the lord of materialism, who works with the Elohim in the creation of solid matter. The task of the backward ahrimanic beings was to lead man to consider as real only those phenomena which can be perceived by the five senses.

The luciferic powers took hold of human nature in an attempt to accelerate human evolution, breaking humanity free from the hold of the spiritual world in order to set him upon the path to an individual adulthood. Since that time Lucifer has appeared as a power calling mankind onwards, back into the spiritual world. Ahrimanic forces incorporated themselves into the human being for a different reason. They wished to bind man for ever to the material earth, and through him to mechanize the universe in their own image. Luciferic illusion, manifesting as a weightless spirituality, became one of the balancing poles of human nature. At the other extreme the forces of soulless death, void of any redeeming spirituality, worked to create the counterbalance to the luciferic impulse.

After a certain point in human evolution there was no way back up the original road that led from Paradise; its gates were firmly shut and overgrown with weeds. The only way for the Logos to re-enter evolution was to descend into matter and enter into such an intimate relationship with humanity that the individual ego could be transformed by a free, subjective recognition of the divine essence within itself and other human beings. 'The God had to descend as deeply into matter as he had allowed man to sink into matter.'[40]

Rudolf Steiner has described how the all-embracing cosmic Logos described in the opening verses of the St John's Gospel was experienced by humanity prior to the Incarnation as the mighty Sun Spirit, the sum total of the six Elohim who had made their home in the sun-sphere. Zechariah, the father of John the Baptist, had prophesied the imminent appearance upon earth of the Sun Spirit: '...because of the tender mercy of our God, by which the rising sun will come to us from heaven to shine on those living in darkness'.[41]

At the Baptism in the Jordan the Sun Spirit descended into the human being who was prepared to receive Him. The man Jesus had been prepared by his life experience to become the first bearer of the higher Ego within the astral, etheric and physical sheaths. In fact, *two* human individuals were directly involved in becoming the bearers of the Christ. For many years biblical scholars have puzzled over the two contrasting and contradictory accounts of the Nativity given in the Matthew and Luke Gospels. The two accounts are so divergent that many honest scholars have had to put their variance down to inept scholarship on the part of the Gospel writers. Such blatant inaccuracies at one of the most crucial points would cast considerable doubt on the reliability of the Gospel texts. However, according to Rudolf Steiner's spiritual research both accounts are accurate, each reflecting the events surrounding one of two separate children. The idea of the two Jesus-children, a common one in art and theology prior to the modern age, was described by Steiner out of his own investigations.

The Jesus-child we read of in the Gospel of St Matthew, who is described as having descended from the house of David through the Solomon line—the child who was visited by kings—is described by Rudolf Steiner as being the reincarnation of the ego of Zarathustra, the inaugurator of the ancient Persian civilization. Zarathustra had perceived the Christ ruling from the sphere of the sun as the great Sun Being, Ahura Mazdao.

The Jesus-child of the Gospel of St Luke is described as having descended through the Nathan line of the house of David, directly from Adam, the son of God. In connection with this Rudolf Steiner describes how the Nathan Jesus was a being of total purity, a part of the 'Adamic-substance' that had not experienced the impact of the Fall. This Nathan child was in every respect the 'Second Adam', truly human but one who still retained the unsullied nature of the original state of humanity—a child who could therefore prepare the way for all of humanity to return to a state of paradisaical innocence. He thus became the first human being incarnated who was free of the effects of the Fall in relation to his control of the totality of the four ethers in the etheric body. As a result of this the blood coursing through his veins was of a different composition to the blood of other human beings; it was vivified with the full power of the chemical and life ethers. Here lies the secret of the redeeming blood of Christ who descended into the body prepared for him by the innocent soul of the Jesus-child.

According to Rudolf Steiner's spiritual researches, the two Jesus-children became one individual at the age of 12 when the ego of Zarathustra, which dwelt in the Matthew child, incorporated itself within the sheaths of the Luke Jesus. The outer story of this event is given in St Luke's Gospel when the previously pure and simple Jesus-child is '...found in the Temple, sitting in the midst of the doctors both hearing them and asking questions...All that heard him were amazed at his understanding and answers.' [42]

The secret of the two Jesus boys was known by Christian initiates in the past. For instance in the Kaiser Friedrich Museum in Berlin there is a picture by Raphael that depicts a Madonna with three little boys (Madonna del Duea Duca di Terranuova). One of the children is depicted lying lovingly on Mary's lap, while the other, radiating wisdom, rests against the mother. The third child is the little John the Baptist.

In the wonderful Roman church of St Ambrosius, in Milan, we see in the north aisle a shining coloured picture by Borgognone (1455–1523) depicting the 12-year old Jesus in the Temple. Raised in the centre in the chair of the teacher sits a boy with a countenance illumined by wisdom. On the left, in the foreground, swathed in shadow, another boy is walking out of the Temple porch. This work of art, whether created in full consciousness or less consciously, is an exact representation of the two boys after the ego of one passed into the sheaths prepared by the other.

Theologian Emil Bock further outlines the theme of the two Jesus-children in his *The Youth and Childhood of Jesus*:

> In the apocryphal *Egyptian Gospel*, of which we know only a few fragments, is the following passage: 'To Solomon's question as to when the Kingdom would come, the lord answered: When the two are one, and the outside as the inside.'
>
> In the book *Sohar*, a part of the Cabbala, there are again and again passages like this: 'The son of David and the son of Joseph are two, not one. The son of Joseph will die a cruel death. Then he will be followed by the son of David. The Messiah, who is the son of Joseph, will not remain alive; he will be killed and will come to life again when the small hill conceives on the large hill'; 'The Messiah, son of David, and the Messiah, son of Joseph, are cast into the abyss. One

of them is a poor man, riding on an ass; and the other is the first-born of a bull.' In the early Christian document, *The Testaments of the Twelve Patriarchs*, '...the Lord will raise up a High Priest out of Levi, and a king out of Judah, God and Man.'[43]

The Zarathustra being—the bearer of all the riches that can be gained through human experience—lived within the innocent sheaths of the Nathan soul until his thirtieth year, when the Logos came into Incarnation and the ego of Zarathustra returned to the spiritual world. This combination of total experience and absolute innocence in one man made Jesus the perfect vessel to hold within it the cosmic Host: the Sun Spirit.

We have reached the point where we can begin to understand the significance of the shedding of the blood on Golgotha. The commonly held assumption that a wrathful God needed to shed blood to appease His anger, with Christ as the brutalized victim, has been rightly rejected by many modern people. But with an understanding of the etheric nature of the blood and its role in human evolution we can begin to discern the occult implications of the Crucifixion.

When the blood flowed from the cross two events of immense evolutionary importance occurred. First of all the influence of Lucifer and Ahriman was cast out from the human sheaths so that the full Tree of Life forces could be safely returned to the human blood. Secondly, the power of these four ethers was returned to the earth. At the Last Supper the Christ had already directed the attention of his followers to the new condition of the earth when he taught them to view the wine and the bread as his body and blood. At the climax of the Crucifixion the Logos passed into the earth.

It is interesting to note here that the Greek word for ratio is Logos, which also means thought, or word. As we have seen, one of the activities of the chemical or sound ether is in establishing ratios between things and is connected with the Music of the Spheres. Clement of Alexandria and the other early Church Fathers who wrote on music could argue that the Pythagorean identification of ratios, or Logos, with the divine principle of universal order harmonized with St John's Gospel's identification of Logos with God, of which Christ was the manifestation.

At the event of Golgotha the Sun Spirit became the Spirit of the Earth so that, just as the human ego works through the bodily sheaths to transform them, so Christ works through the earth's sheaths in the same order. At first this began within the astral sheath of the earth, where Christ could be clairvoyantly perceived permeating the world with the power of the sun, with which it would one day be reunited.

7
Resurrection and Transubstantiation

> We know that in the moment when the blood flowed from the cross upon Golgotha that, there in the interior of the earth, a new sun globe was born.
>
> Rudolf Steiner to Countess Keyserlingk
> after the Koberwitz lectures

In finding a relationship between the transformation of Jesus Christ's physical body and the body of the earth much of what one hears described as the raising of the earth's energy and the transformation of negative energies begins to be clarified. Steiner's interpretation of these events led to a practical understanding of the Mystery of the Last Supper and also began to shed light on the Rosicrucian ideal—the transformation of the earth into a sun. At the so-called Last Supper, Christ had taken bread and wine and stated that these were now His body. If the words of Christ are taken literally they seem not to lead to a new form of ritual—eating a small piece of bread and sipping a mouthful of wine on Sunday mornings—but to a realization that the earth is now, in a totally real sense, the body of Christ. For the earth itself is a Grail, and if we are called to be guardians of the Grail then it is to her that we must direct our efforts. Before delving into the Mystery streams we must take one final step to the completion of the 'Grail cosmology' and look at this theme of the transubstantiation of matter within the stream of teachings derived from esoteric Christianity.

Here in all its transcendent glory is the full motif of the Holy Grail: the descent of the Sun Spirit into the moon chalice. This sublime archetype was realized upon the stage of world history when the Being of the Sun passed into incarnation within the body prepared for it by the Jewish people, the people who had been chosen for this task by the moon spirit, Yahveh.[44]

When the Resurrection was accomplished, the possibility

arose for the transubstantiation of mankind, the earth and all the kingdoms of nature—for the attainment of the New Jerusalem spoken of in the Book of Revelations.[45] When Jesus was approached by Lucifer in the wilderness he represented all of mankind in a repetition of the original 'temptation' when luciferic beings invaded the human astral body. In withstanding these attacks Jesus was able to reverse their effect on the human astral body.[46]

The full permeation and transformation of the astral body is imaginatively pictured in the story of the walking upon the water. The astral body was bestowed upon Old Moon when the watery element was added to the world content. Anthroposophical researcher Sergei O. Prokofieff writes concerning this event: 'In the scene of the walking on the waters, the disciples are borne fully into the elemental, astral world which comes before them in the picture of the watery element. This is where the Apostles—led by Christ—arrive through the awakening of their consciousness in the astral body. This first "awakening" is the result of the union of the macrocosmic Ego of Christ with the astral body of Jesus of Nazareth.'[47] The astral form perceived in clairvoyant vision by the disciples was given the name of Spirit Self by Rudolf Steiner. Just as the astral body was poured out on Old Moon, so will the Spirit Self become a fully realized actuality in a future evolutionary condition that is known in Anthroposophy as the *Jupiter* epoch.

The Gospel event known as the Transfiguration occurred when the Christ Ego fully permeated the etheric body of Jesus. This etheric body was then changed into a 'sun' radiating its own light.* Only three of the Apostles can accompany Christ this far into the macrocosm, into the sphere of the sun itself. Christ's etheric body shines with all the elementary power of the light that was one of the evolutionary developmental goals of Old Sun. This Christ-permeated etheric body was called by Steiner the Life Spirit

* 'There he was transfigured before them. His face shone like the sun, and his clothes became as white as the light.' (Matthew 17: 2. New International Version.)

and will become a fully realized actuality for all of humanity only at the end of an evolutionary transformative period that will follow the Jupiter developmental phase, and is known as the *Venus* epoch of human evolution.

Once the transformation of Jesus' astral and etheric bodies into the Spirit Self and Life Spirit had been completed it became possible for the transubstantiation of the physical to be achieved in only three days. Alfred Heidenreich comments:

> Finally in that sublime event of death the Being of Christ fully permeates the disturbed relationship between the etheric and physical bodies. Rudolf Steiner speaks of certain details here before that inner permeation was actually completed in death; when the processes of decomposition and combustion were finished and all that was left were the salt processes.[48] These, within the body and in connection with the spices, dissolved so quickly that, during those three days when he was in the grave, dematerialization could take place not as a miracle but as the result of the three years of gradual, progressive re-establishment of the paradisaic balance between the four constituent members of the human body.[49]

Only one of the Apostles can accompany Christ this far. This is the disciple John. He alone of the Twelve stands before the cross on Golgotha, participating in Christ's permeation of the physical body. Just as the secrets of Sun and Moon evolution are unveiled to the ego as it penetrates into the etheric and astral sheaths, so does the physical body yield up full knowledge of events on Old Saturn. The fully spiritualized physical body is known in Anthroposophy as the Spirit Man, and its attainment by the whole of humanity will only occur in the most distant reaches of cosmic evolution, a developmental evolutionary epoch that Steiner called the *Vulcan* epoch. This future planetary incarnation will carry human evolution to its completion, after which humanity will join the cosmic Hierarchies as a new spiritual dimension, that of Freedom.

During the three days following the event on Golgotha,

Christ descended to the centre of the earth. Since the Fall this has been the bastion of the centric forces, the region of the fallen ethers, the habitation of their corresponding 'backward' beings. There the Christ, now as 'Spirit of the Earth', together with the human physical body in which the laws of matter are in the process of being reversed, confronts these fallen forces of light ether (electricity) where Lucifer is working, chemical ether (magnetism), which is Ahriman's realm, and the life ether (the Third Force), relating to the Asuras or Rakshasas:

> Christ descended into the forecourts of hell. It was not human beings that He met there; He was confronted by spiritual beings. The Rakshasa beings were brought thereby into a state of paralysis and lethargy. They were at the same time kept in check so that they became unable to move. They could only be lamed in this manner because they were being opposed from two sides. That would not have been possible if there had not been two natures combined together in Jesus of Nazareth: on the one hand the old Chela nature deeply connected with the physical plane, which could also work effectively on the physical plane and through its power could hold it in balance; on the other hand there was Christ Himself who was purely a spiritual being. Something occurred at that time in occult spheres; it was the banishment of the enemies of mankind, which has its echo in the saga of the Anti-Christ, who was put in chains but will make his appearance again if not opposed once more by the Christ principle in its primal form...This tension, this bottled up energy had to be prevented from becoming effective energy. That is the Christ principle against the Anti-Christ...The Asuras are igneous or dynamic in their nature and their power for evil was terrific. It was destroyed for ever by the advent of Jesus Christ, and they now are as St Jude puts it 'reserved in everlasting chains until the judgment of the great day'.[50]

In *The Fifth Gospel* Rudolf Steiner describes how an earthquake followed the darkening of the sun when Jesus's body had been laid in the grave*: 'It shook the grave in which the body of Jesus had been laid and the stone covering it was wrenched away; a fissure was rent in the earth and the corpse was received into it. Another tremor caused the fissure to close again over the corpse. And when the people came in the morning the grave was empty, for the dead body of Jesus had been received into the earth.'[51]

The physical body of Jesus descended into the earth and the transformation of the physical substance took place in those regions where the centric forces predominate, laying the foundation for the future transformation of all 'physical' earthly conditions. The power of those beings particularly concerned with fallen matter was thus held in check and an impulse was then given to the whole of fallen creation by the body of Jesus Christ as it was transformed within the earth. After this the way lay open towards the metamorphosis of the Earth into the next planetary incarnation: Jupiter evolution—the New Jerusalem. Steiner comments:

> The physical body which was laid in the grave was dematerialized to such an extent that it was spread over the whole world, and that is why no body could be found when it was looked for. The Resurrection Body was the ether body which was so densified by the Christ that Thomas was able to touch it, which is as we all know impossible with a normal ether body. It was indicated that it was a different body from the physical one hinted at in the Gospel by the fact that Mary Magdalene and the others didn't at first recognize Him again.[52]

On Easter Monday, when the tomb is found empty, the risen figure of Christ is seen by the two Marys as the first creation of the New Jerusalem, the fully perfected etheric body that has total control over the physical realm, including, Rudolf Steiner often stressed, the human skeleton.

The form of the human skeleton was first established

* 'There was a violent earthquake, for an angel of the Lord came down from heaven and, going to the tomb, rolled back the stone and sat on it.' (Matthew 28: 2. New International Version.)

during Ancient Saturn evolution. The skeleton is now the part of the physical body that has descended furthest into matter:

> In the structure of man there is one element to which the power of a pre-Christian initiation could not penetrate: the subtle physico-chemical processes in the skeleton. Strange as it may sound to you there never had been a human individual in its Earth evolution, either among initiates or elsewhere, with power over the physico-chemical processes in the skeleton. Through the entry of Christ into the body of Jesus of Nazareth the Egohood of Christ acquired domination even over the skeleton. And the result was that, as a unique event, there lived upon earth a body capable of applying its forces in such a way as to incorporate the form of the skeleton—that is, its spiritual form—in Earth evolution. Nothing of all that man passes through in his earth development would endure were he not able to incorporate in Earth evolution as a law the noble form of the skeleton, were he unable to gradually master this law of the skeleton.[53]

When Christ transubstantiated the human skeleton at the Resurrection, He also in a sense empowered the human ego to begin a process of transformation within the sheaths. Man is now able to join forces with Christ in transubstantiating matter into this new substance that is physical, but a physicality that is not subject to the effect of the Fall.

However, the full reality of the Resurrection as an impulse working through human evolution in a *continually* transformative way cannot be grasped unless we pause here to reconsider the work of the ahrimanic beings within the human organism. For Ahriman has brought into evolution the power of the human intellect. This intellect is a *death* force which with its destructive analytic process kills the intimate warmth of the soul's life. Essentially, the intellect is to do with what has died, which belongs to the past as opposed to the living immediacy of the body and soul life.

In the chapters on the new etheric science we considered the need for a new type of thinking, a *living* thinking that is holistic and fully self-conscious right down into the depths of its soul-filled activity. The capacity for this thinking came through the Mystery of Golgotha. It is the working of Christ within the sphere of the heart that creates the possibility for thinking to become a spiritual force within human evolution. We will consider this more fully in the chapter on the northern Mystery stream. For the moment it will suffice to note that the Fall created an inner chasm in humanity, an almost unbridgeable abyss between the human soul and its higher self. The new freedom-filled thinking is the Christ-capacity that will heal the chasm introduced into human consciousness by the Fall.

This understanding was not first put out into the world by Rudolf Steiner, but is in fact the central core of the original, uncorrupted teachings of the Apostle Paul. In his letters and teachings Paul explicated the renewed nature of human consciousness, which will be attained by each man and woman when they absorb into their conscious egos, as a free sacrifice, the overshadowing Ego of Christ. The result of this will be a new faculty of cognition, one that has already begun to manifest in its primal radiance in the works of Goethe and Rudolf Steiner.

If we think of the many selfless hours spent by Goethe studying the sense-perceptible process of plant-formation, of Viktor Schauberger dedicating many long nights to watching the activity of water upon the surface of a pool, we can understand the cognitive dimensions of Paul's teachings on the nature of love: 'Love is patient. Love is kind. It does not envy, it does not boast, it is not proud. It is not rude, it is not self-seeking, it is not easily angered, it keeps no record of wrongs. Love does not delight in evil but rejoices with the truth. It always protects, always trusts, always hopes, always preserves.'[54]

This love is the Christ-cognition that will renew all of human knowledge even as it works transformatively right down into the human physical body, reversing the effects of the Fall that subjected the human body to the effects of centralization and calcification.

The mission of the earth is thus redirected by combating the calcifying effect of the centric forces and restoring the original goal of Earth evolution, a state into which the newly created ego of man can work without the danger of being dragged down into a lower sphere. Then the cosmic Word will once more sound into all the life-forms of creation. The three days in the Underworld marked a turning-point; seeds have been planted for a process that will gradually increase but which can only be accomplished with the cooperation of human individuals working freely out of their own conviction of the necessity and urgency of the task. The intervention of fallen beings in evolution has made it possible for us to act in freedom, but this has had to be paid at a heavy price. All of the entanglements and complications of materialistic civilization, the horror and perversion that faces us daily in the media—where the truth is distorted to goad humanity into further desperation—is the result of our relationship with the same beings who have made it possible to take a giant stride to the next planetary evolution. We shall then move towards Jupiter evolution—the New Jerusalem—as responsible co-workers with the nine Hierarchies above and Christ beside us. Without the intervention of the fallen beings this possibility would not be there. But as a result, the responsibility for mankind is twofold: transformation of evil and the transubstantiation of creation.

8
The Western Mystery Stream: from King Arthur to the Grail

My journey into the 'science of the Grail' had begun with an intuition that the solution to the mysteries of Rennes-le-Château might lie encoded in the area's complex geometrical geography as defined, though in contrasting ways, by Henry Lincoln and David Wood. Certain life-changing experiences had also led me to a deep interest in Wolfram von Eschenbach's version of the Parzival legend. As my interest in Rennes-le-Château had motivated me to read anything I could lay my hands on concerning the Grail I gravitated towards the writings of Walter Johannes Stein, who in his book The Ninth Century—World History in the Light of the Holy Grail *had embarked upon a profound study of the Parzival legend. The authors of* The Holy Blood and the Holy Grail *had related the Grail to a blood-line descending from Jesus down through the Merovingians to modern times, and to a possible 'king of Europe'. Stein mentions a blood-line too when he talks of the Grail Family and its tasks in human evolution. However here there was a parting of the ways, and, backed by my now comprehensive understanding of the Grail cosmology, I was able to begin to discern between the Grail tradition and that anti-Grail tradition which seeks to oppose it. I was also fascinated by Baigent, Leigh and Lincoln's reference to a 'secret Mystery stream' and this prompted me to search deeply into the various European Mystery streams for clues as to the workings of both the Grail and anti-Grail traditions. In many ways the theme of the Mystery streams lies at the heart of this book, and these next four chapters could be seen as the four chambers of the human heart.*

I soon discovered that the Mystery stream flowing into Europe from the West was involved with the secrets of the etheric. The aspect of this stream that most interested me was that connected to King Arthur and his knights. In this chapter on the western Mystery stream I interweave these varied themes, of the Grail and the anti-Grail, of King Arthur, of the earth energy at Rennes-le-Château and of the young knight Parzival who begins within the stream of Arthur but is destined for a much higher goal.

In many of his lecture cycles Rudolf Steiner has indicated how myths and legends embody folk memories concerning spiritual and historical events. This can be seen as one of the reasons why folk tales and sagas appear simultaneously in otherwise separate cultures. Considered from this point of view, ideas and teachings that have their origins in the spiritual world would be expected to appear simultaneously in far-flung geographical locations. Similar methods of pyramid construction, for instance, could have developed at the same time in Egypt and Mexico without the aid of a Kontiki-style odyssey as a means of conveying information.

History, as we know, is written by the victors. Others, wishing to preserve unorthodox spiritual teachings and to record threatened historical information, could adopt the technique of translating the material into *pictorial imagery* familiar to the local culture. In this way 'forbidden knowledge' could be preserved, visible yet concealed, until decoded by those who were wise or knowledgeable enough to divine the hidden meanings.

A modern example of this process are the prophetic poems of William Blake. Blake lived at a time when laws against sedition imposed a strict web of censorship upon the common culture. Blake wrote his poems in a mythological style to record both his spiritual teachings and his thoughts about the historical events of his day.

In his book *The Mystery of Arthur at Tintagel*, Richard Seddon, an innovative Arthurian scholar, comments concerning the legends of King Arthur:

> We know that in 1113 a belief existed in Cornwall that Arthur was not dead but recuperating somewhere, and that his return was awaited, because a riot broke out in Bodmin when visiting French priests dared to question it. We have William of Malmesbury's assurance in 1125 that the belief

> was also widespread in Brittany.[55]

Richard Seddon continues by exploring the implications of this belief. There was, he says:

> an obvious political implication that before long Britain would be freed from foreign yoke, an implication seized on by both Henry I and Henry VII in naming their eldest son Arthur—in both cases to no avail. But the thesis of this study has been that 'Arthur' was a rank, the leader of a Mystery school that existed at Tintagel for many centuries prior to the fifth century AD. In this sense the 'return of Arthur' would point to the renewal of a spiritual impulse, leading to a culture once again based on spiritual-moral values.[56]

In his essay 'Is King Arthur an Historical Character?' Walter Johannes Stein suggests that: 'Behind the historical figure of Arthur works a superhuman spiritual being leading invisibly, but most powerfully, the whole history of the island kingdom. Putting aside all differences of races he seems to embrace Celts, Scots, Normans, French, and even Germans in different epochs of history. He places the island kingdom as the centre not only of a European but of an all-embracing human culture.'[57] Later in the same essay, while discussing the contribution of Thomas Malory to the Arthurian corpus, Stein continues:

> In his preface to Malory's work Caxton says: 'In the Abbey of Westminster, at St Edward's shrine, remaineth the print of his seal in red wax closed in beryl, in which is written Patricius Arturus, Britanniae, Galliae, Germaniae, Daciae, Imperator.' The name of Arthur is given to St Edward in the same way as William of Malmesbury, speaking of Ambrosius Aurelianus, the hero of the Battle of Mons Badonicus, calls this man, having quite another name, 'Arturus'. This is the real hero of the British tales. The name is used as a synonymous term for a certain type of hero. There have been many King Arthurs and the title was

> given to all those who honoured and worked for the continuity of the evolution of the island kingdom in such a way that the progress and evolution of other nations were included. About Edward all these things can be said, so we can therefore understand that he was given this title. Many years after his death, therefore, St Edward received the title 'Patricius Arturus' and it was sealed on his tomb. Those who did this must have had powerful authority behind them to have obtained the necessary permission and the existence of the seal must have been a fact which could be proved by any person who visited Westminster Abbey, Caxton speaking of it as common knowledge. This shows that a society of knights must have existed closely connected with the royal house. The name of Arthur was used by this society because they worked for the historical continuity of the best traditions of the island.[58]

The Arthurian knights utilized a body of symbolism and star knowledge drawn from many different times and cultures, hence emphasizing the cosmopolitan nature of their impulse. Richard Seddon ruminates further on the origin of the name 'Arthur':

> The name would be pre-Celtic in origin, and only later Romanized as 'Arturus', rather than the other way round as commonly supposed. Rhys pointed out last century that the syllable 'Art' is related to the Gaulish goddess Artio, German Etra/Nerthus, English 'Earth'; and that this Brythonic stream led to a group of words in Cornish and Welsh around 'ardu', to plough. The second syllable is likely to derive from the name of the sun-god Hu, the pre-Christian name of Christ. The name 'Arthur' thus expresses accurately the connection between sun and earth as the central experience of the Arthurian knights in the weaving sunlight and nature forces at Tintagel.[59]

According to Rudolf Steiner, before the incarnation of Christ, Hibernian Mystery centres in the West perceived Him approaching as the descending Sun Spirit. The legends of King

Arthur point to a time before the historical king, to a figure who represents these western Mysteries and who knew of the incarnating Christ before the event in Palestine had occurred.

When Rudolf Steiner visited Tintagel Castle in Cornwall he described his impressions of the location:

> Before the Mystery of Golgotha had come to pass, the knights of King Arthur's Round Table stood on these rocks, gazed at the play between the sun-born spirits and the earth-born spirits, and felt that the forces living in this play of nature spirits poured into their hearts and above all through their etheric bodies. Therewith they received into themselves the Christ-impulse which was then streaming away from the sun and was living in everything that is brought into being by the sun-forces. And so, before the Mystery of Golgotha, the knights of King Arthur received into themselves the Sun Spirit, that is to say the Christ as He was in pre-Christian times.[60]

In his Torquay lectures Rudolf Steiner further describes his impressions at the ruins of Tintagel:

> This interplay between the sunlit air and the rippling, foam-crested waves continues to this day; over the sea and the rocky cliffs at this place, nature is still quick with spirit. But to take hold of the spirit-forces working there in nature would have been beyond the power of one individual alone. A group of men was necessary, one of whom felt himself as the representative of the sun at the centre, and whose twelve companions were trained in such a way that in temperament, disposition and manner of acting, all of them together formed a twelvefold whole—twelve individual men grouped as the zodiacal constellations are grouped around the sun. Such was the Round Table: King Arthur was at the centre surrounded by the twelve, above each of whom a zodiacal symbol was displayed, indicating the particular cosmic influence with which he was associated. Civilizing forces went out from this place to Europe. It was here that King Arthur and his twelve knights

> drew into themselves from the sun the strength wherewith to set forth on their mighty expeditions through Europe in order to battle with the wild demonic powers of old still dominating large masses of the population, and to drive them out of men. Under the guidance of King Arthur these twelve were battling for outer civilization.[61]

By preparing these early Europeans to overcome the passions and desires of their lower natures, King Arthur and his knights were paving the way for a much later time when the human individual could become a purified vessel, a Grail, to hold the Christ. This is where legends have originated that tell of the questing knights who ventured forth to slay wild beasts and to save princesses from the clutches of terrible dragons; these are the creatures which rise up out of the wild, untamed astrality of the lower nature.

This 'Arthurian impulse' plays an important role in one of the most important legends of our time—the story of Parzival, particularly in the form developed by Wolfram von Eschenbach. The basis for a definitive study of Wolfram von Eschenbach's *Parzival* was established by the historian and philosopher Walter Johannes Stein in his book *The Ninth Century—World History in the Light of the Holy Grail.*

Stein was born in Vienna on 6 February 1891. He received a superb education at the Schottengymnasium, a school run by Benedictine monks, and later studied mathematics, physics, and the history of philosophy at Vienna University. In 1919 he was employed by Rudolf Steiner to teach history and literature at the first Waldorf school in Stuttgart.

The regular process of teaching and exploring *Parzival* with his pupils led Stein to become intrigued by its strangeness and complexity. Official scholarly views located *Parzival* within the genre of historical romance, an entertaining and innovative, yet essentially straightforward account of the adventures of knights and their ladies set in the Middle Ages. Scholars puzzled over the structure of the poem, however, some even going as far as to publish new editions with vast tracts of the poem excised on the assumption that much of

Dr Walter Johannes Stein

what Eschenbach had written was irrelevant to the plot! But Stein began to find profound meaning in the structure of the book. He noted that the same events often occurred twice, and that such incredible attention was given to detail that nothing, not even the most seemingly irrelevant reference, could be dismissed.

Stein was intrigued by the fact that Eschenbach claimed to be unable to either read or write. The occasional self-pitying reference within the book revealed Eschenbach to be a poor knight with his own share of personal troubles. Yet this impoverished knight had written his *Parzival* from out of supersensible perception. There could be little doubt that despite all outward appearances Wolfram von Eschenbach was an initiate of a high order.

In consultation with Steiner, Stein was given several clues that would catapult him into fevered activity. Steiner pointed out the part in the text which states that Parzival's mother lived eleven generations before Eschenbach himself, locating the events firmly within the ninth century. Steiner suggested that this hidden historical background was a central determining factor of the book's content: 'In the description of Parzival's experiences we can see very well that the conditions of the eighth or ninth centuries are being described. Those were times of bloodshed. Men were accustomed to live among bloodshed. And at that time too there were wild forests everywhere, and there men fought. The amount of blood that was shed is really a characteristic of the eighth and ninth centuries.'[62] Stein later quotes from the poem itself:

> ...This root of all goodness [Parzival's mother Herzeleide]
> From whom the shoot of humility has flowered.
> Woe! that there have not remained to us
> Her children to the eleventh generation
> So much is false around us.[63]

Stein comments: 'Thus according to the statement of Wolfram von Eschenbach, Herzeleide lived eleven generations earlier than Wolfram himself, i.e. about 870.'[64]

Stein soon came to see that while the vivid pictorial events depicted in the poem were of universal spiritual significance, they also pointed to a concrete place and time. Behind the mythical figures in the poem there were actual personalities. By uncovering the exact historical background to the poem Stein would be able to throw new light upon the Mysteries of the Grail.

A logical place to look for the exact historical events behind *Parzival* seemed to be within the context of the courts established by Charles the Great. Stein began to search for a link between these courts and the quest for the Grail. The religion espoused in *Parzival* suggested a variant of Manichaeism, stressing that 'God is Light' and that evil could be redeemed through the activity of human beings. The strong influence of Roman Christianity upon Charlemagne and the Frankish kingdoms seemed to militate against such a heretical influence. However, Stein uncovered several documents that threw light upon a forgotten influence at work in

Charlemagne's environment. These two documents, which are reproduced in the second chapter of *The Ninth Century*, relate legends connected with associates of the king, namely, Waldo, a bishop, and the knight Hugo of Tours. Both come into possession of a blood relic of Christ. In the Tours version the blood relic later comes to the monastery on the Odilienberg, founded by St Odile several centuries earlier.

The crowning of Charles as Roman Emperor in AD 800 pushed the Manichaean stream underground. All historical references to this underground stream were later repressed.

Eschenbach gives us scintillating hints in his poem as to the sources of his work, and the individual from whom he had received his secret knowledge. In the poem, Parzival is a young Arthurian knight who is destined to become the Guardian of the Grail. Stein quotes Steiner on the subject of knighthood: 'From time to time shining forms of light clad in scintillating armour passed through the forest. When they came to inhabited places, the people met together and conferred with one another and no longer went out to fight and plunder. These knight errants, who appeared from time to time in their flashing armour, sought to establish in this bloodthirsty age an order that was based on bloodshed. The central body of these knights was formed by the knights of King Arthur or, as we may also call them, knights of the sword.'[65]

Parzival's father, Gahmuret, is a knight who wishes to serve 'the greatest man in the land' , a cosmopolitan impulse that leads him into the service of the Islamic Caliph. Gahmuret has two children: firstly Feirefis, born of a Muslim princess; later his half-brother Parzival whose Christian mother was Herzeleide. Gahmuret dies in battle and Parzival's heartbroken mother withdraws with her new-born son and brings him up alone and isolated from the world. Parzival grows up in complete ignorance of the traditions of knighthood. When the young Parzival asks his mother 'Who is God?' she instructs him in the Manichaean teachings that God is the Light of the World who took on human form. When at a later date some knights pass through the forest, their armour shining brightly in the sun, Parzival mistakes them for godlike beings.

Wishing to become like them he abandons Herzeleide, and rides off to search for King Arthur. In a final attempt to keep him from harm Herzeleide dresses her son in jester's clothing, and gives him an ass to ride on.

Ignorant of the ways of the world, Parzival inadvertently causes suffering to those he encounters on his journey. After becoming a knight and marrying, he abandons his wife in order to return to visit his mother. He does not know that she had died of heartbreak on the day that he left her. Parzival's mother is now part of the spiritual world, the starry heavens, and in his search for her Parzival enters *unconsciously* into the spiritual realm. Here he discovers the Grail Castle. Few find their way into this castle. However the squire guarding the drawbridge recognizes Parzival's humility and the power of love that slumbers within him, and lowers the drawbridge.

Upon his arrival at the castle, Parzival is greeted with great joy and a banquet is held in his honour. Amfortas, the Grail King, has been wounded by the black magician Klingsor. Klingsor has struck him a blow to the groin with a lance. This spear is shown to new arrivals at the Grail Castle.[66] It is carried, dripping with blood, through the great hall in the hope that the guest, filled with compassion at the immense and tragic sorrow of the Grail King, will rouse his slumbering faculties into action and become a healing force.

Parzival witnesses the immense agony of the Grail King, but remains silent and passive. When he awakens the next morning the castle is deserted and he rides out alone again. The castle closes its doors to him and he experiences this as a kind of 'Fall'. Only after much personal suffering and heartbreak can he return to the castle—this time as a healing force. This second time he also brings with him his Muslim brother, Feirefis, who cannot see the Grail but who falls in love with the maiden who carries the Grail—and so attains to the Grail too.

Parzival's path of development leads him from *Arthurian knight* to *Grail knight*. He unites these two when he becomes capable of compassion and heals the wounded Amfortas. Eschenbach uses his poem to elucidate the Grail motto:

'Through compassion to self-knowledge'.

This brief synopsis has not dealt with all the rich complexities of the Parzival legend, but has brought out several central motifs. The Grail is associated with healing. Parzival and his half-brother are of different religions and blood-lines yet they *both* attain the Grail. Amfortas is healed not by magic but by Parzival's heartfelt compassion for his suffering. The Grail is the embodiment of these healing and reconciling forces.

Parzival joins together two streams. The Arthurian stream proceeding, as explained earlier in this chapter, from the West, and the Grail stream coming from the East. This is the significance of his transition from Arthurian knight to Grail King.[67] This eastern stream found its highest form in what has come to be called Manichaeism. To understand the importance of the Frankish tribes within this, we must take a deeper look into the background of the western Mystery stream.

From the West, the survivors of the Atlantean catastrophe brought with them the secret of the Tree of Life: of the two ethers whose control had been denied to mankind after the Fall. This secret had been preserved in the Atlantean Mystery centres where the Atlantean initiates had for a time kept it well guarded, only using it in a controlled way for the benefit of society. However, after a time, its misuse by certain of these initiates brought about the destruction of Atlantis. This has been described as follows:

> They commanded the elements, made fine weather or storm as it pleased them. There were no children, for by an effort of unnatural power they attained to the great secret of causing life without the material union of the two forces. The soul returned and reincarnated by an effort of will, taking its form from the natural elements without any other medium. This was what ultimately ended their power, for it could not be allowed to continue. It is dimly figured in the late Hebrew legend by the 'Tree of Life'. There was nothing left of progression and therefore the cataclysm had to overtake this civilization and destroy even its memory. They overset the balance of creation and so ruined their

> civilization. The material cause was that they withdrew the life-force of the earth, and exhausted all supplies of the life-current. This caused convulsions of nature and the storm broke irredeemable, terrible and swamped them. [The] earth is a living creature, and if you tap its life-current you can work all miracles. The Atlanteans are the souls of today in some cases but they have been discrowned...They had to return into ordinary life by the simple way of being born as an ordinary infant.[68]

Here is a possible connection with Rennes-le-Château. It would be reasonable to assume that when Atlantis sank below the waves those who had caused the catastrophe would attempt to rescue as much of their land as they could. The western edge of Europe could in fact be a relic of ancient Atlantis. The lines of earth-energy which ran across Atlantis, having been worked from very ancient times, were lost beneath the ocean. Certain sacred sites that were preserved above sea level along this western fringe of Europe, which was salvaged during the Deluge, are places where etheric energy is concentrated allowing the energy of the earth to interchange with the 'formative forces' from the cosmos. In ancient times these sites would have been dedicated to the 'Sacred Marriage'—earth goddess to sky god. Rennes-le-Château could well be an important site of this nature. It is a 'sacral' point of major significance which relates through various lines to a main line of chakras running from Les Saintes Marie de la Mare near Marseilles up through France and England to the north coast of Scotland. It is therefore reasonable to assume that this is a site that was used in Atlantean times to 'incarnate' the rebel Atlantean initiates, where they literally 'siphoned out' the 'energy before matter' rising up from within the earth.

There is a correlation between each of the four ethers and certain geometrical symbols. The exact nature of this connection is still controversial, but there exists at the very least a symbolic correlation between the circle, the triangle, the crescent, the square, and the warmth, light, chemical and life-

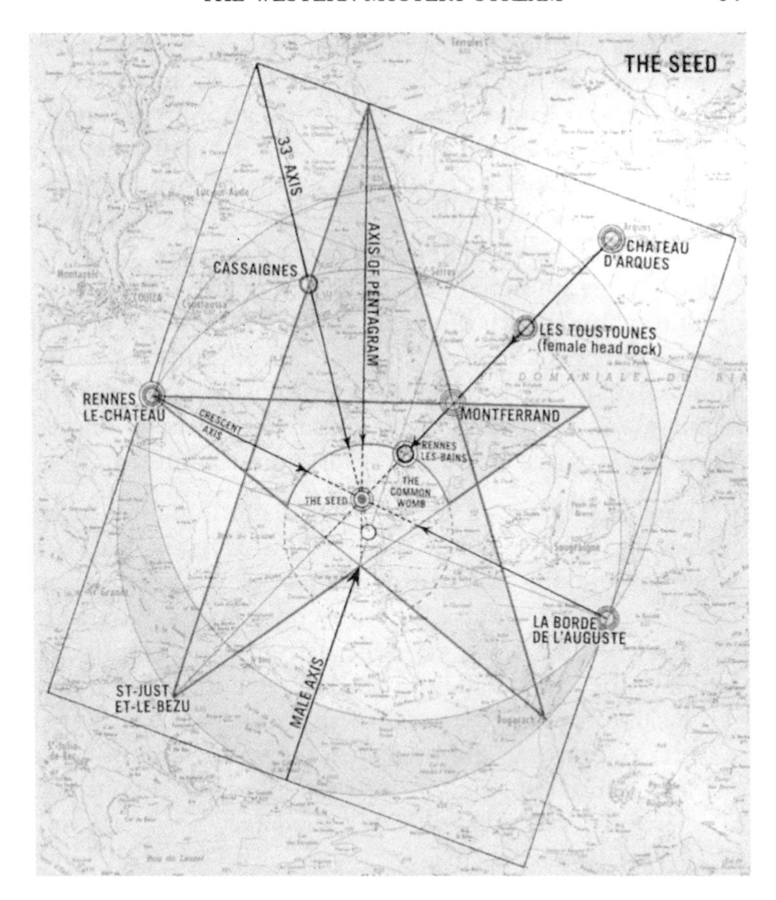

David Wood—an experienced cartographer and surveyor—used precise mathematical and geometrical calculations to uncover the existence of a vast pentagram at Rennes-le-Château. The design of this immense earth temple incorporates the geometrical symbols for the four ethers (see diagram 4), while the pentagram itself relates directly to the working of the etheric.

ethers respectively. In David Wood's *Genisis* the central point of Diagram 105[69] is surrounded by a circle, then by two triangles which he interprets as a five-pointed star; further out there are two crescents, while the entire figure is enclosed by a huge square. These could mark the development of creation from Ancient Saturn to the present earth which is repeated in the development of the human foetus from conception to birth. This seeming representation of the ethers spread over the terrain surrounding Rennes-le-Château recreates the birth of matter from the point of its inception in the spirit.

The constellation that impinges upon the zodiac between Scorpio and Sagittarius—Ophiucus, the Serpent Bearer—has been connected with Rennes-le-Château. In recent years attempts have been made to establish Ophiucus as the so-called 'thirteenth sign' of the zodiac. In reality Ophiucus lies beyond Scorpio, with the 'head' of the Serpent reaching up beyond Virgo and Libra, and the tail beyond Sagittarius. Although it does play a role in esoteric cosmology, Ophiucus is not a zodiacal sign. In an unpublished essay, anthroposophical researcher Margaret Jonas points out that:

> There can be only 12 constellations of the zodiac; occult teaching is clear about this. But at different historical periods the star wisdom of various civilizations has included consideration of the other constellations also. Little is known of this today and most astrologers are indifferent to the other constellations, which do not presumably carry the same formative forces for the earth and the human being as do the 12. For instance, the terrestrial 'zodiac' at Glastonbury consists of a mixture of zodiacal constellations and others lying outside the zodiac.[70]

David Wood has suggested that a line runs between Scorpio and Sagittarius, down through Gemini and Taurus on the opposite side of the zodiacal circle. He calls this the 'serpent' line and relates it to electromagnetic forces. This makes sublime sense if considered in the light of spiritual science. Ophiucus healed by the use of springs and spas, thus he is indicated as having control over the 'water' or chemical ether. It was this ether that, as we have seen, degenerated into magnetism. The term 'serpent line' suggests an association with the terrestrial 'ley' lines which could be seen as carrying currents of etheric force that have descended to the level of sub-ethers. In passing it is worth mentioning that Orion, the constellation just beyond Gemini and Taurus, was used by the ancient priestly astronomers for gauging the alignments used in the building of the stone circles. Orion was supposed to have been given the power to walk on water and is thus related also to the chemical ether.

In the essay quoted above, Margaret Jonas mentions the legend wherein King Amangons raped one of the virginal maidens who protected the springs that often marked key points along the leys. After this act of desecration the land went to waste. King Arthur and his knights had to seek the Holy Grail in order to restore the land. We can trace a set of concepts here that relate back to the fall of Lucifer (the Serpent) who, in falling, brought the power of his wisdom to the earth where it became electrical energy. As a result of the Fall, humanity was divided into separate sexes. An electro-chemical response was incorporated within the human organism to act as the basis of sexual attraction. The Holy Grail sought by King Arthur in this legend is the true knowledge of the ethers, which alone can heal the earth.

With the division of the human race into male and female at the time of the Fall came the need to reproduce. In the microcosm of the human organism Scorpio is the genitals and the reproductive organs. Sagittarius corresponds with the thighs. In between these lies the etheric centre known to esotericists as the four-petalled lotus flower, situated at the base of the spine. Rudolf Steiner informs us that this is associated with the moon, and was implanted during the time of the Fall. From the moon, the Elohim Yahveh implanted the power of love, in the form of heredity, into the human blood. This 'moon force' in the human spine relates to the Kundalini. On the opposite side of the circle, Gemini corresponds in the microcosm to the shoulders and arms, and Taurus to the throat. Between them is the 16-petalled lotus flower associated with Mars. The planet Mars is correlated with the power of sexual desire and speech. Rudolf Steiner has indicated that in the distant future the moon will reunite with the earth. By this time the process of human reproduction will have changed. Humans will reproduce through the power of the word, in imitation of the cosmic Logos. The mouth and vocal chords are metamorphosed from the sexual organs. They are the future bearers of a form of reproduction imbued with genuine love.

We have discussed in relation with the mission of the Christ on earth how the bonds of blood ties were to be replaced by ties based on love and brotherhood. When the human race has learnt to control the 'sound' ether wisely and has evolved into the fullness of objective communal love, then these powers associated with the 'serpent line' will be able to be used wisely. However, Rudolf Steiner has pointed out that there would be those who would wish to take hold of these powers prematurely and use them in their fallen state for unlawful ends. We may be close here to the hidden agenda of those who currently wish to resuscitate Ophiucus as a 'thirteenth sign'. If 12 is deeply associated with the Grail Mysteries we could be looking at an *anti-Grail* current that wishes to preserve the impulses of the past, namely, to keep humanity chained within the matrix of blood ties. These people would wish to see a humanity united under old forms of leadership, replacing individuality and brotherhood with identification with a single unified state. The ruler of this state would need to be someone whose blood-line is of great importance. An article in a magazine published by the Priory of Zion argued for a 13-sign zodiac, and we have already noted their interest in placing a king descended from the Merovingians on the throne of Europe.[71]

Ophiucus is depicted as carrying a caduceus in one hand. The caduceus is constituted by two serpents entwining about a central pole. The caduceus could be seen as a representation of DNA. In the normal process of incarnation, the incoming soul is guided to choose a position somewhere within the 12 signs of the zodiac in order to fulfil his karma, or destiny, in the forthcoming life on earth.

However, if one came into incarnation as a maverick one might need a maverick sign under which to incarnate, and enter brandishing an individualized DNA spiral. It is rather like landing at a large, well-organized airport in one's own home-made aeroplane between flight schedules on one of the official runways, in full view of the horrified officials in the control tower.

It is interesting to note that the birthday connected with this sign, 22 November, is also St Cecilia's Day. St Cecilia is the patron saint of music. We have already seen a connection between the Music of the Spheres and the ethers. In his book *The Music of the Spheres* Jamie James points out that:

> Another departure from the Platonic Model in 'Scipio's Dream' is the emphasis on man, particularly on man the music maker. As we have seen, in the Pythagorean-Platonic cosmos music exists quite independently of man: *musica instrumentalis* is harmonious because it reflects the perfection of the cosmos in the world of ideal forms; an octave sounds harmonious to human ears because the rhythms of the music are in concord with our own internal rhythms, the *musica humana*. Yet Cicero clearly makes the connection between excellent music and the excellent life. 'Skilled men' (*homines docti*) who are able to imitate the Music of the Spheres on stringed instruments or with their voices are permitted to return to heaven. It may also mean 'Those men who have been initiated or indoctrinated'.[72]

With our knowledge of reincarnation we could surmise that certain initiation knowledge in one lifetime could resurface as musical ability in a future life.

Over western Europe, before exoteric Christianity had filtered in from the East, there spread the cultures of the early European tribes: Goths, Visigoths, Lombardi, Suevi, Vandals and Franks. 'In this ancient Europe a group of human beings had been preserved who had not been taken away from sharing in the Tree of Life; in whom there lived on, so to speak, the trees of life: ash and elm. In Europe something was left over as it were, like a treasured remnant of the forces of life.'[73] In these peoples the forces of the Tree of Life to a certain extent still flowed through their blood.

One can here understand how there could be a certain *similarity* between the blood of the Merovingian dynasty in France and the figure of Jesus—the *'Luke'* Jesus-child whose blood was vivified with the full power of the life and chemical ethers, forces of the Tree of Life—an unexpected connection but not a hereditary one.

A clue to this may be concealed in a legend that Merovee, after whom the Merovingian line was named, was born of two fathers. His mother, according to this legend, had been impregnated by both her husband, King Clodio and by a sea monster. The legend then points out that two blood streams flowed in the veins of Merovee, one human and one semi-divine or extraterrestrial.

Baigent, Lincoln and Leigh state that: 'By virtue of his dual blood Merovee was said to have been endowed with an impressive array of superhuman powers. And whatever the historical actuality behind the legend, the Merovingian dynasty continued to be mantled in an aura of magic, sorcery and the supernatural. According to tradition, Merovingian monarchs were occult adepts, initiates in arcane sciences, practitioners of esoteric arts...They were often called "the sorcerer kings" or "thaumaturge kings". By virtue of some miraculous property in their blood they could allegedly heal by laying on of hands; and according to one account the tassels at the fringes of their robes were deemed to possess miraculous curative powers.'[74]

As the survivors of the Atlantean disaster moved eastwards, new Mystery centres were established in their wake. At Chartres in northern France a Mystery centre was established on the site where centuries later the cathedral would be built after the advent of Christianity. An effigy of the Black Virgin was venerated at Chartres in pre-Christian times and was later kept in a cave under the cathedral until it was destroyed in one of the many fires which it has suffered in its long history.

There are clues to be found at Chartres which lead one to believe that in the early traditions of its founders, both pre-Christian and Christian, there was knowledge of the life force and of its connection with the Christ Being. The relic around which the cathedral is built—the veil worn by the Virgin Mary when she gave birth to Jesus—is refreshingly unusual, being a symbol of life instead of death. There are strange stories of how all efforts to bury the dead there were thwarted; the cathedral itself rejected the bodies, and strange rumbling noises were heard when the attempt was made.

Chartres is located over Granite. Granite manifests a preponderance of the effect of the life ether as it is thrust up from the deepest rock layers of the earth which, as we saw in a previous chapter, is the realm of the life ether which also manifests its fallen quality. Pierre Morizot writes about Chartres from this point of view in his article *The School at Chartres*:

> Again we may ask: why were those places chosen? The study of etheric forces has provided Rudolf Steiner with the answer. In some regions of the globe the crust of the earth has subsided to a marked degree, while the emergence of powerful chains of mountains has distributed the concentric layers of the etheric forces which, from the core of our planet, rise up to the highest reaches of our atmosphere. Thus gigantic fissures have enabled man to come into close contact with etheric influences differing from those of his natural surroundings. Such are the deep valleys which form the bed of the river Jordan, the Dead Sea, the lakes of the upper Engadine, and the clefts where are to be found the caves of Chartres, Lourdes and Delphi. Our physical frame has lost its elasticity and become rigid, but, in the distant past, man was highly sensitive to these differences in etheric activity...Where there is a cavity of characteristic form and geological nature, the forces issuing from the earth escape from the ground and enable the inhabitants to put into use faculties which, normally, are dormant in man. Chartres had no Pythia dwelling at the foot of a cliff, as in Delphi, no Sybil living in a cavern-like Cumae, but it had its priests, who prophesied or, to use the Latin word, vaticinated.[75]

There are also indications that the Knights Templar incorporated their knowledge into the construction of the Gothic building on the site, bringing back certain secrets connected with the 'Cosmic Word' from their time spent in the vicinity of Solomon's Temple in Jerusalem.

Chartres became an established centre for the original, vibrant Christianity which had been strongly influenced by Platonism and the impulses of the lively Celtic Christianity which emanated from Ireland and which in turn owed much to Gnosticism and the Coptic Church in Egypt. Chartres became a centre for the Cistercians who worked creatively with agriculture and healing, sending this knowledge from Chartres to communities all over Europe.

The School of Chartres was renowned throughout the medieval world; among its great teachers were Bishop Fulbertius, Alanus ab Insulis, John of Salisbury (a friend of Thomas à Becket), Bernardus Silvestris and Joachim de Flora.

The Extern Stones in the Teutoberg forest near Paderborn in eastern Germany stand in another Mystery centre founded by the migrating Atlanteans.

> This temple was 80 feet above ground because it was on a sandstone rock extending that height above the general level. The people do not realize that they have there one of the deepest and holiest Mystery places. This is shown by the fact that through the opening between the outer and the inner area there runs a streetcar line. There is a hole in the stone with an altar in front of it. When you stand before the altar and look through the hole in the stone you see some hills on the far horizon. About 15000 BC, the sun set over the central hill on the day of the winter solstice. This shows when the centre was founded. At the foot of this rock there is another rock with a grave hewn in it. Here in the dark men could lie for three days in the Temple Sleep of initiation. These rocks are the oldest documents that man has of the original Mysteries of the sun as they were brought from Atlantis. When these men under the leadership of Skythianos landed in Europe they founded this centre and practised there the Temple Sleep and the resurrection from the grave.[76]

It has already been mentioned that the neighbourhood of south-eastern France around Rennes-le-Château was a

Mystery centre in ancient times, and also that it was possibly misused by the Atlantean initiates at an even earlier time. Those familiar with earth energies have identified the area as being particularly powerful. Montségur, the fortress which sheltered the Cathars during the penultimate siege before their obliteration at the hands of Pope Innocent IV's army, was built on a place where in former times there was a solar temple.

In his book *The Templars* the French anthroposophist Pierre Morizot speaks of the Montsalvat of the Grail Legend:

> This magical name was applied to several centres where the knights dedicated to the 'Quest of the Grail', as it was called, could develop the forces and receive the teachings needed for their purposes. Tintagel on the Cornish coast may have been a Montsalvat, just as a castle hidden in the forest of Broceliande or a forbidding dungeon on top of some Vosgian hill. Rugged Montserrat towering above the Catalan plains, proud Montségur in the heart of the Pyrenees were perhaps such sanctuaries. Some places seem to be predestined by etheric geography to become centres where supersensible impulses meet the external conditions necessary for their realization on the plane of history and it is an inspiring thought that one of them indirectly connected with the impulse emanating from Saint Odile and the tradition of Parsival was selected by Rudolf Steiner for the centre of the Anthroposophical Movement.[77]

Earlier in this chapter it was described how the earthly body of man could be seen as the chalice of the Grail developing towards the possibility of holding the Christ within. So too these Mystery centres, which have already been considerably transformed, are waiting, together with other places of intensified etheric activity, for sufficiently developed human beings to bring about their transformation through taking the Christ into themselves. In both cases, within the human being and within the earth, the chalice begins to hold the Host.

9
The Eastern Mystery Stream

> Against the earth Cain sinned, with the earth he remained united, and the earth he must redeem.
>
> Walter Johannes Stein

My discovery of Walter Johannes Stein's book The Ninth Century *furnished me with much inspiration, but especially in dealing with the eastern Mystery stream which holds the essence of Manichaeism—the transformation of the dark by the light. I came to see that the eastern Mysteries are the Mysteries of the Host which descended to the chalice of the Grail. In the following chapter we explore the theme of the redemption of evil, and look closer into the activities of the Grail family as they reached out to the East in order to rescue from there the original wisdom of Aristotle and of esoteric Christianity.*

According to the teachings of esoteric Christianity, the fallen powers—the spirits of darkness—are incorporated into the human structure, there awaiting redemption. This spiritual fact, of such profound consequence for human life, was meant to have become an integral part of all Christian teaching via the Persian, Manichaean impulse coming from the East. However, the content of the original eastern Mystery stream was destined to be changed by what Walter Johannes Stein has described as 'the Arabianizing of Aristotelianism'.

In Rudolf Steiner's spiritual research it is shown how Plato had passed on to his pupil Aristotle the task of translating into conceptual form the substance of the ancient primeval Mysteries. Walter Johannes Stein mentions that:

> Preserved as it was in the oriental Mysteries this primeval wisdom found its last pictorial expression in the magnificent mythical pictures of Platonic philosophy. In the

Symposium, in the Banquet of Plato, there still live Grail Mysteries. Plato is the last oriental, his pupil Aristotle the first westerner. We know from the spiritual investigations of Rudolf Steiner that an important conversation took place between Plato and Aristotle, in which Plato demanded from Aristotle that he should henceforth transmit the whole of the primeval wisdom divested of pictures in the form of concepts used in the West.[78]

This process was the earthly reflection, within the consciousness of humanity, of the descent of the cosmic Logos from the spiritual heights. Christ came to redeem evil, and we can find a reflection of this process in the ideas of Aristotle. Walter Johannes Stein continues:

> What has Aristotle to do with evil? If we study his philosophy in this light we find in it the thought of transubstantiation. It is the idea of the transformation and spiritualization of the substance of nature. The thoughts of Aristotle have the power of spiritualizing matter and evil and changing them. That is why Christianity absorbed the thought world of Aristotle, for the central point of the Christian Mystery, the transubstantiation of substance in the Mass, can only be grasped with Aristotelian ideas. While the Logos Himself was descending there grew within humanity the faculty of knowledge to comprehend the Logos. It was with the thought-structure of Aristotle, that is with the metamorphosed primeval wisdom, that the Middle Ages sought to understand the Christ impulse. At first of course the world evolution was such that no people on earth were so adapted to understand Jesus of Nazareth as the Persians who had prophesied of Him. Christ the Risen One however could be understood in a grand way by the Greeks. By a union of the Persian and Greek nature an understanding for the divine-human was rendered possible. But that which had been prepared by a wise world guidance did not come to pass. The Greek nature did not unite with the Persian impulse but with the

Arabs. And Arabism came to the West via the Arabs.[79]

It was this conceptualized wisdom of Aristotle that the Arab philosophers took hold of, introducing into it a greater materialism and rigidity. This 'contamination' of the eastern stream was to have far-reaching consequences.

We have already mentioned that the eastern stream was essentially Manichaean. Rudolf Steiner speaks of Manichaeism as 'a spiritual movement which although at first only a small sect became a mighty spiritual current. The Albigensians, Waldenses and Cathars of the Middle Ages are a continuation of this current to which also belong the Knights Templar...and also by a remarkable chain of circumstances—the Freemasons.'[80]

Manichaeism arose in Asia Minor in the third century AD. Mani, its founder, was born in AD 216 in Babylon and lived mostly in Iran. On his mother's side he was connected with Iranian royalty who had been overthrown by the Sassanian dynasty. His real name was probably Kurkat or Kubricios. Mani was brought up as a Christian in a Jewish-Christian community—El Kasai. There had been very little exoteric knowledge of him until the beginning of the twentieth century when archaeological finds, especially by German teams, unearthed information from central Asia where a Manichaean settlement was found in the Turfan depression near the Gobi desert.

One reason for the misunderstanding of Mani's teachings may have been that they have only been passed down in fragmented documents. Rudolf Steiner's spiritual research has, however, made it possible to obtain a much clearer and more extensive understanding of these teachings. Walter Johannes Stein quotes extensively from the Manichaean teachings:

> Evil has not existed as evil from the beginning but only in the elements. For what is good and right is different for different times. Thus, what at first worked for good because it belonged to the time later works injuriously. Taken merely in the elements then, evil is of the same origin as

good, and it too therefore is without end. As evil it does end. But it determines its own end, being placed in a position to do so by the sacrificial act of the good which freely mingled with it. In order that good shall be able to redeem evil, it develops to the extent that, while separated from it, it has the power through partly uniting with evil to place it in the position of becoming good also, out of free will, stimulated by the radiant light of the good. Now because evil has five members while good has seven, the good only remains by itself at the beginning and end. But during the middle period of its evolution it dips down into the five and redeems the harmony of the twelvefoldness. [Here reference is made to the seven light and the five dark constellations in the sun's course.] Therefore the Godhead, King of the Paradise of Light, adopts five members. His members are Gentleness, Knowledge, Understanding, Silence and Penetration. Five other members are, however, concerned with the heart: Love, Faith, Fidelity, Bravery, Wisdom. As the evolution of the world brought about the severance of the world of light, of the heights, from the dark flood of the depths, there arose Satan from the depths. He was not himself without beginning but was nevertheless without beginning in his parts and elements; thus it was these parts which came together out of the elements and formed themselves into Satan. His head was that of a lion, his trunk was that of a dragon, his wings were like those of a great bird, his tail was that of a water animal, his four feet, however, resembled those of a land animal. As this being had formed itself out of the darkness it was called the Dragon, the Old Serpent. Then he began to destroy, to swallow and to injure other beings, stalking hither and thither to right and left and penetrating below into the depths where he continually brought injury and destruction to all who sought to overpower him. Thereafter he darted upwards into the heights and catching sight of the radiance of the light felt a repugnance towards it. When he further saw that this radiance was only strengthened by coming into contact with its opposite, he was alarmed, crumpled up together limb by limb, and withdrew into his basic elements.

But now once again he darted up into the heights, and now the Light-Earth observed the activity of Satan and his intention to attack and destroy. And as the Earth observed this, behold the world of Insight, the world of Knowledge, then the world of Silence, then the world of Understanding, then the world of Gentleness also observed it. Thereupon the King of the Paradise of Light observed it and considered by what means Satan might be met.

His hosts truly were powerful enough, but in the realms of light there was only good. Therefore He with His righteous Spirit, with His five worlds and with His twelve elements, created a race—the original race of men. This race he sent below that it might mix itself with the darkness. And this race was to fight the Dragon. Then primeval man armed himself with his five supporters, the five gods—with the lightly fluttering breath, with the wind, with the light, with the water and with the fire. The first thing with which he clothed himself was the breath. Over the fluttering breath he wrapped the mantle of light that undulated downwards, and over the light he drew the veil of welling water and protected himself with the blowing wind. Then he took the fire as a shield and lance in his hand and he hastened to descend from Paradise. Then the Dragon armed himself with his five supporters—with the smoke, the flame, the darkness, the scorching wind, the suffocating fumes—he armed himself with them, took them for his shield and went forth against primeval man. They fought for a long time and the Dragon won the victory over man, devoured some of his light and surrounded him with his supporters and his Elements. Then arose the storm, the whirling dance and death, and hell consumed itself. Thus arose the human race. Man however recognized the Friend of Light, the King of the Paradise of Light, and this radiance filled him with delight. For the light of primeval man that the Dragon had swallowed caused the Dragon to feel pleasure in light. 'May light be kindled by light' rejoiced

> man, and the abyss rose even higher and higher, radiating, sparkling, shining and emitting light like a sun. Thus were the spirits of darkness together with all their dependents and their substances redeemed, uplifted, illuminated and warmed, so that the gentleness proved stronger than hatred. In man gentleness redeemed the Dragon from hell.[81]

For Manichaeism, the fallen spirits of darkness were not lost to cosmic evolution for ever. Esoteric Christianity describes how the falling luciferic Powers were incorporated into the human head by the Archangel Michael: 'It is Michael who sent his opponents to man in order that, through taking into himself this luciferic element of opposition, man might acquire his power of reason and all that corresponds to the human head.'[82]

For the Manichaean, as for the later alchemists, evil was to be considered under the sign of the black coal, or carbon. The coal is the unrefined form of the diamond. Carbon is the basis of the human organism, and the process of metamorphosis that turns the coal into the diamond is symbolic of the transformation of the fallen, carbon-based human body and the Powers incorporated into it, into a higher, redeemed form.

Stein says of Mani's teachings that: 'In the true Manichaeism there lives a wonderful moral impulse, a true Christianity; but with a special and peculiar concept of sin. That sin is something that can be made good again, that is the faith of Manichaeism.'[83] Had this stream united with the true teachings of Aristotle, 'we may imagine what a turn history would have taken...We can depict to ourselves what a complete synthesis would have come about between the heathen religions and Christianity.'[84]

It is described how 'as time went on, the esoteric stream was followed by a current which, in the forms of Arabian thought, was becoming increasingly exoteric and formal. What men over in Asia had made of Aristotelian teachings, that too flowed over in the wake of what had been a very spiritual understanding, and under this influence the content of this esoteric stream became more and more materialistic.'[85]

In *The Ninth Century*, Walter Johannes Stein describes the meeting of the western and eastern Mystery streams as they are depicted in the legend of *Flore and Blanscheflur*. Stein devotes a chapter of his book to this poem, which is laced with alchemical symbolism. Wolfram's epic is set against the background of the ninth century and the courts of Charlemagne. *Flore and Blanscheflur* takes place earlier. It deals with a spiritual and political mission inspired by Charlemagne's grandparents. Stein says of it: 'So the legend of Blanscheflur, grandmother of Charles the Great on the mother's side, likewise belongs to the circle of those documents with which we are here concerned. We shall see that in the form of a charming story the greatest world-historic impulse of the eighth and ninth centuries comes to expression.'[86]

In an essay, entitled 'Basilius Valentinus in the Context of Arthurian Legend', Stein relates some of the basics of alchemy: 'According to the alchemists and to the teachings of the Mysteries, human beings are not constituted in the way they should be and must therefore be guided back to their original state. The alchemist sees the occurrence of the Fall as the cause of human deviation from the divine plan of creation, introducing not just moral but also a physiological transformation which has to be reversed.'[87]

In essence, human wisdom and experience were to be renewed through the purification of the astral body. The alchemist sought to attain to the pure innocence that pulsates through the plant world whose etheric forces were not subject to the Fall. For this reason: 'People who were aiming for such goals took plant names such as "Flos" or "Blanscheflur". Or a plant was chosen as a symbol, a rose or a lily for example, when the secrets of higher development were revealed in fairy-tales.'[88]

We have seen how an esoteric Grail-imbued current was at work within the courts of Charlemagne, and how one individual working with this was able to take it to a greater height of realization. The historical figure behind Parzival was living in the last third of the ninth century. He was able to unite the western and eastern streams for the first time. So the Manichaean impulse must have been brought West at an earlier date for its substance to have been available to this individual. Stein shows how *Flore and Blanscheflur* relate to the Carolingian dynasty: 'Charibert de Laon, the maternal grandfather of Charlemagne, longed for the Mysteries of the East. These Mysteries were influenced by Zoroastrianism, the Ancient Persian religion in which the great initiate Zarathustra had given knowledge of the Great Sun Being Ahura Mazdao.'[89]

In the legend, Flore, a young knight, goes to an Arabian court to rescue the maiden betrothed to him who has been sent away to work in the courts as a slave. The pure love of Flore and Blanscheflur eventually melts even the hardened heart of the Caliph who has imprisoned the young girl, and they are allowed to return together to the West. According to Stein, Flore symbolically represents Charibert who inspired his daughter Bertha and King Pippin her husband to send ambassadors to the court of Mansur in Baghdad. This embassy departed from the land of the Franks during Christmas 765 and returned in 768. What they brought back from the court of Al Mansur was symbolized by Blanscheflur: the true soul of Europe, the teachings of Aristotle.

Tragedy befell the Zoroastrian impulse after this embassy left for Europe. The wisdom which had been preserved by the Persian Barmacides was lost when Al Mansur was succeeded as Caliph by Harun-al-Rashid who was painfully aware of the importance of the Persian element and of the power of the Barmacides. Harun-al-Rashid gave orders for the Persian prime minister to be seized from his home and beheaded. Stein relates:

> They tore him violently from his seat and dragged him outside. When half an hour later the Christian physician Gabriel came before the Caliph, he observed that the severed head of the Barmacide lay on a dish before the chief of believers. This was the downfall of the family. All who belonged to it were taken into captivity that evening and

> thrown into prison. Messengers were sent in haste and by order to overthrow their authority in the provinces and all their possessions were taken from them...through the beheading of the Persian leader, through the extermination of the family of the Barmacides, a stream of culture was destroyed. It is the stream of the continued influence of the Zarathustra element which Manichaeism wished to renew, to Christianize, and which in its union with the Greek wisdom would have brought about a synthesis between Christianity and the ancient Mystery wisdom.[90]

A spirit-denying materialism had been injected into the Arabic intellectual world many centuries before this event. It was the anti-Grail stream that continually sought to eliminate the Persian impulse with its deep teachings concerning the spiritualization of matter. According to Rudolf Steiner it was this Arabic impulse which became the basis of modern materialistic science:[91]

> In the days when everything in Europe was extremely primitive, over in Asia much brilliant spiritual culture was personified in Harun-al-Rashid whom Charlemagne held in great veneration. But this was a kind of culture which knew nothing of Christ nor wished to have anything to do with Christianity; it preserved and cultivated the best elements of Arabism and also kept alive the ancient forms of ... Aristotelian logic and dialectic which had spread so widely in the West and were the principles upon which the work of the Church Fathers and later the Schoolmen were based...Thus in our own time we have on the one side the direct, unbroken line of Christian development and on the other, the penetration of Arabism, first and foremost in abstract science.[92]

This materialistic impulse was not confined to the domains of science and intellect, but infiltrated the Catholic Church via the Eighth Ecumenical Council of 869 in Constantinople: 'The living spirit died when doubts of the Trinity arose. The

Council of 869, through which Trichotomy was abolished—the teaching that body, soul and spirit are to be considered as distinct from one another in man—is only a completion of a long series of events. The Council merely expressed what had been accomplished within human evolution. The path to the spirit was no longer accessible in the old way. At the same time Ahriman, the spirit of lies, was drawing near—that spirit of untruth then entering humanity. But upon this fact hangs world history; for how could the modern age approach—the age of the machine, of printing, of the power of the newspaper—without the entry of this spirit? It had to enter.'[93]

What then was the significance of this embassy from the Franks to the court of Baghdad as symbolized in the legend of Flore and Blanscheflur? 'The soul of Europe had to rescue from the court of the Caliphs what was really its own soul bride. The wisdom that had passed down from Zarathustra had been prevented from joining with the Greek Mystery wisdom at the court of Harun-al-Rashid in Baghdad. So it was then taken to Europe, to the lands of the Franks where it was preserved as a Mystery since at that time it must not become the universal property of all mankind because humanity was not yet prepared to receive it in the right way.'[94]

In this way the eastern Mysteries came to join the western Mysteries, particularly in the south-western corner of France on the borders of Spain. The Zoroastrian/Manichaean impulse was later absorbed by the Cathar movement, which grew prevalent in south-western France in the eleventh and twelfth centuries. Parzival is esoterically connected with the eastern stream although he stands exoterically within the western stream. What was the essence of the eastern Mysteries that were brought from Baghdad? Stein:

> The Mystery of Golgotha came to pass at the moment when Christ's blood flowed down upon the earth. Then the Spirit of the Sun passed over into the earth. Then the heavenly Logos had not only become flesh but it had also passed from Jesus, the man, into the whole earth-organism. What occurred at that point had been in preparation for a

long time, and the whole pre-Christian history is the history of the descent of the Divine down to earth. When the Persian looked up to heaven then he knew that behind the surface of the sky, hidden behind the darkness of the heavens, shines the Spiritual Sun. At one spot it becomes visible, where the sun's disc appears. Out of this wonderful radiant background of gold appear the coloured forms of the Gods seen in imagination. This experience is reflected in Persian art, for example in the Persian mosaics, where the most beautifully coloured pictures appear on a golden background. The sun is the door, but is also the Guardian before the door, for in looking up to this Guardian the earthly glance perishes. But He who later spoke the words, 'I am the door,' and 'No man comes to the golden radiance of the world foundation (to the Father) but by Me,' He was still experienced in cosmic space as the Sun Spirit in the most ancient Persian time. Stepwise, *gradalis*, He descended thence to earth, and His descent, the descent of the World Saviour down into the darkness, is reflected in the history of the oriental religions. What then descended was experienced as the cosmic Word, sounding from all directions of space, which in shining sounded, and in sounding shone. This light radiating in the depths must penetrate the forces of nature and these forces were felt in the image of the Bull. Mithras conquering the Bull is one of the imaginations of the primal Word in its descent. This Bull was experienced as spreading through the whole space of heaven, for its head was where the constellation of the Bull is and its tail where the constellation is of the Virgin bearing the ears of corn. This tail ended in three ears of corn. From below, from the constellation of the Scorpion, the subearthly forces of the Scorpion lay hold of the Bull. So, to begin with, the heavenly Bull was spread out in the zodiac. Later we find as a picture of heavenly events on earth the gleaming plough thrust into the earth's neck.[95]

Walter Johannes Stein continues by pointing out that the descent of the primal 'Word' which was preserved in the ancient Mysteries here mentioned re-emerges in later times in the Parzival story as related by Wolfram von Eschenbach, where he describes the whole corona of beings who form the 'crown of Lucifer' as it fell from heaven to earth. He describes how:

> Michael with his flaming sword strikes *one* spirit out of the corona of spirits...One spirit took the path from the heights to the depths, not as one falling, but accompanying the falling spirits out of free will in order to bring salvation to the men who were to be delivered over to these spirits. This being of angelic nature prepared the way for the Lord who followed him, for the World Logos Himself took the same path which the falling spirits took whom Michael trod underfoot. Concerning this being who prepared the way for the World Logos, the legend says that He had shone as a wondrous jewel in the crown of Lucifer. Michael struck this stone from Lucifer's crown; he then came down to men, formed himself into a vessel, became indeed the vessel destined to receive the blood of Christ. This became the sacred chalice which held within it the Sun Host...Thus the history of the Grail is the history of the wisdom descending from above downwards, the wisdom which was to become the vessel of love, and which became so the more as it took its way from East to West.[96]

Here in pictorial language the Grail legend describes how the 'Luke' Jesus-child was not involved in the 'dynamic' of the Fall; how when he descended into incarnation, it was by divine intervention. Michael 'struck him from the crown of Lucifer'; he did not fall together with the rest of us but remained a 'being of angelic nature'. Thus when he prepared the body for the Christ Being during the first 30 years of His life, the body was already a Grail ready to receive the Christ. The blood which flowed through the veins of the physical body of the Luke Jesus-child carried the *full force* of the life and chemical ethers. And it is in St Luke's Gospel that the motif of the redemption of evil is expressed in the story of the two criminals crucified with Christ:

> One of the criminals who hung there hurled insults at Him: 'Aren't you the Christ? Save yourself and us!' But the other criminal rebuked him. 'Don't you fear God,' he said, 'since you are under the same sentence? We are punished justly, for we are getting what our deeds deserve. But this man has done nothing wrong.' Then he said, 'Jesus, remember me when you come into your kingdom.'[97]

These criminals are imaginative pictures of Lucifer and Ahriman and of the redemption of evil that is so central to the Grail legends. At the time of Golgotha it was possible for Lucifer to be redeemed. Ahriman's redemption would have to wait for a later date. How then does the entire theme of the redemption of evil come to expression within Eschenbach's poem?

Parzival is an Arthurian knight, a sharer in the fallen nature of humanity. The power of redemption is carried by the eastern stream, and it is Parzival's destiny to realize this impulse from within himself.

The Arthurian Mysteries were based upon the power of the sword. They were a community-building impulse that sought to subdue and tame the astral forces. The eastern stream in the meantime belonged, and still belongs, very much to humanity's evolutionary future. This was based on the individual, and on the making good of evil. Only a unique and entirely new inner capacity could bring these two opposite impulses together in a balanced union. Rudolf Steiner has called this capacity the 'consciousness soul'. He has described this soul as being filled with the forces of brotherly love and compassion, forces born out of inner loneliness and despair. In the consciousness soul the individual awakens to full self-awareness, and experiences the realization of his own uniqueness as a shearing separation from the universe and from other men. This 'Garden of Gethsemane' experience must come to men and women as a totally necessary experience on their path. Without it the individual would remain for ever part of the group soul.

In Chapter 9 of Wolfram's epic, the now adult Parzival arrives at the hermitage of the man who is to be his spiritual teacher. Much time has passed since Parzival first left the Grail Castle in disgrace, as detailed in the last chapter. For years Parzival has been a wanderer, hoping to find his way back to the castle but unable to do so, sinking deeper into doubt and despair. In despairing rebellion against his destiny, Parzival had cried out against God:

> ...Who is He, this mighty God?
> Had He Power, then methinks our portion had ne'er been this shame abhorred!
> Small power shall be His! I served Him from the day I first knew His grace.
> Henceforth I renounce His service.[98]

Mourning his loss of the Grail, and anguished at the continuing separation from his wife, Parzival rides through the snows on Good Friday. He has reached the depths of personal loss. Letting go of his horse's reins he wrings his hands, and his thoughts turn to God:

> If today be His Day of Redemption! Let Him help me, if help he can.[99]

The horse that Parzival is riding by this point in the poem is a Grail horse, and as Parzival releases his grip on the reins the horse begins to trot and carries Parzival to the place of his healing.

Parzival arrives at the hermitage that is the simple home of his uncle, Trevrizent. We learn that Trevrizent is the brother of Amfortas. Trevrizent had withdrawn from the world with a pledge to live a life of austere simplicity and total purity. He is attempting to create the counterbalance to the sin of Amfortas.

Parzival tells the elderly recluse of his loss of faith in God. Trevrizent admonishes him that one can get nothing from God by anger. Then he tells him of the hindering powers whose role in world evolution is to lead man into temptation and seduce him from his path. Humanity was born at the same time that Lucifer was cast out of heaven. Trevrizent specifically focuses on Cain's sin against the earth:

> For the earth was Adam's mother, of the earth was Adam fed,
> And I ween, tho' a man she bare here, yet still was the earth a maid.
> And here will I read the riddle, he who robbed her of her maidenhood
> Was Cain the son of Adam, who in wrath shed his brother's blood.[100]

Parzival has inherited the strife and discord that has come down the generations through this act:

> For wrath of man and envy, thro' Cain did they wake to life,
> And ever from that day forward thro' his sin there ariseth strife.[101]

Through this highest evil came in time the highest good, as the cosmic Logos chose to descend and unite Himself with humanity and the fallen earth. Trevrizent informs Parzival that the power of the Godhead can penetrate into the thinking of the human heart, into the deepest motives and impulses of the individual, and that those who wish to make good their transgressions win God's favour. Parzival is heartened to hear that God is faithful and that he has not been abandoned, that his suffering has not been in vain.

When Trevrizent discovers that Parzival is mourning for the Grail he reprimands him. It is not right to bear longing for the Grail. Walter Johannes Stein expresses the meaning of this passage well: 'The hermit wishes to say to Parzival that there is no sense in seeking for the Grail. The only sense is in fulfilling with enthusiasm the demands of the Grail—to work upon oneself and to serve the world. Whether one comes to the Grail or not, that one must leave in the hands of God, that is a grace.'[102]

Trevrizent is then moved to instruct Parzival in some of the deeper secrets of the Grail in relation to the fallen spirits:

When the battle was fought between Trinity and Lucifer
The whole heavenly host with its shining wings
Had to descend to the stone, there to serve the same stone[103]

The luciferic Angels with their 'shining wings' were sent to tempt Jesus in the wilderness. We are told in Chapter 4 of the Gospel of St Matthew that after the temptation Jesus was protected and ministered to by angelic beings. Trevrizent's teachings point to the fact that the *same* forces that had attempted to seduce Jesus and gain power over him were made into his servants. Trevrizent misleads Parzival at this point by teaching him that the fallen powers can win salvation for themselves through their exertion. He later admits to this deception. The fallen spirits cannot be redeemed through strife. The true conditions for their redemption are given in the story of the two criminals in the Luke passage quoted above. The Grail cannot be striven for, it only comes to the pure of heart who have transcended strife.

Through its very nature Manichaeism condemned itself to be stamped out. The belief that evil must be transformed, not combated, led the movement to bow its head and dwindle to almost nothing when faced with the immaturity of human understanding. According to Manichaean thinking, the opponents of spiritual progress rise up in our path so that we may ultimately transform fallen creation more effectively. But in a time when the newly developing human ego had to cope with the wild astrality in which it found itself, like a novice cowboy astride a bucking bronco, there was very little hope of facing that opposition, let alone of transforming it. Every nerve was tensed to avoid the machinations of the evil ones who were waiting to lure unsuspecting souls to ghastly regions of hell. The Seven Deadly Sins were constantly kept in mind in case of being tripped and pitched down to the waiting depths. Not only were the senses invaded by luciferic beings but also the mind was eventually captured by Ahriman. Ahriman could be described as attacking in the wake of Lucifer like a hyaena feeding off the prey of other predators. Lucifer encourages insular individuality by appealing to selfish desires springing from the senses; once participation in the unity of creation has been thus sacrificed Ahriman moves in to draw a blind of insensitivity and disbelief over anything that is not encompassed by sense-bound experience.

This has been brilliantly illustrated by Hans Andersen in his story 'The Snow Queen', which gives an accurate picture of Ahriman's effect on mankind. An evil magician creates a magic mirror that distorts all that is true and good so that it appears stupid and meaningless. The mirror breaks and the pieces enter the hearts and eyes of human beings, who react by viewing the world from a cynical point of view which is dictated by mathematical rigidity. When Kay gets a piece stuck in his eye he is whisked away to the Snow Queen's palace where Gerda finds him attempting to write 'Eternity', in blocks of ice.

This accurately describes our computer-orientated society redirecting the wonders of creation to cold, clinical predictability. Only Gerda's love, sacrifice and determination to find Kay again can remove the piece of glass from his eye and the ice from his heart, which had been frozen by the Snow Queen. In those early centuries of Christianity the way was not yet clear for the impulse of Manichaeism to take root. The 'descent of the Dragon' had not yet gone far enough. Humanity still had to experience what had been prepared at the court of Harun-al-Rashid in Baghdad. As a result Aristotelianism would not meet with the eastern Mystery stream for many centuries; instead it would ride westward in a different garb.

With the increasing influence of the Muslim advance into Europe a new age was born. Henceforth man's intellect would flower independently from the inspiration and wisdom it had previously received from the spiritual world. Manichaeism would be destined to enter evolution after the point where the descent had reached its lowest level. Now the latest moment has arrived. Now we have the opportunity to redeem creation with the freedom which we have won at such a price. The task is very dangerous. The way leads not 'up the old road' but right through the centre of everything that has risen up around us as a result of the Fall.

Manichaeism can be seen as a vital component of the eastern Mysteries, which were brought from the court of Baghdad to western France before that stream was obliterated by the Muslim influence. Here it met with the Mysteries of the West.

In the south-western corner of France these Mysteries may have been preserved in the custody of the Cathars and early Templars. Manichaeism can thus be seen as a stream within the Cathar movement—but not the Catharism of which we hear most today, a stream which wishes to return to the pre-Fall state, overleaping matter to instant spirituality. It may be that when they faced the fire the Cathars ended their incarnations with a feeling of outrage at the extinguishing of esoteric Christianity. The modern Manichaean, however, accepts that, having descended the Grand Canyon, we now have to lighten our packs to face the steep climb up the other side; we are at the very bottom.

10
The Southern Mystery Stream: The Mysteries of the Word in Matter

> Yet the Most High does not dwell in houses made with hands; as the prophet says, 'Heaven is my throne, and earth my footstool. What house will you build for me, says the Lord, or what is the place of my rest? Did not my hands make all things?'
>
> Acts 7:48–50

Here in the southern Mystery stream we finally reach the secret stream referred to in The Holy Blood and the Holy Grail*—the 'secrets of the Word in matter' which was central to Cathars, Templars and Rosicrucians. This theme is central to this book, winding its way, as it does, through the depths of the Grail tradition. While I was able to find confirmation for the contents of this chapter in both Steiner and Wachsmuth, the information itself came through unexpected meetings with many individuals who felt themselves to be linked in a karmic sense with this southern stream.*

Like many who have read the book The Holy Blood and the Holy Grail *I was both moved and fascinated by the story of the destruction of the Cathars by the Roman Catholic Church. In a brutal act of genocide an entire culture was suppressed and Catharism seemingly totally destroyed. However, on the last night of the final siege, according to Baigent, Leigh and Lincoln, four Cathar priests escaped from the mountain stronghold of Montségur. Legend hints that they carried with them some treasure of immense import, perhaps even the Grail itself. Hints dropped here and there suggested that Montségur was a Grail castle and, being connected with the area surrounding Rennes-le-Château, it undoubtedly had some connection with the etheric forces that had been tapped there. In the following chapter we not only move into the heart of the Grail tradition but we also attempt to suggest a resolution to one of history's most enigmatic mysteries—the nature of the treasure removed from Montségur on the eve of the fall of the Cathars.*

In his book *Mystery Streams and the New Mysteries*, Bernard Lievegoed refers to the southern Mystery stream as the 'Mysteries of man in his earthly physical form of incarnation. They are the Mysteries of material death and of the resurrected body. The secrets of the pure physical body filled with matter.' Lievegoed also refers to it as the stream of *Johannine* Christianity, because it is the figure of John the Gospel writer who leads the southern Mystery stream from age to age.[104]

One of the texts found at Nag Hammadi, 'The Secret Book of John', is described by Andrew Welburn as 'a primary Gnostic cosmological treatise giving an account of the earliest, purely spiritual phases of world evolution, followed by the origin of the material world and the moulding of man's physical body'.[105]

John the Divine's intimate connection with the southern Mystery stream has been detailed in full by Rudolf Steiner. Steiner identified John as the foremost leader of the *Rosicrucian* stream of initiation, one who bore within himself the desire to experience in full the initiation of Christ. According to Bernard Lievegoed:

> The best known Rosicrucian incarnation in antiquity is that of Hiram Abiff, the master builder of the temple of Solomon. Solomon had the ability, within his spiritual vision, to determine the measures and proportions of the temple. He could observe the way the spiritual powers required the temple to look. But he could not make the specific, precise calculations for the construction. He needed an architect for that who could handle earthly matter, who could build something which in the sphere of the earth would not remain a vision but a lasting reality.[106]

Rudolf Steiner has indicated how the Mysteries of the human physical body were incorporated in the dimensions of the temple: 'The temple had to be the symbol illustrating man's body. Therefore builders were sent for—Hiram Abif—who understood the practical arts that could transform man himself into a God.'[107]

It is recounted in John's Gospel how Jesus drove the money

lenders and the sacrificial animals from the temple. The Jews challenged him, demanding to know on whose authority he acted. Jesus replied with a reference to his own transformative working within the physical body: 'Destroy this temple and in three days I will raise it up.'[108] The temple was the microcosmic reflection of the 'human form divine'—to borrow a phrase from Blake—the Logos through whom the cosmos had been brought into being. Now Jesus was declaring that the temple had been replaced by his own body into which the Logos had begun to penetrate.

It was Solomon who was given the task of building the temple. Solomon was imbued with the pure, clear wisdom of the Elohim Yahveh. Yahveh created Adam who united with Eve to give birth to Abel. Abel is described as a 'keeper of flocks'. He is the spiritual force that accepts passively what is given to him from the spiritual world. He offers back to the Elohim their own substance and his gift is accepted. Cain on the other hand is the creation of those Elohim who had made the sacrifice of remaining behind when the sun left the earth. Cain works upon the ground. While Abel is still a spiritual being, Cain descends onto the physical plane to work upon matter with his own will-power and intelligence. His offering is alien to Yahveh because it is made not of spirit but of man's own will force. Rejected by Yahveh, Cain sets off alone to found his own race.

One of Cain's descendants is Tubal-Cain who was master of the use and working of metal ores. Hiram too is a descendent of Cain. He is the great architect, the worldly-wise man who works out of his own energies upon the physical world. Solomon has wisdom but he is not productive. We are told in legend how Hiram, during the construction of the temple, descended to the centre of the earth there to meet his great forefather Cain. Cain gives him a hammer and a golden triangle. Hiram returned with these tools to complete the construction of the temple. This was achieved through the correct melding of fire and water. The water is the pure, clear wisdom and love that was later taken to its full development by the Christ. The fire is the force coming from Cain, the astral forces of desire and self-will.[109]

It is the 'fallen' Elohim who create matter. They also work on humanity to create the division of the sexes. In the understanding of their workings lies the secrets of human sexuality, from which will be derived the alchemical science of the future. The aim of this science will be the reunification of the sexes.

Along with the separation of the sexes at the time of the Fall came the enlightenment of consciousness. Wachsmuth quotes from Steiner's *Occult Science*:

> There occurred that event which gave a different turn to the whole of evolution. Everything which could contribute to the hardening of the solid earth-material was cast out. At that time our present moon left the earth; and what had formerly contributed directly with the earth to the production of permanent form now worked indirectly and with less strength from the moon. As a result of this a difference appeared in the form of the human body, which must be regarded as the beginning of the cleavage into male and female sex. The diaphanous human form, which hitherto had inhabited the earth, brought into being their descendants, the new human race through a collaboration within themselves of the two forces—the germ and the life-giving force. In one group of these descendants the germ force of the spiritual and psychical, in the other group the life-giving force prevailed.[110]

Wachsmuth describes this further in Chapter XII of the same book:

> Mankind hitherto androgynous and unisexual, with all four formative forces working harmoniously within him, is subjugated by the new, inflowing warmth and light forces which disturb the existing harmony; now one part of mankind allows these to penetrate right into the substance, thus making use of active recreative forces for the purposes of physical productivity. Yet, in so far as these forces are active in the psycho-spiritual domain, man experiences

hereby an alteration of his organs of perception and consciousness. 'And the eyes of them both were opened' (Genesis 3:7). Mankind has always had the idea of luciferic beings, not only as an impulse behind the forces of cleavage, of bi-sexualism, of the Fall, but also as agents of the enlightening consciousness in the illuminating of man's perceptions of the universe around him. After he has partaken of the virtues of the 'Tree of Knowledge', man loses the harmony of the four formative forces (four ethers) in his etheric body; he becomes not only bi-sexual, but also altered and illuminated in his active powers of perception. Yet the strengthening of one kind of etheric force sometimes displaces others. Light and life ethers, which hitherto produced in man's etheric body a life process enlightened by consciousness, a living light, a living wisdom, now part company, and there remains to him only a life process no longer illuminated by consciousness, a light no longer permeated by life forces, a dead wisdom. Since that time the actual life processes in the human organism have no longer been illuminated by the light of consciousness; they have sunk into the subconscious. The sense organs, though they are still permeated by the light of consciousness, are now only able to perceive what is physical; they see and feel light and warmth, but can no longer discern the work of the life ether.[111]

The situation resulting from the Fall therefore divides humanity into two separate groups where the male organism is so constructed that:

Warmth and light-ether prevail at the physically creative pole.
Chemical and life-ether prevail at the spiritually creative pole.

While the female organism is so constructed that:

Chemical and life-ether prevail at the physically creative pole.
Warmth and light-ether prevail at the spiritually creative pole.

From this we can begin to understand how a small proportion of people who have developed ahead of us have reached this future state which is no longer hampered with problems caused by gender. We can also see that another problem involved in reversing the effect of the Fall is the overcoming of limitations set by this division. Part of the Mystery secret of transubstantiation lies in the unification of the two separated pairs of etheric forces at both the physical and spiritual poles of the human being: 'Only when man unites all etheric forces in spiritual harmony at the higher pole can he engender within himself the harmony already ruling in the cosmos around him.'[112]

These events, the changes caused by the Fall, occurred during a stage of evolution which Rudolf Steiner has set in Lemuria. Lievegoed has described how the southern Mystery stream 'originated in Lemuria and came via Egypt and Rome into Europe'.[113] It is possible to suggest an alternative to this.

The Mysteries of the southern stream pass through the Egyptian Mysteries where preoccupation with the physical body is evident in the skill that the Egyptians used in the process of mummification and in the development of surgery. These Mysteries were incorporated into the Hebrew schools of initiation by two individuals: the Thrice Great Hermes—Hermes Trismegistus—and Moses.

Rudolf Steiner describes the karma of Egypt being fulfilled in such a way that not only was Moses initiated into the Mysteries of Egypt, but he also took them with him when he went into exile. Lievegoed says: 'It is told of Solomon that he was able to build his temple because he possessed Egyptian wisdom...he carried within him all the cosmic wisdom of the previous Mysteries. He could conceive the true temple—he knew the cosmic secrets of the physical body—and he knew the divine measures and secrets of the "Ark of the Covenant", which was also a symbol for the mathematical secret of the physical body.'[114] And it was the 'Thrice Great Hermes, the inspirer of the Egyptian culture who brought the Mysteries of the physical, the temple in which the soul and spirit found their way home'.

In a Christmas lecture of 1916 Rudolf Steiner describes how 'the spiritual eyes of those who were guiding incarnating souls to the earth from cosmic worlds gazed downwards and beheld the temple of Solomon with its symbols. The temple was like a star whose light enabled them to guide the souls into bodies who would be capable of understanding its meaning.[115]

The Mystery of the cosmic Word is incorporated into the southern Mystery stream both from Egypt and through Hiram. Thus the influence of the 'John being' can be traced back through the southern Mystery stream to a very early time. Christ was able to reverse the laws of matter and 'rebuild' the human physical body in the three days following his Crucifixion and death. This was prefigured by Hiram with his 'Cain knowledge'.

In his lectures published under the title *The Temple Legend*, Rudolf Steiner indicates how this 'Cain knowledge' became the basis of Freemasonry. The ideal of the original Freemasons was to transform the solid substance of stone and metal into a building whose form would be an expression of the spirit:

> In the original occult brotherhoods the thought lived that man has a task to fulfil; the task of restructuring the inanimate world, of not being satisfied with what is already there. Wisdom thus becomes deed through its penetration of the inanimate world, so that the world should become a reflection of the original and eternal spirituality. Wisdom, Beauty, Strength are the three fundamental words of all Freemasonry. So to change the outer world that it becomes a garment for the spiritual—that is its task.[116]

In her book *Masonry and Medieval Mysticism*, Isabel Cooper-Oakley connects Manichaeism with early Freemasonry:

> Herman had spread his teaching in Egypt, where the Coptic priests and the Christians mingled it with the Mysteries adopted from the Jews...It was through these

same Coptic priests that both the Mysteries of the 'Children of the Widow' (Manichaeans) and the cult of the Great Architect (Freemasonry) came to us in consequence of unforeseen events, and it will be seen that they obtained a sure footing in the West. The Mysteries maintained their existence under the name of the cult of the Great Architect of the Universe, a name that has its origins in the allegory of Hiram, which represented the Mysteries of 'the unknown God', the eternal and sole creator of all things and the regenerator of all beings.[117]

The Order of the Knights Templar also incorporated this 'Cain impulse'. Founded in 1118 by Hughes de Payen, the Order originally consisted of only nine knights and there are very few exoteric records of their early existence and activities. It has been claimed that the Templars received a secret doctrine transmitted from St John.

In *The Mysteries of Chartres Cathedral*, Louis Charpentier finds extensive evidence to prove that the nine knights were originally sent to the Holy Land for a particular purpose by Bernard of Clairvaux, head of the Cistercian order. Charpentier describes how the Ark of the Covenant containing the Tables of the Law may have been the object of their mission in the Holy Land. Charpentier also says of the Tables of the Law:

> They are the Tables of the Law, the Logos, the Word; of reason, measure, relationship, number. 'I have made everything with number, measure and weight,' says the Lord God in Genesis. The divine law is the law of number, measure and weight. In the language of today we should call the Tables of the Law the tables of the Cosmic Equation. To possess the tables then is to have the possibility of access to the great law of unity that rules the worlds, of relating effects with their causes and consequently of acting on the phenomena that the causes produce as they diversify into plurality...One sees that Moses was not deceiving the Hebrew people when in the name of the Eternal he promised them power and dominion through

> the Tables of the Law. But it goes without saying that he would only present the possibility of using this instrument of power to those who had made themselves worthy of it; and that is why he not only forbade access to the Tables but also took the greatest care to hide the light under a bushel.[118]

Charpentier continues by saying that a man would:

> ...be unable to make use of the Tables unless he had been initiated into the secret of reading them. Moses gave such an initiation in a commentary in Semitic language and in a writing that he perhaps devised; a cryptic writing in a numerical system that was later called the Cabbala. The secret then was well sealed up. More so even than it seems.
>
> Since his commentaries, which constitute the sacred books, are in cipher, they must in no case be modified even by an iota. Change would render the cryptography indecipherable. Thus one begins to see why Etienne Harding, Saint Etienne, Abbot of Citeaux, although his Order was an Order of 'contemplatives', put the whole of his abbey, after the conquest of Jerusalem, with such ardour to the study of Hebraic texts with the help of learned Rabbis from High Burgundy; and why Saint Bernard made a special journey across the Rhine to calm the anti-Semitical fury of those who had lived in that region who were, already, organizing bloody pogroms.
>
> It was because the Hebraic books constitute a 'treatise on the interpretation' of the Stone and the Jews are the depositories of it.
>
> ...Moses was a man of the temple and was learned in all the wisdom of the Egyptians (Acts 7:22).
>
> ...Knowledge, in no matter what kind, has only a speculative interest. If it is to be of use to mankind, it must be translated into action. To bring a work into being there must be workers. Israel forgot this obvious principle, which is why it was never given to Israel itself to realize the work in detail which is to be found in the Tables of the Law. Solomon, King of Jerusalem, had to appeal to

Hiram, King of Tyre, to build his temple.

The sons of Saint Benoit will not forget this.

...The alacrity with which the temple of Solomon was put at the Templars' disposal shows plainly enough where the key to the riddle is to be sought. Otherwise it would seem unlikely that there should have been handed over to nine knights an establishment that accommodated at the same time the king, his household and the canons of Saint Sepulchre. They were certainly afforded every comfort, these poor knights; comforts which exceeded the needs of men whose job was to safeguard roads and communications. If the nine wished to live by themselves it was necessary because they were engaged, not on the roads but in the temple itself, in some secret activity...the nine knights went there to seek, keep and take away something of such importance that the mission called for men who were above human passion; something so precious and dangerous that it must be kept in absolute secrecy.[119]

Isobel Cooper-Oakley relates how 'the Crusaders who had been admitted to the Mysteries of the Children of the Widow and initiated therein imparted them on their return home to their pupils in Europe'.[120]

Here we have two separate references to knowledge that Templars or Crusaders have brought back from the Holy Land to France. The Knights Templar maintained a presence in the area immediately surrounding Montségur. The Knights Templar could have brought these powerful secrets to the Cathars. Catharism, like the teachings of Mani before it, has been little understood by historians and theologians. Failing to grasp the intricate esoteric background to their teachings, many have seen in them a simplistic, life-denying dualism. For a more accurate perspective we must first trace in greater detail some of the esoteric threads outlined above.

Two primal streams, those of Cain and Abel, flow through all of human history. Purity of wisdom, a deep inner connection with the good powers of the spiritual world, flowed through the Abel stream. Abel lived out the will of the Gods in total obedience. The Cain stream was that of the self-willed human, seeking to transform the whole world into his own image and to become fully independent. It was the forward-moving activities of the Sons of Cain that produced the catastrophes of Atlantis. It makes sense to suggest that some of those involved in these occurrences took it upon themselves to bear a deep awareness of the outcome of the 'Fall'. As a fulfilment of their karmic debt to the rest of humanity they may have pledged to work through history, creating the counterbalance to the effects of their own actions. They would need to work with the dangerous etheric forces that had otherwise been removed from human grasp. The burden of this work coupled with a profound awareness of the suffering of humanity often led them to being seen as 'dualists', imbued with a thoroughly negative view of the world.

This stream is indicated in the *Parzival* legend in the figure of Trevrizent who lives a life of austere purity in order to act as counterbalance to his brother Amfortas. Trevrizent is possessed of a deep awareness of the nature of the Fall and the unredeemed activity of the Backward Spirits. In essence Trevrizent is an extremist, and we have already noted that to some extent he led Parzival astray. In other times Trevrizent might have found it necessary to throw himself into the activities of the world, to become a soldier or statesman. The essence of his activity is to move to the opposite pole of the official spirit of his time. In this he was a true Manichaean.

The Manichaeans were often called the 'Children of the Widow'. The 'Father' is the spiritual world, the realm of power and authority. The Children of the Widow could not take their wisdom and understanding from this realm via the authority of the Church. They had to derive it for themselves from their own being. When large Manichaean groups gathered—as did the Cathars in southern France—they become visible to the temporal rulers, the power of Church and state. These temporal rulers could not allow humanity to move beyond the structures of the present time. They were forced to curb the activities of those who were pressing ahead of the mass. The Cathars on the other hand felt that the given social order and its sacraments were imprisoning. Their work demanded that they should press on towards the transformation of evil.

The brutal suppression of the Cathars by the Roman Church was motivated at least in part by the desire on the part of Rome to claim for themselves the legendary 'treasure of the Cathars'. No such treasure was ever forthcoming, and rumours have spread down through the ages of some secret knowledge, whose resonances have permeated the Rennes landscape, soaking it in mystery.

It is possible that the 'Cathar treasure' was in fact the 'wisdom' which passed through the southern Mystery stream, the Mysteries which were brought back from the temple of Jerusalem by the Knights Templar. These were the secrets of the Logos referred to by Charpentier, which included 'the great symbols of Solomon's temple' to which Steiner refers in his Christmas lecture of 1916. Both Mysteries concern the mirroring of the cosmos in physical manifestation, the Logos permeating matter. This is the Mystery of the southern stream, of Johannine esoteric Christianity to which Cathars, Templars and, later, Rosicrucians belonged. This form of Christianity was not destined to survive in the open. It had to be temporarily forgotten in order to make way for the advance of materialistic scientific thought. As we saw in the previous chapter, the descent into matter had to take a final plunge before the full mission of Joannine Christianity could be fulfilled.

The accepted historical account of the siege of Montségur relates how after a prolonged siege the defenders requested a two-week truce, during which hostilities were halted to enable them to consider the terms of surrender offered by the 'Crusaders'. Full pardon was offered to any who would recant their heretical beliefs, and in return the defenders voluntarily agreed to provide hostages as a guarantee against any of them attempting an escape during the period of truce. On 15 March the truce expired. Early the following morning the *parfaits*, none of whom had recanted, were taken down and burned at

The castle stronghold of Montségur

the foot of the mountain. That night, 16 March, four of the *parfaits* who remained hidden escaped on ropes down the steep cliff-face. They took with them something so important and precious that no danger was too great to face in its protection. It has been suggested that the two-week truce period was intended to provide time for a ritual to be performed, and that only after this had been done could the Cathar secret be removed.

While the clouds of the future age were gathering it was necessary that the Mysteries of the south should be brought to meet the unified eastern and western streams. It is possible that a ceremony was performed at Montségur on 14 March

1244, which symbolically brought the Mysteries of the southern stream together with those of West and East. The Mystery secrets which once radiated into the cosmos from the temple of Solomon, 'central star of the earth, shining out into the spiritual heights', now turned this stronghold on its high peak in the Pyrenees into a location which for a few brief hours held the promise of a future time. On the site of an ancient sun temple all the 'treasure' of the ancient Mystery wisdom, all the 'riches' of Joannine Christianity began to enter a long sleep that was to last through the following centuries of increasing materialism.

11
The Northern Mystery Stream

If God was able to become man, he can also become stone, plant, animal and element, and perhaps there is in this way a perpetual redemptive power in nature.

Novalis

For any student of Rudolf Steiner his founding of the new Anthroposophical Society at Dornach on 25 December 1923 has great personal significance. However, as I looked into the last of the four great Mystery streams, the northern stream, connected with the evolution of individual human ego consciousness, I began to suspect that something of greater import had happened than just the founding of a new esoteric community. Steiner himself had made clear that the aim of his work, and its culmination in what has come to be known as the Christmas Conference, *was to open up the Mysteries to all of humanity. What had been nurtured in secret places could now be made public. Streams and impulses that had been long suppressed by the authoritarian powers of the present age would now need to work their way back into the light of day.*

The northern Mysteries are the Mysteries of the human ego. This ego is a fructifying seed because it contains, working within its very depths, the universal power of the Christ Being. Many who consider themselves to be Christians are unaware that Christ, as the Cosmic Ego, is humanity's elder brother. He united Himself with the earth in order to become its Spirit at the moment of the shedding of the blood on Golgotha. 'The blood streaming to the earth from the wound was the vehicle through which the Spirit of the Sun passed into Incarnation within the body of the earth itself...in promise of the reanimation of the whole dying earth existence and its reintegration into the solar dominion of the macrocosm.'[121]

Bernard Lievegoed characterizes the essence of the Mysteries of the northern stream: 'The Germanic-Celtic Mysteries were Mysteries in which the pupil was led not inward into his own subjective world, but outward into the cosmos, the world of the Hierarchies, which guide the development of humanity.'[122]

The youthful Germanic tribes—in whose blood still flowed the powers of the chemical and life ethers—were still at their sentient-soul stage when the rest of humanity had reached the level of the intellectual soul. Within the Germanic tribes was maintained a blood-based group consciousness, each member of the tribe feeling himself at one with the total identity of his clan. The group ego of the Germanic peoples was felt to be the thunder god, Thor. Each member of the Germanic tribes felt a close relationship to Thor. Rudolf Steiner describes Thor as one of the mightiest of the Angels. Thor is the bestower of individual human consciousness. In the macrocosm, lightning is the ego-force working within the blood, thunder the ego-substance of thinking. Thor as the storm god worked within these elements and their microcosmic reflection within humanity.

The Germanic peoples advanced swiftly through the stage of the intellectual soul under the guidance of the Church during the Middle Ages and with the advent of the consciousness-soul age they took on their role of representatives and pioneers of the ego. Their intimate relationship with the thunder god manifested as a rapid ego-development, that was also consciously cosmopolitan.[123]

This Germanic element gave a characteristic stamp to the substance of the Middle Ages. The Germanic peoples expressed their awakening into ego-hood not in the form of alienated isolation but in the form of trade and craft associations and so on. Their ego was not one that shut itself off within a private world, but one that joined together with others. This working together was not based on personal sacrifice or coercion, but on the willing co-operation that flowed as moral substance from the depths of their soul natures.

It is among the German and Austrian idealists of the eighteenth and nineteenth centuries that the sense of the ego first attains to total *conceptual* clarity. When dealing with these thinkers Steiner emphasized that what lives in their thinking is a *soul-content* of life experience open to *all* human beings. This warm, *life-filled* soul-content had to be taken hold of by 'ice-cold abstract thoughts'.[124]

Describing a lecture given by Fichte, Steiner says: 'In the course of his lecture Fichte calls upon his listeners: "Think about the wall!" His listeners made every effort to think about the wall. After they had done this for a while Fichte's next demand follows: "And now think about the one who thought about the wall!" For Fichte, within the self-awakening inner activity of the human soul there lies the power of self-knowledge. And within this activity he also finds the place in the soul where the spirit of the world reveals itself in the spirit of the soul. In Fichte's world-view the world-will weaves and works in all existence; and within the willing of its own being the soul can live this world-will within itself.'[125]

In philosophical terms Fichte describes the now fully conscious and internalized relationship between the macrocosm and the microcosm: 'In all the fullness of life, order and growth that I see in it, this world is still only the curtain by which an infinitely more perfect world is hidden from me—and the seed from which this more perfect world is to evolve. My belief goes behind this curtain and warms and enlivens this seed. My belief does not see anything definite, but expects more than it can grasp here below or will ever be able to grasp in the realm of time.'[126]

The moral duty of humanity is revealed, for Fichte, within this act of self-awakening. The world is the realm into which the supersensible wishes to pour itself through human moral activity. The human soul looking out into the world feels that its inner content is richer than that which can be brought to birth within the world, but that to bring such a content to birth is its supreme task and purpose. The spiritual world can be seen as an infinite and *infinitely potent* seed. Human ego-consciousness is the nutrient-rich field in which it must be brought to birth. That *such a task is itself infinite* points to the fact of the immortality of the human spirit.

Inspired by the need to become the vocal point of a

universal world content, the German and Austrian Idealists experienced, at the very centre of their inner, conceptually determined world, and in the most profound intuition, the indwelling macrocosmic presence —the Ego of Christ. This led Schelling to declare that Christianity was not a doctrine or creed, but instead the very substance of Christ, intuitively apprehended.

In the ego—in Christ—humanity becomes one race. The Parzival legend culminates with Parzival's second arrival at the Grail Castle, where he heals the wounded Amfortas and replaces him as the Guardian of the Grail. Amfortas, as we will recall, has been mortally wounded, but is kept alive by the power of the Grail. He wishes for death, but it never comes. This is the present condition of many modern people who believe that death will bring the solution to all their problems by bringing a final end to their existence. Unaware that they are immortal souls, they do not know that there is no end, that the spiritual world is ever renewed and never at rest. Like Parzival every person must put to right the wrongs they have done and complete down to the smallest detail the task that destiny has laid upon them.

But now, at the end of the poem, Parzival returns to the Grail Castle. He is not alone this time. He brings with him his half-brother Feirefis. Half black and half white, Feirefis represents the mass of humanity who have not awoken to their individual ego-hood, who are ignorant of the Grail. When they first meet, in Adventure 15 of the poem, the two brothers fight. Each does not comprehend the identity of the other, and their strife is fierce. Here Wolfram is describing the 'War of All against All' that must inevitably consume mankind unless a higher force intervenes:

Then on high flashed the sword of the heathen, and many such blow had slain,
To his knee Parzival was beaten—Now see how they fought, the twain,
If twain ye will still account them, yet in sooth they shall be but one,

For my brother and I are one body, e'en as husband and wife are one![127]

Walter Johannes Stein comments on this verse: 'That is man's Cain nature, that will not be its brother's keeper. He who wishes to approach the Grail must be willing to lead his brother to the Grail.'[128]

At last, after an immense struggle, the two men stop fighting. Then they each realize the identity of the other and that they share a single father. Their mother—the Earth—has made them different, but in the *Father* they are one. Now Parzival also learns about the death of his earthly father. The laws of iron necessity and karma are to be replaced by the inner laws of brotherhood and love, given out of freedom.

So Parzival returns to the Grail Castle with his human brother. Feirefis cannot see the Grail but he falls in love with the Grail bearer. In this way he too comes to the Grail. Parzival asks the question that heals Amfortas. The attainment of the kingship of ego-hood bears within it the seed for the reunification of humanity above and beyond all that would keep human beings in enmity. This is not achieved at the cost of diversity, but on the growing understanding that we all come from a common source, that our Father is the divine spiritual world.

The northern Mysteries re-emerged at the turn of the century in the form of Anthroposophy, which Steiner defined as 'a path of knowledge that leads the spiritual in man to the spiritual in the universe'. Anthroposophy is the culminating fruit of *all* the Mysteries of antiquity, but within it the Mysteries of the ego are central, and are, indeed, taken to the highest levels of perfection.

How were the northern Mysteries, the Mysteries of the ego, the eternal spirit of man united with the other three which had been joined at Montségur? The four Cathars who were chosen to leave there in secret on the night of 16 March 1244 may have been given the solemn task of preserving and maintaining the link which had been made between the Mysteries of West, East and South. In the early hours before dawn they silently descended the steep walls of the fortress and out through the sleeping lines of the Pope's army, taking with them the seed that had been sown during the 'ceremony' performed at Montségur. These four would then have been free to scatter north, south, east and west but particularly east where this seed could lie almost dormant with those who would preserve its potency until the time came when there would be fertile ground out of which it might spring: the Rosicrucian movement.

Students of Anthroposophy are familiar with Rudolf Steiner's interpretation of the so-called 'Second Coming' of Christ. In the Gospels Christ Himself refers to this event saying: '...and they shall see the Son of Man coming in the clouds of heaven with great glory.'[129] The phenomenon of cloud activity is closely connected with the etheric world. Since the Mystery of Golgotha Christ's presence is to be found as a reality within the etheric realm of the earth. Paul's experience on the road to Damascus was the first objective example of experiences which have increased since the second half of this century.

Rudolf Steiner has explained how the human etheric body once extended further from the boundaries of the physical body than it does now. At the beginning of the Atlantean epoch the etheric head protruded outside the physical head, then withdrew to coincide with the physical head from the middle of the Atlantean epoch until very recently when, from the beginning of this century, the etheric body has begun to expand outwards again so that it is once more becoming increasingly possible for human beings to perceive the etheric world. This is not a return to the previous faculty of clairvoyance, when dreamy Atlantean vision of the etheric world gave rise to the later myths, legends and fairy-tales. The new faculty, which is beginning to arise, is experienced in clear, wide-awake consciousness. Because of the dimming of earlier spiritual vision, the presence of Christ began to radiate into the etheric world at a time when awareness of the event was least possible to mankind. Only in this century can we begin to attain a faculty that leads to full consciousness of the fact that Christ never left the earth after the Mystery of Golgotha: 'Lo I am with you always even unto the end of the world.'[130]

The significance of the disciples' experience of the Ascension has been explained by Steiner. The vision of Christ rising up through the clouds at His Ascension was not, as conventional Christianity teaches, of His leaving the earth but was an imagination that was given to the disciples to illustrate to them an event which would have occurred to all of mankind had Christ's Incarnation not taken place on earth.

> What they witnessed revealed to them, as in a picture, the prospect of what would have come about for men had the Mystery of Golgotha not taken place. They beheld as a concrete spiritual happening what would have then befallen, namely, that the physical bodies of men would have so deteriorated that the whole future of humanity would have been endangered. For the consequence of this physical deterioration would have been that the human etheric body would have obeyed the forces of attraction which properly belong to it. The etheric body is being drawn all the time to the sun, not towards the earth. Our constitution as human beings is such that our physical body has earthly heaviness, gravity, but our etheric body sun levity. Had the human physical body become what it must have become if the Mystery of Golgotha had not taken place, the etheric bodies of men would have followed their own urge towards the sun and have left the physical body. The existence of mankind on earth would inevitably have come to an end...In spiritual vision the disciples see the Christ Himself rising heavenwards. A vision is conjured before them of how the power, the impulse of Christ unites itself with the etheric nature of man in its upward striving: of how at the time of the Mystery of Golgotha man was facing the danger of his etheric body being drawn out into the sun like a cloud, but how in its sunward streaming it was held together by Christ.[131]

In a lecture given in New York on 22 April 1949, the Christian Community priest Alfred Heidenreich reiterates this by clearly stating that 'there is no such expression in the...New Testament...as "Second Coming". It just does not exist. It has gradually crept into the popular use of religious language, but otherwise does not exist. There is one term in the so-called apocalyptic passages of the New Testament which can, among other things, mean "coming". But nowhere do you find the adjective "second".' Heidenreich then proceeded to write the Greek word *parousia* on the blackboard. This is the word from which 'coming' has been translated; in the dictionary *four* different meanings for this word are given. 'Its first meaning is presence and that is the original meaning. Then comes the second, which may mean advent or coming. Thirdly it means indwelling, and then also aid or help. In the original text of the New Testament this word is used for prophecies which speak of a future, new presence of Christ in human evolution. Nothing less than the comprehensive fullness of the fourfold meaning is adequate for translating those passages.'[132]

Previously Heidenreich had described how in the two thousand years between the Mystery of Golgotha and the middle of this century Christ's 'presence' ebbed slightly but now intensifies as we draw close to the end of the century. He quotes an anthroposophical friend who describes this event in the light of cosmic rhythms: 'Think of a pond, a quiet bit of water, and a stone thrown into its centre; then the ripples travel out until they reach the shore when they are thrown back again to its centre. The Incarnation of Christ is like a stone thrown into the ocean of humanity. The effects of it spread from the earth into the cosmos in the Saturn rhythm until they reached the furthest point in the Saturn sphere, travelled back, and began striking onto the shore of human history in 1935.'[133]

One of the central concerns of Anthroposophy is to awaken humanity to the reality of the presence of Christ in our midst, to indicate how a conscious entry to the etheric world is now possible for the first time since the closing of the Gates of Paradise after the Fall of Man. Steiner outlined some futuristic perspectives on this subject while in conversation:

> Let us now picture the vision of Christ as it will appear to the first forerunners during the next 2,500 years and as it appeared to Paul on the way to Damascus. Man will ascend to the knowledge of the spiritual world permeated by *a new country, a new realm*. Man will enter an etheric region which is here now, but which he must first learn to perceive. This etheric region is even now spread out before the eyes of those who have carried their esoteric training as far as 'illumination'. It is visible for the initiate up to its lofty heights, and he draws thence at certain intervals the forces that he requires. Thus, when he has to carry out some special work, he draws forces from this realm within the earth's circuit—*which is here*, but only for the human beings who can see into it. A part of that land will be spread before a great portion of humanity during the next 2,500 years. Formerly, in the days of a primeval clairvoyance, man could see into the spiritual world, so that he has already been able to see what he will now see again, but with his new self-consciousness.[134]

The experience of crossing the Threshold is not an easy one. Rudolf Steiner predicted that many people would be caused great distress towards the end of this century because they would not possess the necessary spiritual faculties to understand what they were experiencing. The opposing powers have anticipated this event with great cunning so that psychedelic drugs made their appearance just at a time when the possibility of attaining to this new dimension was beginning to be experienced. Crossing the borders of the spiritual world is rather like being cast out into the ocean in a boat without oars or compass. To know where one is and to be able to stay on course makes great demands on that part of our being which is still in its infancy: the ego, our eternal spiritual core, which only came into existence during the present Earth Evolution.

The northern Mysteries re-emerged at the turn of the century in the form of Anthroposophy. Rudolf Steiner constantly spoke of the urgency for each individual human being to begin to strengthen these forces of the ego so that humanity would be able to cross this frontier without losing itself. All individuals will experience this whether or not they are prepared. Therefore it is a matter of the greatest urgency that they are ready to face it in clear consciousness and with the strength to fulfil their individual destinies. 'Christ is the medium through which we find our own total individual humanity, our own unique being. The more we find that, the less we need to focus on Christ. We become focused in our own centre. Christ is an activity; He is the becoming of the highest in oneself.'[135] Recognition of the reality of Christ is therefore a personal experience which cannot be forced on humanity; we must all find Christ in our own time.

To say 'I am a Christian' is merely lip service if the recognition of Christ is not a *personal* experience. Turning the message of Christ into 'fire insurance' and frightening people into accepting Christianity is a direct example of how the opposing powers operate.

Steiner has described how, after death, regions of the spiritual world are reached where a certain aspect of Christ can be perceived, but that those individuals who on earth have as yet had no inner experience of Christ cannot see Him there. When the individual moves into the spiritual region of the sun between one life and the next they 'find the throne of the sun empty' and enter a cosmic sleep which lasts until the beginning of their next incarnation. From this it can be understood why there is so little true understanding of the Christ prevalent in the world as yet.

On Tuesday, 25 December 1923, at Dornach in Switzerland, Rudolf Steiner laid the Foundation Stone for the Anthroposophical Society in the form of a verse which he spoke to the assembled members.

> From the way Rudolf Steiner delivered the opening address, beginning by making a special sign, it was immediately apparent that a deed would be performed which would introduce a new phase in the development of the Mysteries of mankind. When the Foundation Stone Meditation had

been spoken out, few realized immediately the intimate connection of its contents with that which had begun to live on earth through the laying of the first Foundation Stone and the building of the Goetheanum. On this occasion, the Foundation Stone was laid in the form of a meditation verse into the hearts of those present. The laying of this Foundation Stone can thus be described as an almost public Mystery deed. For it is certain that not only official representatives of their groups had come but also others; some of them had only recently become members, and could hardly yet have become connected with the actual destiny of the Society on earth.[136]

Thus, on 25 December 1923 Rudolf Steiner opened the Mysteries to all of mankind. During the speaking of the Foundation Stone meditation it has been related that some of those present supersensibly perceived Christian Rosenkreutz and his host entering the hall to join the Anthroposophists gathered there. The southern stream, which had been passed on to and secretly preserved by the Rosicrucians through the intervening centuries, having now met the Mysteries of East and West at Montségur on the night of 14 March 1244, was brought to join the northern Mysteries represented by Anthroposophy on 25 December 1923. The northern Mysteries, the Mysteries of the ego, are added to those of the South. The four Mystery streams were now united and made available to all of humanity. From that time onward it has been possible for any individual, without being initiated into any secret organization, to bring their ego into such a relationship with the physical body through the progressive transformation of astral and etheric principles, that finally the transubstantiation of matter can begin—the transubstantiation of both the individual and of the earth itself. North, East, South and West: four Mystery streams, four human principles. Four square: the foundations of the temple and of the New Jerusalem.

12
The Grail Chalice

'And is the interior of the earth of that gold that originates from the hollow space of the sun and goes back to it again?'
'Yes, the interior of the earth is of gold.'

Countess Keyserlingk
in conversation with Rudolf Steiner

'If you want to find the Holy Grail, you might look into the depths of a Norwegian fjord!' These words were spoken by someone who was unaware of their great significance. For what lies buried in the northern fjords and lakes on winter nights? The reflected radiance of the aurora borealis!

With my research into the Mystery streams complete I felt that I had come a long way towards resolving some of the questions raised by the Grail tradition in the book The Holy Blood and the Holy Grail. *And now I felt that I needed to look more deeply into the theme of earth energy as a potential manifestation of the Grail. I found wonderful confirmation of my intuitions in Harald Falck-Ytter's book* The Aurora, *which forms the basis of the following chapter. The magnetic field of the earth in relation to solar activity exactly echoes the Grail theme which we are exploring. The following chapter is largely scientific in nature, and the chapters that follow expand upon it, introducing correlative themes from the Grail legends and from the Gnostic gospels to fully demonstrate the intimate interweaving of science, legend and cosmology which forms the substance of the Grail tradition.*

In his beautiful book *The Aurora*, Harald Falck-Ytter describes how 'the aurora is a phenomenon taking place whenever the high-speed plasma of the solar-wind interacts with the electro-magnetic field of the earth. It is justifiable within the meaning of present-day science to look for the aurora's origin in the neighbouring regions of the earth. In this case the decisive question arises as to whether the solar wind's outgoing effect is not so much the cause of the aurora as rather the occasion for an as yet unknown, sun-related structure within the terrestrial organism, including its surrounding spheres, that gives rise to the aurora's mysterious revelation.'[137]

And elsewhere: 'The solar wind with the solar plasma issues from the events within the corona [of the sun] without transition. It streams through the whole planetary system and fills it. Planetary space remains dark, for the plasma is not light and not even, like the corona, light related. On the contrary, this stream of ions and protons is related to matter. The solar wind carries ionized material particles such as hydrogen and helium along with it, and moves with fluctuating velocity according to the forces of its expulsion and the opposition it encounters.'[138]

The etheric implications of this description can be brought out through reference to a statement made by Wachsmuth: 'Experimental research establishes the fact that the substance which makes its appearance in the *vanishing* of matter, in its spontaneous radioactive decay, is the same as that which we discover at the boundaries of our earth organism, in the coming into existence of matter; that is helium (He). When the forces radiated inward into the earth organism penetrate more deeply into the material world, the sun-force then forms ozone, the threefold oxygen.'[139]

This 'sun-force' we will recall as being the life ether, the fallen form of which is known as the mysterious 'Third Force'. With the life ether we are dealing with the mystery of 'energy before matter'. We continue the quote from Falck-Ytter begun above: 'The [solar winds] relationship to all material existence is demonstrated by its being bound to magnetic forces. The plasma carries along these forces which, on the photosphere, are already all-embracingly and intensively united with the sun-spots. In this way, the direction of the plasma-stream is diverted from the magnetic fields of other planets. As plasma in the earth's magnetosphere it produces light and colour in the terrestrial darkness in the form of the aurora by colliding with the highly refined terrestrial matter.'[140]

The aurora is created when the sun forces come into contact with the earth's magnetism, which we can also understand to be the concentrated realm of fallen life ether at the poles. As Wachsmuth points out: 'There must be points within the earth organism where the constant concentration of life ether and its unmodified action reach their maximum. Such points, then, of the heightened activity of the life ether are the magnetic poles.'[141]

Falck-Ytter continues: 'The stream of solar particles now penetrate into the regions of the open lines of magnetic force above the geomagnetic pole directly into the terrestrial environment; in so doing it fuses with the funnel-shaped converging lines of force which act as a powerful brake on it. This gives rise to a barely perceptible, high aurora which fits into the vault of heaven like a delicate pink cupola in the far north around Spitsbergen, even during the polar day, in winter.'[142]

We seem to be in the realm of the continual cosmic re-enactment of the Grail ceremony in the following description: 'Shining auroral ovals take form as light and coloured blossoms above the earth's polar regions. Into the centre of these blossom structures, pale red plasma flows into the high realms of the sun. It fills the chalice structure, invisible to the naked eye, with the solar processes which pass out of the heights into the depths.'[143]

Both the chalice and the 'plasma' which fills it are depicted by the aurora phenomenon as arising through interaction between the sun and earth forces. The sun is the realm to which the pure forces of the life ether were removed, the moon subsequently becoming the refuge of pure chemical-ether forces when the dynamic of the Fall created a realm of centric forces within the earth: electricity, magnetism, and the Third Force.

We can also regard electrical and magnetic phenomena above the earth's surface as having been created by the Fall. Therefore, in this context, the chalice of the Grail is formed by the as yet unredeemed etheric forces and the Host within the Grail as that which issues from the sun itself, a manifestation of the original pure life ether: solar plasma and the solar wind.

Here we can see that the 'sun-related structure' referred to at the beginning of this chapter is being suggested as the pure life ether from the sun. How can this intensification of the etheric forces proceeding from the sun be described in relation to the findings of modern science?

In his book *The Sun—Ancient Mysteries and a New Physics*, Georg Blattman tells how a friend of his, 'an advisor to NASA and the US Air Force, a man with several degrees and expert in these fields [sunspot activity etc], said to the author one would not like to admit what observation has shown in the last years, namely, that the sun is not a body at all, as previously understood, but consists of plasma (the term plasma means a non-material state).' Blattman adds that 'this sounds too evasive; fundamental rethinking is necessary for a true understanding of the sun, but this is avoided. Yet to speak of a plasma sphere and use ideas far removed from the earthly phenomenon leads close to a non-material position.'[144]

From this statement onwards we only have to achieve a slight shift in understanding to absorb Rudolf Steiner's indication that the interior of the sun creates the centre of a vortex around which the planets circle as in a great cosmic whirlpool. The centre of the sun is a cavity not filled with substance but is instead emptier than empty—negative or counter-space. Blattman graphically describes the surface of the sun as the boundary between matter and spirit:

> The surface, which appears so smooth and shining to the naked eye, appears through the telescope as a bubbling boiling cauldron, and very grainy. These bubbles are called 'granules', but the expression is too neutral for the activity taking place over there. A mighty seething of currents, a conglomeration of furnaces, a clashing together of darkness and light, a collision of foaming tidal waves towering up one moment and thrusting down the next, a wild ebullience of thunder and lightning; all of which must be accompanied by the sound of a roaring hurricane in terms of terrestrial experience. That is what is shown where the

> opposing worlds of matter and anti-matter rub against one another, collide and separate in eternal incompatible turbulence.[145]

This realm of 'anti-matter' is the etheric realm. It is a type of space that is devoid of all material substance, an emptiness that is formative in its activity. The etheric realm has been described as both the source of life and the region into which the dead first pass after leaving their earthly bodies and from which the newly incarnating spirit descends at the time of birth. With this in mind it is fascinating to read of the Eskimo traditions concerning the aurora: 'The influence of the aurora in the sphere of birth is often emphasized...children playing would often be seen in the image of the aurora.' And 'By far the most common is...the widespread idea that the dead are present in the aurora borealis...an example of this is a tradition from the Eskimos in Labrador (Hawkes 1916, 153): "The ends of the land and sea are bounded by an immense abyss, over which a narrow and dangerous pathway leads to the heavenly regions. The sky is a great dome of hard material arched over the earth. There is a hole through which the spirits pass to the true heavens...The spirits who live here light torches to guide the feet of new arrivals. This is the light of the aurora. They can be seen there feasting and playing football with a walrus skull." '[146]

We can also trace the influence of the aurora phenomenon upon the Mystery centres of antiquity. To do this we must first return to the subject of magnetism. Wachsmuth: 'It has been shown by recent research that terrestrial magnetism is not as had been mistakenly supposed—fixed to the shell of the earth or a characteristic of this—but that it is a result of the action of a truly variable field of force.'[147]

This field of force is described as moving freely over the surface of the earth, not emanating from within the fixed shell. In the next chapter we will see how Harald Falck-Ytter compares this action with the grinding action of the 'Sampo' in the Finnish epic *The Kalevala*. This free moving field of force above the earth's surface was described earlier in this chapter as having been less affected by the Fall than the centric forces trapped at the centre. It unites with the solar wind to demonstrate the original splendour of the etheric world in the colours of the aurora, thus forming a physically visible picture of the 'pre-Fall' conditions of the earth towards which all of those who wish to attain the Grail are striving.

In earlier chapters several early European Mystery centres were mentioned—centres which had been established by the emigrating survivors of Atlantis in their progress from west to east across the continent. Steiner describes one more of these 'north of today's Russia' where sacred 'Grail knowledge was connected with the "power" which brings new plant life into being in the spring, a power which is innocent in the plant kingdom but entangled with passion and desire in the animal and human kingdoms.' Here one can assume that Steiner is referring to the secret of the Tree of Life, of the chemical and life ethers, particularly the life ether. In lecture 20 of *The Temple Legend* he mentions the Grail again in the same connection:

> What then is the Holy Grail? For those who understand this legend correctly, it signifies—as can even be proved by literary means—the following. Until now, man has only mastered the inanimate in nature. The transformation of the living forces, the transformation of what sprouts and grows in the plants, and of what manifests itself in animal and human reproduction—that is beyond his power. Man has to leave these mysterious powers of nature untouched. There he cannot encroach. What results from these forces cannot be fully comprehended by him.[148]

We learned earlier that Steiner has also mentioned how in certain 'post-Atlantean Mysteries the initiates looked forward to a distant time when animal nature bound by the Fall would be transformed to a state where as the ray from the sun goes right down into the plant so will man's now purified power unite itself with this divine chalice which will manifest like a blossom hanging down from the sky—a reversal of the "chalice" of the earthly plant: man's transformed energy rising up from the earth like the sun's ray.'[149] It is then remembered that the future goal of mankind is to further Christ's deed in transforming the earth into a sun.

Very little is known of this centre. If it was north of Russia, it would be situated near or within the Arctic Circle, north of Latitude 60 and in an area which at the time of Parzival (the ninth century) would have been in the area in which the aurora was most visible!

The centre of the northern lights shifts slowly in relation to the North Pole. It is assumed today that in about 700 BC this centre lay somewhat north of Spitsbergen and in about AD 1200 lay near to the Novosibirskiye Ostrova (New Siberian Islands). During the ninth century this centre would have been situated between these two points in an area corresponding to northern Russia. In northern Russia the aurora was a frequent phenomenon. Exact descriptions go back to the year AD 919.

Here we can possibly make a connection between the above-mentioned Mystery centre and the aurora. In his book Falck-Ytter relates the three natural phenomena—lightning, the rainbow and the aurora—to God the Father, God the Son and the Holy Spirit respectively. Like the aurora, the spirit has always been hidden and unknown in the historical periods of human evolution. Before the Christian era the spirit could only be found in the secrecy of the world beyond. And since that time it is only slowly penetrating this sphere of human experience. In the same way the aurora shows itself to human beings; it was only in the twentieth century, when humanity became a comprehensive and interrelated society, that the being of the aurora came fully into appearance. The aurora's nature is like the yet unveiled spirit of the future.

In the Grail legend the Dove of the Spirit hovers over the Grail chalice. The pre-Christian initiates waited in secret dark caves to perceive the Spiritual Sun, shining at the midnight hour on the deepest night in winter. This was not a physical manifestation of the sun's light but its spiritual counterpart, which to be seen needs an inner effort of human activity.

A further possible reference to this invisible solar plasma

can be found in Rudolf Steiner's lecture cycle *The Search for the Holy Grail.* Steiner describes how:

> In the gold gleaming sickle of the moon—as any close observer can see—the dark part of the moon emerges and is as though marked off from the bright sickle...The gold gleaming sickle becomes apparent because the physical rays of the sun fall on the moon. The illuminated part of the moon shines out as the gold-gleaming vessel. Within it rests the dark Host. Physically, this is the dark part not reached by the sun's rays; spiritually there is something else. When the rays of the sun fall on part of the moon and are reflected in gold gleaming light, something does nevertheless pass through the physical matter. This something is the spiritual element that lives in the sun's rays. The spiritual power of the sun is not held back and reflected as the sun's physical power is; it goes through and, because it is resisted by the power of the moon, what we see at rest in the golden vessel is actually the spiritual power of the sun.[150]

Is Steiner here speaking of the solar plasma when it is becoming physically discernible both in the way he mentions above and in the manner in which science describes the creation of the aurora borealis?

The Poles are the least inhabited areas on the earth's surface; therefore the phenomenon of the aurora has rarely been observed by human beings until comparatively recently, when the Mysteries are secret no longer. In the dark sky over the Poles the inverted chalice is openly displayed over sparsely inhabited territory. It can be seen and reported by any human being who journeys there. As a result of the progress of modern science, travel to the remote corners of the earth is now possible for anyone if they can afford the fare. Could the aurora be the 'inverted blossom'—the 'Grail'—seen by the very few Atlantean initiates inhabiting the terrain north of Latitude 60? The word 'plasma' is used both in this context and in connection with the blood. If the Grail legend is connected with this ancient Mystery centre north of Russia, one could imagine, as we have mentioned before, that the cup, the chalice itself, is a symbol for the forces of the life and chemical ethers retained in the earth after the Fall, together with the chemical ether which still proceeds from the moon. The awesome music of the Grail theme in Wagner's *Parsifal* hints at the depths in which the fallen ethers lie, not only in the earth but in human nature as well. At the Poles the still unredeemed earthly forces rise up to meet the life ether as it streams down from the sun, or from within the magnetosphere. The force that rises up from the earth and from our lower nature must be transformed by human effort. The deepest, darkest energy both in ourselves and in the earth can then become a light that will shine out into the cosmos from the earth whose depths have become a sun.

On his way to the Grail Castle the innocent Parzival is put through many temptations by the beautiful Flower Maidens who, together with Kundry, were held in thrall by the evil Klingsor—his aim being to lure the Grail knights from their high goal of purity. By themselves they are the innocent vessels of energy which would only become a threat if the one aspiring to the Grail falls prey to the frailty of his lower nature. This lower nature can be recognized as a residue of moon influences left behind both in the human being and in the earth at the time of the Fall. At the beginning of Earth evolution the forces of sun and moon worked harmoniously through the planet from within. At the Fall the subtler life ether was withdrawn to ray down to the earth from the direction of the present sun; the moon forces were also withdrawn to the present moon-sphere. These forces also left a residue in the earth; they are forces which date back to the previous Moon evolution of the earth. Rudolf Steiner elaborates on this in a course of lectures given on the Holy Grail at Leipzig, 28 December 1913 to 2 January 1914:

> In the moon festivals of the Jews it was made clear that the Lord of the Earth shines down symbolically in its reflection from the moon...When all that has come over into Earth evolution from Saturn, Sun and Moon periods is grasped in its natural aspect, then we find it symbolized in the old

> Hebrew tradition through Eve. EVE—the vowels are never clearly pronounced—EVE! Add to it the sign for the divine being of Hebrew antiquity who is the Ruler of earth history, and we have a form which is quite as valid as any other—JEHVE-YAHVEH—the ruler of the earth who has his symbol in the moon. If we bring this into conjunction with what has come over from the Moon period and with its outcome for Earth evolution, we have the Ruler of the Earth united with the Earth Mother whose powers are a result of the Moon period...YAHVEH! Hence out of the Hebrew antiquity there emerges this mysterious connection with the Moon forces which have left their remains in the moon known to astronomy and their human form in the female element in human life. The connection of the Ruler of the Earth with the Moon Mother is given to us in the name YAHVEH.[151]

Here the Moon forces are described as the 'human forces in the female element of human life'. In a lecture given at Dornach, on 27 January 1923, Steiner explains this further:

> What the moon is able to reflect from the whole universe forms the sum total of forces which sustain the animal element in man and are connected with his sexual nature in its physical aspect. So the lower nature of man is a product of what radiates from the moon, while the highest wisdom once possessed by the earth lies concealed within the moon fortress.[152]

In the Leipzig Grail lectures previously quoted Rudolf Steiner gives us a picture of the forces of sun and moon united once more: '...the gold-gleaming sickle of the moon as it appeared in the heavens, with the dark moon like a great disk dimly visible within it...' where 'in truth the Spirit of the Sun rests in the vessel of the moon'. Earlier in the lecture Steiner describes this in such a way that we can see the chalice of the Grail—the 'moon' nature of the earth personified by the 'Earth Mother'. He reflects how, when he was...

> ...coming out of St Peter's in Rome under the strong influences made on me by Michaelangelo's work that you find on the right side when you enter—the mother with Jesus, the mother who looks so young, with Jesus dead already on her knees—and under the after-effect of looking at his work of art, there came to meet me, not as a vision but as a true imagination from the spiritual world...showing how Parzival, after he has gone away for the first time from the Castle of the Grail, where he had failed to ask about the Mysteries which prevail there, meets in the forest a young woman who is holding her bridegroom in her lap and weeping over him. But I knew that whether it is the mother or the bride whose bridegroom is dead (Christ is often called the bridegroom), the picture had a meaning, and that the connection thus established...had a meaning also.[153]

The way forward to the Grail Castle, the high goal of the Templars, is found through the re-establishing of sun and moon together, through the moon forces of the lower nature which are transformed to hold the Host. These are the deepest forces both within the earth and within the human nature which undergo catharsis so that the depths into which Earth evolution has descended becomes the Grail through which the Host, the transforming power of Christ can shine.

13
The Changing Face of the Goddess

> I am she that is the natural mother of all things, mistress and governess of all the elements, the initial progeny of worlds, chief of the powers divine, queen of heaven, the principal of the gods celestial, the light of the goddesses. At my will the planets of the air, the wholesome winds of the sea and the silences of hell be disposed. My name, my divinity, is adored throughout all the world, in divers manners, in variable customs and in many names, for the Phrygians call me the mother of the gods; the Athenians, Minerva; the Cyprians, Venus; the Candians, Diana; the Sicilians, Proserpina; the Eleusians Ceres; some Juno, others Bellona, others Hecate...
>
> Lucius Apuleius, *The Golden Ass*

We have seen that in the Grail the pagan and Christian traditions greatly enhance each other. The 'orthodox' forms of Christianity that were created as the esoteric stream went underground were totally complicit with the suppression of women in patriarchal culture. Orthodox theology saw the living world of sensual energies as being evil, and divided women into two categories: the virginal and pure Mary, and the fallen, sensual Magdalene. On the other hand, the pagan traditions revered the feminine powers in nature and saw them as being primal to the evolution of the complementary masculine aspects. The Goddess was both the Earth Mother and the energetic manifestation of the cosmic whole. This pagan attitude was maintained in the Grail tradition, as a reading of the Parzival legend will reveal.

The main inspiration for the following chapter came from my oldest friend, the brilliant mime-artist and story-teller Peri Aston.[154] *Peri's life journey had moved in tandem with my own ever since we had been drama students together, encouraging each other to explore the evolutionary frontiers of the imagination. Peri went on to become a performance artist within the Celtic-pagan traditions, while I found my natural home in Anthroposophy. However, an ongoing exploration of the deep connections between these two traditions resulted in the material contained in the following chapter. Here we show how the pagan and Christian Grail streams interweave in exploring the theme of the Goddess as the expression of the etheric realm in all its rich complexity.*

In a lecture given at RILKO early in 1995 on the subject of symbolic landscapes and the ley-line system, leading earth mysteries investigator and best-selling author Paul Devereaux argued that one should not speak of the leys as being charged with 'energy'. He suggested that if we do so we are interpreting them with our modern consciousness, which is steeped in constant references to electricity, computer chips and circuit boards. We are all too ready to apply our knowledge of these 'energies' to the mysterious properties of phenomena which were either found or fashioned by peoples who lived in distant times and whose preoccupation with them was governed by very different modes of consciousness.

Devereaux suggested that these ancient peoples may have known of something 'other' that was involved in the manifestation of these lines, and he warned against being in a hurry to resolve the unknown with a glib explanation culled from contemporary consciousness. He detailed how he had conducted a close reading of the ley phenomena, and had been led to view them as 'spirit paths' guiding the out-of-body travels of the ancient shamans.

From the perspective of this book, we can suggest that the use of the leys has left a *residue* of recordable energy, but that this is a mere *after-effect* of their function. Modern ley-hunters and occultists whose reductionist approach debases all spiritual phenomena to electromagnetic force are in fact merely rummaging about in the debris left on the building site and ignoring, at great personal cost, the magnificent building erected there.

The something 'other' of the leys could be the qualitative, negative space of the etheric realm. We have already seen that complementing the etheric as counter-space are its fallen manifestations: electricity, magnetism and the 'Third Force'.

In a lecture given by Walter Johannes Stein on the theme

of the interrelation of man and cosmos, on 1 February 1947, he correlated electricity, magnetism and the Third Force with the three concentric layers within the earth—realms described as the domain of the 'Mothers' in Goethe's *Faust*. According to a report of this lecture:

> Dr Stein said that these three layers are the earth's past, the relic of its past evolution still buried within it. At the central core lies Old Saturn, above it the stratum which is Old Sun, and the outermost layer, coming beneath the mineral earthly surface, is the relic of Old Moon evolution...Mephistopheles spoke of the Mothers with the greatest awe as goddesses unknown to men, and told Faust that he 'must burrow to the uttermost Profound' if he would find them in the 'ever-empty Far'.[155]

Stein further described how the Mothers correlated with the stages of planetary metamorphosis prior to Earth evolution. He related Demeter to Moon evolution, Persephone to Sun evolution, and Rhea to Saturn evolution. Later he speaks of the 'Third Force':

> From the innermost layer there will arise the as yet undiscovered Third Force. Dr Stein denied emphatically that this was atomic power...He connected this Third Force with the creative Word. In the Primal Beginnings (in the Archai) was the Word. The undiscovered force is to come from the backward Archai...Saturn spirits at the Earth's centre. Their realm is the realm of the negative life ether.[156]

Did Stein mean that the 'Mothers' of Ancient Greek tradition only represent the 'fallen' counterpart of the ethers, or could one see them also as representing the *potential for transformation* into the pure etheric condition as it was before the luciferic intervention? In a lecture on *Faust* Rudolf Steiner describes the Mothers as personifications of the pure life force in its different aspects as it originated on Ancient Saturn, Ancient Sun and Ancient Moon respectively:

> Let us ask ourselves what the Greeks looked for in their

> three Mothers, Rhea, Demeter and Persephone. In these three Mothers they saw a picture of those forces that, working down out of the cosmos, prepare the human cell. These forces however do not come from the part of the cosmos that belongs to the physical but to the supersensible. The Mothers Demeter, Rhea and Persephone belong to the supersensible world. No wonder then that Faust has the feeling that an unknown kingdom is making its presence felt when the word 'Mothers' is spoken...When we look from this earth to Saturn, Sun and Moon, there we find the 'Mothers' that figure in another form in the Greek Mysteries under the names Persephone, Demeter and Rhea. For all the forces that are in Saturn, Sun and Moon are still working—working on into our own time.[157]

The Goddess is the creative impulse behind the coming into being of creation. This power moves from spiritual cause to material manifestation but can also be an ominous destructive force in its 'fallen' aspect. In the three Mothers we have the Triple Goddess evolving in creative strength from Persephone to Demeter—spring forces to summer forces—to the Crone when the laws of matter release their hold and the spiritual forms return to their source—as summer turns to autumn and then winter.

A connection can also be made between the Mothers and their Christian counterparts: the Virgin Mary, Mary Magdalene, and the enigmatic figure behind the Black Madonna—whose identity it is hard establish. She could be Anne, traditional mother of the Virgin, which echoes the relationship between Demeter and Persephone. But she also possesses an ancient quality which identifies her with Rhea, namely, her *blackness* which is reminiscent of the darkness of Ancient Saturn, the primal origin of matter.

We have seen how Rudolf Steiner's research uncovered the existence of the two Jesus-children, described in the Gospels of St Matthew and St Luke. These two children with their differing early life histories (as can be seen in the Gospels) imply the existence of *two* mothers, one for each child. Rudolf

Steiner has described how the young, fair-haired mother of the *Luke* Jesus-child was an innocent and virginal girl who mirrored the paradisaical qualities of the child she bore. In contrast was the mother of the *Solomon* Jesus, dark and gifted with profound wisdom. These two Marys were recognized in the Coptic Church as the 'White' and 'Black' Madonnas.

The Black Virgin is a powerful archetype for the Ancient Saturn forces, and has many names. In Ireland, according to Hutton in his book *The Pagan Religions of the Ancient British Isles*: 'The Danu who gave her name to the Tuatha de Danaan is presumably the same as "Ana" described in Sanas Charmaic, Cormac's glossary written around AD 900. There she is called the mother of all deities.'[158]

In *The Religion of the Ancient Celts*, J. A. MacCulloch describes how 'Danu gave her name to the whole group of gods and is called their mother—like the Egyptian Neith or the Semitic Ishtar...'[159] Goddesses like Demeter and Persephone were associated with the underworld, the dead being Demeter's folk. The fruits of the earth are then the gifts of the earth or under-earth goddess. This may have been the case with Dana, for in Celtic belief the gifts of civilization came from the underworld or from the gods. This archetype was then turned into St Anne by the Christians, some of whom believed her to be the mother of the Solomon Mary. On a symbolic level she is both Anne, mother of the Solomon Mary and the Solomon Mary herself.

We know that cathedrals, abbeys and churches have been built over areas of concentrated etheric activity ever since the time that the 'Christianizing' of sacred pagan sites took place. The energies in these places were often transformed by pagan acts of worship long before they were rededicated to Christian saints. Their original 'fallen' quality would have been gradually raised by constant religious practices and devotion so that one could describe them as having changed back to the original pure etheric state—the 'Paradise' condition which prevailed at the beginning of Earth evolution. Rudolf Steiner has related that 'such places were...sought after by the Druids—places where imaginations lingered long in the atmosphere, and where the influence of nature on human beings was stronger owing to archaic layers having come to the surface. Wherever there is or has been a Black Madonna, etheric forces have issued from deeper levels, making the region a quite special place for connection with the elements and through them for communion with the cosmos.'[160]

The Goddess was recognized at these sites by the early Christians who followed their pagan predecessors. Both they and the churches sometimes built over them were often dedicated to the Virgin Mary; in some cases (as in the area around Rennes-le-Château) they were dedicated to the Magdalene, and with some sites to the Black Virgin.

In *The Myth of the Goddess*, Anne Baring and Jules Cashford link the Black Virgin with the Magdalene: 'Statues of the Black Virgin are often found on the sites of the ancient goddesses, or where the Cathars lived, or where there was a cult of Mary Magdalene, with whom she was significantly associated.'[161] The existence of images of the Magdalene with a baby could be seen to add fuel to the claim that Jesus and the Magdalene were married. However, if the image here is that of the Virgin's mother then the child could be the infant Mary.

The connection between Anne and the Magdalene could be seen to be similar to the connection between the life and chemical ethers, one that is so close that it is difficult to tell them apart. The chemical ether and the Magdalene are the energy that works into the material realm as 'magnetism', and this can also be interpreted as sexual magnetism. Anne represents the oldest energy, which in its latest form brings matter into being.

Ancient Saturn gives birth to Ancient Sun, where the etheric realm has its point of origin. Anne bears the Virgin Mary who can be related to the etheric. At Chartres Cathedral this progression from Ancient Saturn to Ancient Sun, Anne to Virgin Mary, is acknowledged in the presence of the Black Virgin in the crypt, and also in the beautiful stained glass windows. Here, too, as is often the case, the Black Virgin is found represented in the same building as the Green Man—another personification of the concentrated life-force.

In his beautifully produced book *The Green Man*, William Anderson unknowingly gives a living picture of the quality of Ancient Saturn evolution and its subsequent repetitions in the later planetary states when he describes the Black Virgin of Notre-Dame d'Espoir in Dijon:

> There is another link between the Black Virgins and many representations of the Green Man in this period [eleventh and twelfth centuries]. All the ancient Black Virgins I have seen have a numinous and hieratic calm, as with the Virgin of Notre-Dame d'Espoir in Dijon. She is a manifestation of a level of being and experience infinitely beyond human failings and sufferings and it is precisely because she possesses this freedom from misery that she is able to comfort and bless through her presence. The atmosphere she generates is the evidence that there is a truth, a level of peace that is attainable and is full of succour for human griefs and hopes. Many of the Green Men possess something of her calm and independence of the vicissitudes of ordinary mortals.[162]

Here surely is the description of a time before even the most potent 'backward' being had fallen, long before unwitting humanity had been caught up in the 'wars among the gods'. In her archetypal beauty the Black Virgin persists in a time before evil began.

In *The White Goddess*, Robert Graves describes a 'Black Annis of Leicester who had a bower in the Dane hills and used to devour children, whose skins she hung on an oak to dry'. Here there seems to be a resonance with the 'crone' aspect of the Goddess, of the fallen life ether—most ominous of the fallen ethers—and also with the Indian Kali. Later Graves quotes Mr E. M. Parr who describes the name Mariamnne: 'a word of triple power. But the basic word is *Anna*, which confers divinity on mere parturition and which also seems to form part of Arianrhod's name. *Arianrhod* in fact may not be a debasement of *Argentum* and *rota* "silver wheel" but *Ar-ri-an*, "High fruitful mother", who turns the wheel of heaven; if so, Arianrhod's Cretan counterpart Ariadne would be Ar-ri-an-de, the *de* meaning barley, as in Demeter.'[163]

Here we have two connections with the life ether: Arianrhod whom we can connect with the etheric counterpart of the forces that swirl above the Poles as electromagnetism, and Demeter, the oldest of the Mothers mentioned in *Faust*. The 'triple power' mentioned above beautifully reflects their interdependence, which is a picture of the ethers or fallen ethers operating in concert.

Robert Graves also connects Rhea with the northern territories, which we investigated when we connected the aurora borealis with the chalice of the Grail. The sacred oak-king was killed at midsummer and translated to the corona borealis, presided over by the White Goddess, which was then just dipping over the northern horizon. But from the song ascribed by Apollonius Rhodium to Orpheus, we know that the queen of the circling universe, Eurynome, alias Cardea, was identical with Rhea of Crete. Thus Rhea lived at the axle of the mill, whirling around without motion, as well as on the Galaxy. Ross Nichols describes how Cardea and her mate Janus form the axle of the millstone of the universe which is at the back of the north wind and which is turned by the strength of the two bears in the heavens.[164]

In Chapter 6 of Harald Falck-Ytter's *Aurora* the 'grinding mill' is described scientifically both through Guenther Wachsmuth's knowledge of the ethers and in traditional scientific terms. In this way we can understand how Rhea also fits into the picture as described by Robert Graves, who continues his description: 'In a later mythological tradition the sacred king went to serve her at the mill, not in the castle; for Samson after his blinding and enervation turned a mill in Delilah's prison house.'[165]

In Goethe's *Faust*, Margarethe sings of a king in Thule who lived in a castle on the edge of the sea and who received a golden goblet on his death-bed. Thule is at present the geomagnetic pole of the northern hemisphere, the centre of the aurora zone, 'the axle of the mill, whirling around without motion' where Rhea lived.

Artemis Caliste was also known as the goddess of the mill. The she-bear was sacred to her and in Arcadia and Athens a girl of 10 years old and a girl of 5, dressed in saffron yellow robes in honour of the moon, played the part of sacred bears at the festival of Artemis Brauronia. The names of the two constellations that circle the North Pole, that 'turn the mill around', are the Great Bear and the Little Bear. The Great Bear, Callisto, was also known as Helice, which translates as both 'that which turns' and 'willow branch'.

The revolution of the constellations of the Great and Little Bears around the Pole, the two constellations that 'turn the mill around', have been further described by Joscelyn Godwin in his book *Arktos*:

> For inhabitants of the northern hemisphere during the last 6,000 years, the most prominent constellation in the north part of the sky has been Arktos, otherwise known as the Great Bear, the Plough, the Big Dipper, and Charlie's Wain. Each night these stars are seen to swing counter-clockwise around the polar point, which is currently close to the star Polaris. Naturally the whole circle can only be inferred, as the sun's rising obscures the daytime motion of the stars. Nearby there is another seven-star group of remarkably similar shape, but reversed: the Little Bear. This also swings around Polaris, which is the last star in its tail. If one wanted to record in graphic form the nightly or yearly cycle of the Great and Little Bears, it would be enough to show them in four positions, corresponding to the four directions of space and the four seasons, strongly suggestive of the swastika in all its varieties, so that it is not surprising that the latter has been used as a symbol of the Pole and of the motion around it.[166]

The swastika, in its uncorrupted form, can then be seen as a symbol for the functioning of the life force. The theme of the mill describing the life-realm at the Pole is illustrated in the *Kalevala*, an epic of the Finno-Ugrian peoples. At the centre of this epic there is a mysterious thing: the Sampo. It is created by the divine-human smith Ilmarinen in dark Sariola, the land of the North. In the epic, it is said of the creation of the Sampo

(X, 414–22):

> Forged with cunning art the Sampo
> And on one side was the corn-mill
> On another side a salt-mill
> And upon the third a coin mill.
> Now was grinding the new Sampo
> And revolved the pictured cover,
> Chestfuls did it grind till evening.
> First for food it ground a chestful,
> And another ground for barter,
> And a third it ground for storage.[167]

This miraculous entity not only grinds substances but also *creates* them. Further on we are told that the Sampo is roofed over by a many-coloured lid which also revolves. In Finnish it is called Kirokansi. This word signifies 'the vault of the heavens'.

As a source of abundance and wealth, the Grail has much in common with the cosmic mills of Scandinavian tradition. The Eddic poem Grottasongr and Snorri's Skaldskapamal tell of a mill that comes into the possession of King Frodi of Denmark, which can grind out whatever its owner wishes for. Turned by two giant women, the mill Grotti grinds out gold for Frodi. But when it falls into the hands of the sea-king Mysing it is used to grind out salt—in such quantities that the giant-women, displeased at being overworked, grind out Mysing's doom as well. The mill then bursts asunder and sinks into the sea, where a whirlpool is formed by the water rushing through the hole in the millstone.

In the *Kalevala*, the enigmatic Sampo is a three-sided mill; one part grinds out meal, one grinds salt, and the other produces coins. As with the mill Grotti, the Sampo is destroyed as the result of its being stolen; its remains sink into the sea, giving rise to the sea's bounty. The cosmic nature of the Sampo is indicated by its revolving, pictured cover representing the constellations, and its roots that greatly resemble those of Yggdrasil (the Norse Tree of Life); and also by its one-time location in the northern otherworld of Finnish tradition, Pohjola. Wachsmuth:

> This area due to its proximity to the magnetic pole would also be very strongly affected by the forces of the life ether. If we apply here the explanation already given that the phenomenon of gravitation is due to the suctional action of the life ether, then it will follow that the terrestrial magnetism directed towards the pole is only a special instance of the universal magnetism, the cause of which is identical with that of so called 'gravitation', that is, the suctional action of the life ether acting from the interior of the earth. The magnetism operating from the magnetic pole is only a plus in the suctional pull operating from points where the life ether within the earth is least disturbed, that is, points of greater activity in the force-sphere belonging to the life ether. As such these are shifting points; that is, they are centres of force in the etheric earth.[168]

This unique peculiarity of the polar cap is described by Wachsmuth as follows. 'The cupola of forces, which is only slightly arched over the polar region, embraces a compressed body of air. The effect exerted by this field of force moves in an east-west direction during the course of the day; that is to say, counter to the earth's rotation about the Pole. There arises thereby a kind of circling, gliding movement around the edge of the polar cap...'[169] In this way, this cupola of forces moulds ever anew the air body contained in it with its impulses as it moves round the polar caps. On the edge of the body of air a contour-forming and structuring impulse occurs, while this contoured body of air is moulded continually from without towards the inside, plastically formed and guided to structural changes. The moulding activity of such spheres of force from outside inwards presents a graphic image of the efficacy of the formative forces described above. These forces lead here to the formation of elastic structures and to the fashioning of contoured organs inwardly changeable. Here grinding and plastically forming events are described which, in the *Kalevala*, are handed down through the special language of myth in almost the same manner as in the Sampo story. In these imaginative accounts, the production of different inorganic and organic structures and substances is described during, as well as after, the Sampo forging. The concentrated life-processes within the polar caps are accompanied by heightened electric and magnetic occurrences. Wherever living things arise, electricity and magnetism are incorporated; they are a preposition for every embodiment and also its sequence and belong, therefore, to all terrestrial organisms.

In certain respects it is understandable that Mary Magdalene has been identified with the Black Madonna. But with our knowledge of the ethers and their interaction, and also their relationship to the previous planetary evolutions, we can begin to differentiate between the qualities and functions of, for example, the chemical ether as opposed to the life ether and through this to the goddesses who represent each of them. Mary Magdalene/Demeter could be seen to belong to Ancient Moon evolution, together with astrality and the activity of the chemical ether. The moon and the chemical ether are also related to the element water. With these two connections in mind it is interesting to read that 'the image of weeping was also one of her defining qualities, for the word "maudlin", which passed into the English language via the French, derived from her name.'[170]

In the Bible one of the views we are given of her is an archetype for the 'fallen' aspect of the female sex. It will be remembered that magnetism, the fallen chemical ether, is the dynamic which works together with the life ether at the female 'physically creative pole' as was demonstrated in the quotation from Wachsmuth in Chapter 10. When the Church lost its understanding of the true nature of the Fall the apparent involvement of the female sex in its relationship to this event led to misunderstanding and mistreatment:

> If secondary creation and inferior substance are accepted, it follows that there is in Eve an image of a flaw in creation. From the history of scapegoats and sacrifice, we might

> expect that Eve would receive those accusations of imperfection that human beings with *unconscious* demands for perfection cannot make to themselves and so project outwards onto a figure who can be blamed instead. The worse the figure can be made out to be, the better the accusers, by contrast, feel themselves to be.[171]

It is paradoxical then that the blame for the Fall has fallen squarely on the shoulders of the sex that has *most deeply* paid for it. Is it therefore surprising that the woman's movement has risen in a tide of outrage now that the hold of four thousand years of patriarchal culture has begun to relax? From the perspective of Anthroposophy one can point out to fellow members of the female sex that Rudolf Steiner has offered us great solace in the laws of karma which organize usually alternating male and female incarnations. As we have already seen in earlier chapters, the original human being was not divided into sexes; the split between male and female came as a direct result of the Fall; the rift will eventually be overcome through the deed of Christ. Therefore it is interesting to note that Mary Magdalene, who seems to belong to the same archetype as Eve, is the individual who first meets the Risen Christ.

The journey through Eve, the earlier version of Magdalene, leads to a woman who represents future humanity in a new state where the laws of matter no longer apply and where the sexes are no longer separate. In this context one can relate the Magdalene to the Divine Sophia.

In this sense Mary Magdalene belongs to the same archetype as Parzival. They are 'humanity' which has gone through the mill and attained to a position beside the Risen Christ. This is a humanity no longer divided by the restrictions of gender. We can see this on the *archetypal* level as a *marriage* between *humanity* (the Magdalene) and *Christ.*

At this point one is sufficiently prepared to understand that the claim made by the authors of *The Holy Blood and the Holy Grail* that Jesus married Mary Magdalene is irrelevant to the authenticity or otherwise of Christianity.

In 'Day Five' of *The Chymical Wedding* (attributed to Johann Valentin Andreae) the Magdalene can be seen as the Lady Venus discovered lying naked in a deep sepulchre. Here the fallen forces of the ethers could be indicated, lying waiting for redemption in the depths of the earth and in the fallen nature of the human being. The Magdalene is also the fallen one with whom all of us can identify—the individual who suffers with all of us in paying the great price involved in the attainment of individual maturity and consciousness.

Rudolf Steiner has spoken of the five-pointed star, the pentagram, in connection with present Earth evolution where,

The 'V ... e zodiac by the planet
Ve ... Venus comes into
... mic intervals.

through the Fall, the independent ego first comes into being. Earth evolution is also spoken of by Steiner as the 'Cosmos of Love'. Steiner has illustrated how the pentagram is a fitting symbol for the activity of the ego working through matter. The combined pentagon-pentagram figure may recall a five-petalled rose about to open. This beautiful figure is a spiritual reality. As its rhythms evolve the patterns in time, they reveal the harmonious relations and proportions recognized on earth in many spatial and organic forms such as those of the Golden Mean. In olden days this invisible star of Venus was more important than the visible planet in its orbit.

The Rose is the flower sacred to Mary Magdalene. The rose was also a symbol which was used frequently by the Cathar troubadours and which was then taken up by the Rosicrucians, both for the name of their Order and it's founder—Christian Rosenkreutz. Both of these groups, as we have seen, continued the impulse of Manichaeism, whose greatest aim was the transformation of evil to bring about the transubstantiation of matter. It is not surprising therefore that the Magdalene should be so closely connected with a region of France that bears the image of the pentagram. This south-western area of France, which sheltered Cathars and Templars, still today manifests 'energy before matter'. The Cathars and Templars belonged to the southern stream which was concerned with the mysteries of matter. Both they and the Rosicrucians guarded the secrets of the life and chemical ethers, the mysteries of female energy. This radiated upwards to both these groups, who populated the Languedoc in the twelfth and thirteenth centuries, and later to those concerned with the secrets of the Rosicrucians. The pentagram connects in a very realistic way with the planet Venus as will be seen in the following passage:

> If the positions of Venus in the zodiac at the times of conjunction are observed and recorded, it can be realized how, by the interacting rhythms, particular patterns are constantly created in the cosmos in the course of time. One

> such pattern is of vital significance for our Earth evolution. We find it if we imagine (or draw) a path not following the orbit but in straight lines, between the points where meetings of similar kind occur, namely, the points of five inferior and five superior conjunctions. This path traces five diagonals across the zodiac, inscribing there over a period of eight years an almost but not quite exact, five-pointed star in the zodiac—as if rotating upon the sun at its centre. To follow one single revolution of this pentagram round the zodiac, we may join the points in an enclosing figure—a pentagon. Twelve hundred years must pass before the pentagram performs one complete rotation through the zodiac. The meetings between Venus and earth continue for about a century in each constellation; the period varies according to the direction of the zodiac in which they are taking place.[172]

The interaction of Venus (occult Mercury) with the sun facilitates the introduction of 'form' into matter. The pentagram bears within it a beautiful form-principle, the Golden Section or the Golden Mean, which demonstrates a proportion found in nature, in the human being and in traditional art. Edward Mann in his *Sacred Architecture* states: 'The mathematician Filius Bonacci (called Fibonacci) wrote a treatise on the number series related to the Golden Mean... Pythagoras claimed that its proportions were musical, and it is true that the harmonious blending of musical intervals is governed by the series.'[173]

This relationship of Venus to the Sun is also a very fitting illustration of the same relationship that the human ego has to the Christ. Both the higher ego of man and Christ bring the formative forces from the cosmos to introduce 'form' and 'differentiation' to the life ether as it creates matter. This function of the planet Venus helps one to understand how it was long ago recognized as the 'healing' planet: 'In ancient times Venus, as understood by modern astronomy, was called Mercury. Venus has a mercurial character in an occult or esoteric sense, and the task of the beings whose symbol she is consists in uniting and healing.'[174]

A description of the properties of the metal mercury by Zeylmans van Emmichoven causes one to wonder at the possibility that not only the names of the planets Venus and Mercury have been reversed since early times, but also the qualities of the metals connected with them. Van Emmichoven describes mercury as 'a force which is concerned above all to assert its own nature. A drop of quicksilver can be divided into ever tinier droplets, all equally round; and they can all just as easily run together to form a big drop. Mercury provides an eloquent, convincing picture of the way a divine unity and multiplicity can arise, all parts resembling the original unity. This also points towards another fact which has already been mentioned: there lives in mercury something of an original principle, not derived from anything else but which exists through itself alone.'[175] This description could also apply to the human ego which has the potential of emulating the Christ and, by so doing, bringing the redemptive quality of the Logos into matter.

It is also interesting that Zeylmans van Emmichoven comments: 'There is a duality in mercury. The sign is the same as that for the planet, a moon and sun sign together, anchored in the earth through the small cross beneath the sun symbol. This points to something in man himself which is hard to understand—the middle part of a threefold man. Where two polarities meet, a centre arises; but it is more important to realize how the central part of the being of man was implicit and intended from the first: "The two arise from sun and moon/ From which doth spring the Son of Man" the Rosicrucian verse says. This points to the highest goal of man's evolution—to bring Christ to birth within himself.'[176] This Rosicrucian verse not only points to the mediating power of Mercury/Venus but also reminds us of the significance of the Grail in relation to the joining of sun and moon forces.

In the Fifth Day of the Rosicrucian text *The Chymical Wedding*, an inscription on the copper door leading to the Lady Venus in a deep sepulchre announces:

Poussin's painting *The Shepherds of Arcadia* which features prominently in the mysteries surrounding Rennes-le-Château

Here lies buried
Venus
that beauty which hath undone
many a great man
both in fortune, honour, blessing
and prosperity.[177]

The Tree of Life is mentioned in the account in connection with Venus, who symbolizes the challenge of those deep 'Magdalene' forces connected with it, etheric forces which have become entangled in matter and which are waiting for redemption.

When the fruit of my
tree shall be quite melted down
then I shall awake and
be the mother of a
King.[178]

When 'The Tree of Life' (the chemical and life ethers) in its fallen state has been totally transformed, then the lower nature of man will realize its true goal and give birth to the higher ego—the Christ.

Is it possible that the enigmatic 'Shepherdess' figure standing behind the kneeling shepherds around the tomb in Poussin's painting *Les Bergères d'Arcady* is both the Magdalene and the Lady Venus strangely risen from her deep chamber? Might *In Arcadia Ego* hint at some secret which the group shares in connection with her unexpected release from those depths, but in this case a release that does not lead to a union with the Christ Being? David Wood has suggested that the figure is Isis. She could also have a relationship with the attributes of Anne/Rhea and even the Indian Kali. Once an area is sacred to one goddess several others seem to take up residence there as well, as in the case of Ephesus which was sacred to Artemis. At Ephesus there was also an Isis connection, and the Virgin Mary spent the last years of her life there in company with John the Divine. John we recognize as that individual who constantly leads the Mystery stream concerned with the secrets of matter. Both Cathars and Templars belonged to this stream, and shared a recognition of the feminine principle in religion and seemed to be drawn to settle in geographical locations where the 'Goddess' is variously manifest in the energies that rise up from the fallen etheric domain beneath their feet.

The terrible Indian goddess of destruction, Kali, could be seen to personify the counterpart of Ancient Saturn evolution in our present earth where the once-innocent Saturn force has become the fallen counterpart of 'energy before matter': the Third Force. It was described earlier as 'a powerful force, as yet unknown to mankind'. Over the door of the church at Rennes-le-Château Saunière has inscribed the words *Terriblis est locus iste*: 'This place is terrible'. 'Terrible' could also be interpreted as 'awesome'. The energy that manifests at Rennes-le-Château, particularly within the church, seems to be a definite example of the deepest of the 'fallen' ethers which are personified by Kali. The Egyptian version of the same archetype is Nepthys, who is the consort of Set. Set can be considered as belonging to the same archetype as the backward Archai on Ancient Saturn—'Time Spirits'—who it will be remembered are involved in the upbuilding of matter in the darkness of night which echoes the darkness of Ancient Saturn. Set has also appeared in David Wood's research on the Rennes mystery together with Isis. Rennes-le-Château has previously been referred to as the sacral chakra in a line of chakras leading up from the Mediterranean through France and England to the north of Scotland. As we know, specialists on the subject of earth energy bear witness to the fact that this particular location in France emanates a concentration of 'earth energy', which in this case seems to manifest the fallen counterpart of the life ether.

Palaeontologists have noticed that in reconstructing the skeletons of certain prehistoric animals the delicate construction of the framework of some of them would have made standing upright impossible unless they were immersed in water and thus supported. It has been proved that they were land animals, therefore one could deduce that gravitation was not as strong then as at a later date. Wachsmuth refers to this in relationship to the changing symbols of the Earth Mother: 'The forms used here for the chemical and life ether [the half moon and the square] were employed for the name of the Goddess "Isis", whereas in the Peruvian texts the forms here assigned to warmth and light ether [the circle and the triangle] were employed for the name of the corresponding goddess. The American Mystery places related to earlier cultural centres are thus seen to have used symbols for the creative principle, the forms of the formative forces (ethers), *phylogenetically* earlier, whereas the Egyptian places belonging later used the forms of those forces *phylogenically* later.'[179]

Here maybe Wachsmuth is indicating that the dynamic of the Fall took time to take effect, that in an earlier age the fallen chemical and life ethers did not yet predominate, or maybe geological changes thrust 'core rock' up from the centre so that the earth's gravitational pull was intensified by a 'churning up' of centric forces. Granite is a rock that manifests the life ether and originates from the layer below the earth's crust (lithosphere) in the form of magma. Where this has risen from below under volcanic pressure it has brought with it centric forces from deeper regions.

If Rhea, Persephone, Demeter/Anne, the Virgin Mary and Magdalene relate to Ancient Saturn, Sun and Moon evolutions—to the physical, etheric and astral principles in turn—then who personifies this Earth evolution for which the goddesses have prepared? This is the Being who is the Higher Ego of all of mankind and who rescues the lower ego, which was entangled in the dynamic of the Fall at a time when it was not strong enough to withstand the intervention of first luciferic and then later ahrimanic beings. Our earth occupies the central position in a progression of seven planetary incarnations; it is the turning-point in evolution. Through the Goddess, whose face has constantly changed, the development towards physical incarnation is achieved. This is consolidated by the 'divine accident' already mentioned. Once this density has been reached, the way back again can begin through the activity of the human ego which, as we have seen, makes its first appearance during Earth evolution. The centre of the labyrinth has been reached. If the thread that has been brought to this point in time by the Goddess is once more traced outwards the whole of creation can be turned inside-out and taken forward to a completely new, gradually spiritualizing state, through the next three incarnations of the earth. The Goddess has given birth to matter. 'Woman' has borne 'Man', or humanity, into Earth evolution. Now, during the remaining half of the earth's incarnations, 'Man' must give birth to 'Woman'—the eternal source of creation within himself.

14
Knights Templar: Guardians of the Grail

> I saw heaven standing open and there before me was a white horse, whose rider is called Faithful and True. With justice he judges and makes war. His eyes are like blazing fire, and on his head are many crowns. He has a name written on him that no one knows but he himself. He is dressed in a robe dipped in blood, and his name is the Word of God. Out of his mouth comes a sharp sword with which to strike down the nations.
>
> Revelations 19: verses 11–13

It did not take long for the Templars to come riding into my research, and many seemingly chance encounters with modern-day 'Templars' led me to consider more deeply Wolfram von Eschenbach's assertion that the Templars were the Guardians of the Grail. If this were true, then it meant that in some way the Templars would be connected with the question of the etheric energies. I also expected that the motifs of the Grail that I had already discovered would manifest clearly within their history. While there has been much outlandish speculation about the Templars of late, I found that they fit into the picture puzzle I was gradually assembling—at a very specific place. And also that, when positioned correctly, many of the mysteries surrounding them and their activity fell into place. Pursuing Rudolf Steiner's many comments on the Templars, I was able to demonstrate the exact nature of their role as Guardians of the Grail and how the realization of the Grail motif within the realms of history was a motivating impulse in much of their otherwise puzzling activity.

The following chapter is not in any way an exhaustive account of the theme of the Templars as Guardians of the Grail, but will build a bridge from the theme of the Goddess to the chapters on alchemy that are to follow.

'I have come not to bring peace, but a sword.' These words of Christ undermine the notion of a pacifist Jesus 'meek and mild'. The Christ of the Book of Revelation, the Christ encountered by humanity in the spiritual world, is far removed from the passive being worshipped in many churches. In the cosmic imaginations of John the Divine, Christ appears as the bearer of a sword—but it is the sword transformed through the process of human evolution.

In its primal state the sword is a principle of division and destruction, a tool of power to mould the world according to instinct and desire. It was transformed in the hands of the Arthurian knights. They turned the sword into an instrument of peace, attempting, as Rudolf Steiner has described, to create order in a world dominated by the blood-lust and tribal bonds of luciferic astrality. In later times, in certain cultures, the sword was to bear the image of a heart, an indication that the time was near when the world-taming power of the sword was to be replaced by the power of human *thinking*.

In the imaginative picture of the Archangel Michael conquering the dragon, the Archangel holds his mighty sword aloft, while the dragon is pinned helpless yet untamed beneath his feet. This Michaelic sword is forged of cosmic iron and represents the power of a world-embracing, *thoroughly cosmopolitan* thinking. As the spiritual personification of such a thinking, Michael has full power over the dragon of materialistic thought and untamed passion. *He does not kill the dragon*. The sword is no longer a tool of division, but a symbol of reunification and healing. It has become the Word-sword which is communal, a *shared* power, an infinite resource that does not mould from *without* but is a source of *power* from *within*.

This process is reflected in the Grail sagas. In the legend of the knight Hugo as recounted in Walter Johannes Stein's *The Ninth Century* we read of how the attempt to execute the innocent knight Hugo of Tours fails when the arm of the executioner seizes up just as the sword is raised. Charles the Great draws his own sword to dispatch Hugo but he too is immobilized. Charles realizes that Hugo is under the protection of God, and must therefore be innocent of the crime attributed to him. His anger against Hugo vanishes instantly.

A similar event occurs in the legend of *Flore and Blanscheflur* when the young couple are brought before the Amiral for execution. Seeing the pure and sacrificial love they have for each other:

> A memory came into his mind
> Of all her [Blanscheflur's] service and his love,
> And how she once had pleased him well!
> And so in *thought's reaction*
> *There fell the sword from out his hand.*[180]

The awakening of his heart forces produces a new type of thinking within the Amiral and the power of the sword falls away from him in the same moment.

The Knights Templar lived at a time when the power of the sword—in its intermediate phase—was still at work. They inherited the Mysteries of the Grail, which are the 'Mysteries of the purified blood of Christ'. In a lecture given in Dornach on 2 October 1916, Rudolf Steiner speaks with great emphasis of how:

> Inwardly considered, the order of the Knights Templar express a specially deep approach to the Mystery of Golgotha on the part of modern humanity. [They] knew how to stand in real inward livingness in that life which, ever since Golgotha, the innermost forces of men are living through the fact that Christ has united himself with earthly existence...The blood of the Templars belonged to Christ Jesus... Every moment of their life was to be filled with the perpetual consciousness of how in their soul there dwelt 'Not I, but Christ in Me!'[181]

In his lecture cycle *Manifestations of Karma* Rudolf Steiner describes how an intense contemplative preoccupation with the life of Christ, inwardly maintained as a free act of the spirit, causes the nerves to withdraw from the blood:

> In ordinary life the process that takes place is such that each influence transmitted by means of the nerves inscribes itself in the blood as on a tablet, and in doing so records

> itself in the instrument of the ego. (This connection can be artificially interrupted so that nerves and blood no longer interact upon each other.) But let us suppose that in spite of the interrupting of the connection between the nerves and the blood a certain impression is made upon the nerve. This can be brought to pass through an external experiment by stimulating the nerve through an electric current. (Through certain spiritual scientific practices this can be brought about also.) When man practises a rigorous inner concentration of the soul on such imaginative concepts, forming these into symbols... It then happens, if he does them in fully awake consciousness, that he takes complete control of the nerve and, as a result of this concentration, draws it back to a certain extent from the course of the blood. (When this experiment takes place, one no longer lives in his ordinary ego.)[182]

If the 'external impression' made upon the nerves was brought about by the Templars in their constant contemplation and devotion to the example of Jesus Christ, then it may have eventually come about that the Templar 'no longer lived in his ordinary consciousness', but that his ego was replaced by the Christ. When this came about a further effect may have become possible: of spreading this penetration of the Christ in the human individual to the body of the earth itself. This may have been a direct effect of the Templar's spiritual work, whether effected consciously or unconsciously by them. The nervous system as the vehicle for consciousness and intellectual thought has attained its present deathly and hardened state through the incorporation of ahrimanic forces. The blood and tissues remain alive, an organic part of the wider world process. However, the blood is inscribed by the nerves with which it interacts in the normal state. In this way the ahrimanic forces within the human structure can inscribe themselves upon the inner nature of man. When the blood and the nerves are withdrawn from each other, access to the inner nature is denied; the death forces and the blood become available to the spirit.

Taking this into account it becomes easier to understand Rudolf Steiner's statement that the blood of the Templars belonged fully to Christ. The Templars were not occult initiates in the usual sense of belonging to a guarded Mystery school, but through their very life style they attained to a *naturally won initiation*. The power of the Tree of Life that had been returned to earth by the Christ and brought to perfection within the body of Jesus became available to the Templars. With this personal initiation came the possibility of extending this permeation of the individual human blood-stream to the earth itself. In his lecture 'The Face of the Earth and the Destiny of Mankind', Guenther Wachsmuth gives us an insight into how such a process could occur:

> We have seen that certain forces mould the body of the earth and of man in accordance with uniform, harmonious laws. In conclusion, we will consider yet another deeply illuminating phenomenon that can tell us how and why the destiny of man is bound up with the earth; why, in effect, the face of the earth becomes part of the destiny of man. Let us now pass from the horizontal to the vertical plane of the body of the earth. We will start, for the sake of simplicity, from the classification of substances given by Empedocles, and apply this to the earth. The earth has a solid body over which we move. This solid body is surrounded by the so-called hydrosphere, the watery sphere, this again by an air sheath, and as Dr Steiner has taught us, this air sheath is enclosed with a 'mantle' of warmth. This is a picture of the realm outside the earth, but passing from thence to the earth's interior we find something very remarkable. The outer is reflected in the inner! The most recent geological investigations confirm what has already been taught by spiritual science, namely, that below the solid body over which we move there is a watery sphere, the magma; further inwards the substance assumes a gaseous form, finally passing over into a condition of warmth, of fire. This is a remarkable phenomenon. Enumerating these spheres, we have: 1) mantle of warmth; 2) air sheath 3) hydro-

sphere; 4) solid earth surface; 5) interior fluidic earth; 6) interior gaseous earth; 7) interior earth warmth. Thus these seven spheres of the body of the earth, governed by the formative forces, are of such a nature that the seventh corresponds to the first, the sixth to the second, the fifth to the third, but the fourth represents something entirely new and unique. There is a most wonderful correspondence between the interior and exterior of the earth, and furthermore, there is a correspondence in another sphere, that of the consciousness of humanity.

When we study this interior nature of the earth we find yet another profound and far-reaching connection with the inner being of man. If the modern investigator will turn his gaze for a moment away from outer nature and direct it to man himself, to the most significant element living within the human being, namely, the blood, he will find when he thus penetrates into a blood corpuscle that it has a body of a peculiar kind, again divided into four spheres. Outside there is a highly transparent sphere, then a more opaque sphere peculiarly saturated and, as it were, inflated with the watery element, then again a somewhat more transparent sphere and, fourthly, again a less transparent. This is the form revealed by a section of a blood corpuscle. A study of the etheric formative forces which on the one hand are responsible for the formation of the interior body of the earth, and on the other for the structure of the human blood corpuscle, will reveal the fact that the solid earth is ruled by the life ether, the fluid elements by the chemical ether, the airy elements by the light ether, and the warmth process by the warmth ether. We find exactly the same thing in the corpuscle of human blood! Thus, we can study the configuration of the etheric body of the earth which is a reflection of our own inner being and we must realize that the etheric forces moulding the body of the earth are the same as those in our blood corpuscles. Today, it is not possible to say anything more of this phenomenon. It can only live within us as a deeply significant cosmic mystery, of which we may perhaps become fully conscious in the course of time. The

> etheric world, with the same forces, moulds and governs the interior of the earth in a wonderful harmony. Furthermore, it now also becomes clear that if new etheric forces arise within the earth in the course of cosmic 'becoming' this reflects itself right into the corpuscles of the human blood; on the other hand, when a change takes place in the etheric structure of human blood, this will be reflected into the etheric sphere of the earth, because, in effect, the earth and the blood corpuscles are formed according to the same laws.
>
> When we are able to perceive this unity between the body of the earth, the configuration of the earth, and the forces of consciousness, we shall live with quite different feelings. As we walk about, we shall set our feet with greater reverence on the body of the earth; we shall feel the body of the earth to be 'holy ground'...We are thus led into a quite different relationship with the earth, a truly Christian knowledge of the spirituality of the earth, to a Gaia-Sophia. More and more we shall realize the connection between the body of the earth and the destiny of mankind.[183]

There is a consistent correlation between this etheric geography and the activity of the Templars who developed settlements where the etheric forces, in both their pure and fallen states, were most powerfully at work. Such far-flung locations as Chartres, Rosslyn and the Rennes-le-Château area itself have been host to the Templars. Ely is another location where the Templars were active. Symbols of the four ethers are inscribed on the paving stones of Ely Cathedral, and a door in the cathedral bears a carving of the Tree of Life. We suggest that the Templars were particularly concerned with the life ether.

The Knights Templar guard the Grail, which has often been described as being fashioned of pure gold. The Templars are famous for their connection with gold, and with money in general. They first engineered the banking system, introducing the use of cheques. It has been described by Steiner how, because of their involvement with gold, they met their downfall at the hands of King Philippe le Bel of France who had an unconquerable and even pathological passion for gold and silver. This was directed less to economic value than to the metallic quality of these elements:

> With every material substance, in particular with every metal, are connected spiritual forces responsible for its structure and formation. In the case of precious metals like gold and silver these forces are specially powerful. A man permeated by them develops extremely lucid and penetrating powers of the brain. Thus Philippe had become the subject and lieutenant of Ahriman. From him he received his cold, calculating mind which was never troubled by sentiment but made straight for its goal, crushing all resistance to its will. The supersensible forces connected with gold and silver added to its sharpness. It can even be said that the king throve on them. He took special delight in handling gold and silver coins, in experiencing their physical nature, and when there was enough bullion in the royal treasury he would walk into it, stirring it up with hands and feet.[184]

As we have already seen the fallen energy of the ethers can be transubstantiated into its higher counterpart, but this would entail engaging with the fallen beings residing within the earth. This process began when Christ 'descended into the forecourts of hell'. There these potentially destructive beings were 'chained' and held down by the power of the Christ who simultaneously began to effect the transformation of physical substance. The centre of the earth, which had been their sphere of action, from then on began to radiate the 'Christ Sun'. But responsibility for the remaining work of transformation now lies with the remainder of humanity. Maybe this points to the significance of the statement made by Christ Jesus: 'This shall you do and more.'

Within the etheric our notions of distance and separation vanish. The concept of *kinship* replaces the concepts of spatial distance. Those things which are akin are joined in unity in the etheric, *irrespective of the distance between their physical manifestations*. If there is a kinship between the blood cell and the earth organism, changes in the one will reflect in the other.

The rigorous discipline and renunciation practised by the Templars was aimed at achieving a purity well above the normal level of those times; their writings 'radiate an almost desperate goodness'.[185] As this human realm is transformed, the higher nature, the Christ, is increasingly present: 'Not I, but Christ in me.' Thus a beginning was made by Templars and Cathars together in those early centuries to continue the process begun by Christ Jesus in the 'harrowing of hell' during the two days preceding the Resurrection. When this happens those individuals who have been able to raise the energy within themselves in turn cause the same effect within the earth itself. In both instances the dragon is transformed from within.

Eight hundred years ago this could only be achieved as a result of rigorous tests and experiences. The shocking practices which the Templars were supposed to have admitted to were in fact a token of the transformation of the lower energy centres which they were attempting to purify. The confessions obtained from the Templars concerning these practices in their initiation ceremonies were extracted under torture and the nature of Templar initiation was far too subtle and esoteric to be understood by those who questioned them.

In *Parzival* we have a picture of the relationship between the Templars and the moon cultures with which they attempted a synthesis. As we have seen, when Parzival is approaching the Grail Castle for the second time he meets the black and white knight Feirefis. At first Parzival engages in combat with him but then realizes that the knight with whom he is fighting is in fact his Moslem half-brother. The two knights embrace one another, and enter the Grail Castle.

When Parzival becomes the Grail King, Feirefis marries the Grail Maiden. The first child of this marriage is Prester John, an enigmatic figure who lives somewhere in the East and who in some legends is mentioned as the founder of the Templars. At a time when the Church had become visibly corrupt, the legend of Prester John abounded. He was a wise king in whose kingdom there was neither injustice nor poverty. One can see in this figure a prophetic dream of the time when religious intolerance has ended through a synthesis of all that is noble in Islam, Judaism and Christianity. Towards *this* goal many of the Templars worked, forging a union between the religion of the sun (Christianity) and that of the moon (Islam), reminding us that on one level the Grail motif shows the fully realized interpenetration of sun and moon.

The moon forces that remained in the earth after the moon's departure began to cause matter to crystallize and harden. This is the definition-forming activity of the chemical ether that calcifies matter when the vivifying activity of the life ether is absent. On the other hand the life ether cannot function effectively without the chemical ether to add definition and form to the profusion of emerging life. The two activities are mutually inter-creative, but destructive if isolated.

Evolution will bring sun and moon together once more. The Grail must first be won, then Feirefis can wed the Grail Maiden. The moon impulse permeating Islam was instrumental in bringing materialism and scientific thinking into evolution. Just as the moon forces bring crystallization and definition to matter—as the chemical ether adds differentiation to emerging life by drawing in the formative influences of the planets and the zodiac—so Islamic culture has brought evolution to a much deeper involvement in matter than would have been the case if esoteric Christianity had prevailed.

The descent into materialism had to reach a nadir point before esoteric Christianity could blossom in full force. This descent culminated in the materialism of the nineteenth century. Only with the close of that century and with the dawn of the twentieth does it become possible for the aims of the Cathars and Templars to be finally realized. Eight hundred years ago they did not have the chance to experience the depths to which the Christ in Jesus had descended when he harrowed hell. Could their purported revulsion of the Cross have been an outward sign of refusal to accept that the great Cosmic Architect had been so deeply connected with matter that He had passed through death itself? Did the Templars deny the Cross because they belonged to the stream of dualism which had not had a chance to understand the Incarnation of Christ in Jesus? Eight hundred years ago human understanding could not encompass the concept. The early Church appealed to the realm of human feeling; understanding of the event remained an act of faith. Celtic Christianity demonstrates that there was a possibility of accepting this deepest mystery of Christianity untroubled by Gnostic reservations. But, '...in the fusion of Christianity with the declining culture of Rome, the influence of western materialism begins to take effect. And under this influence there appeared a picture of Christ Jesus which at the beginning simply was not there, was not part of Christianity in its original form; the picture of Christ Jesus the crucified one, the Man of Sorrows, brought to His death by the indescribable suffering that was His lot.'[186]

Although the Templars are described as Guardians of the Grail, one can well understand that the story of Parzival is really set in a future time when the materialistic age has run its course. Only when the effects of Arabism have fulfilled their purpose in evolution can the mystery of the spirit working in matter be fully understood. The Templars of 800 years ago could effect the beginning of a task that can only be achieved from now onwards.

Patriarchal culture still clings to the old outworn hereditary tradition that has been dominant for the last 4,000 years.[187] Because the original innocent state of mankind has declined since the passing of the old matriarchal culture, it is understandable that any practice which involved a knowledge of the feminine powers in creation should have been strenuously stifled except where they were connected with the closely supervised continuation of the blood-linked generations. The Archangel Gabriel, whose emblem is the lily, has been the protector of these hereditary forces.

At the beginning of Earth evolution when all that had been achieved during the Ancient Moon period was recapitulated, the creation of the new Earth was brought about by the

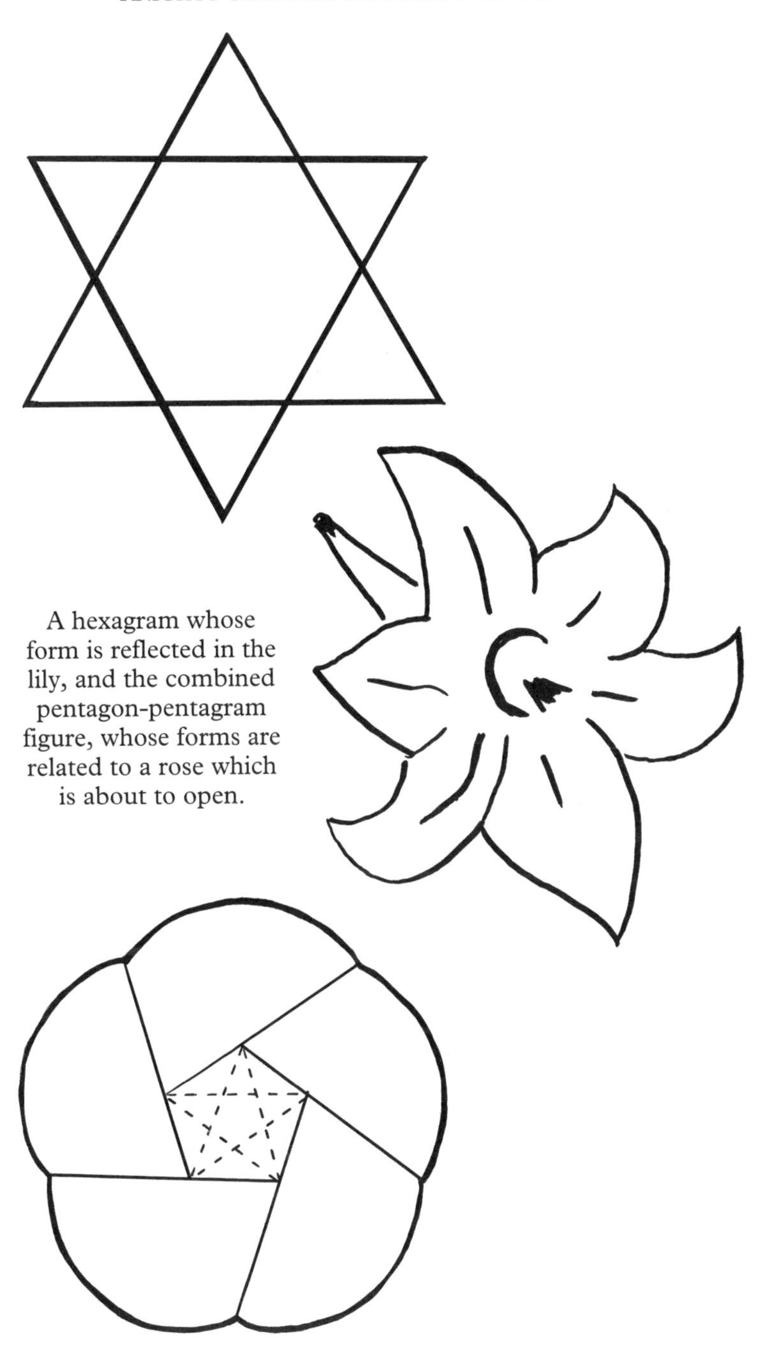

A hexagram whose form is reflected in the lily, and the combined pentagon-pentagram figure, whose forms are related to a rose which is about to open.

'Cosmos of Wisdom'—the Father principle. The symbol of the Cosmos of Wisdom originates from the dynamics of a six-pointed star. In outlining a six-pointed star one travels around the periphery; the centre remains untouched. A six-pointed star is recreated in the petals of Gabriel's flower, the lily, which is also sometimes associated with the Virgin Mary, representative of the lost innocence of creation. In a strange sense the Virgin Mary is interchangeable with the Father principle.

The six-pointed star of David is a symbol of Judaism, the patriarchal religion that had the task of linking its followers to the Godhead, to the Father principle, when as a result of the Fall the blood of generations became the only link with the spiritual world. Heredity and blood ties were the last fading connection that mankind had with the creative principle of the Father. As this connection diminished mankind was faced with severance from the spiritual world unless the effect of the Fall could be reversed. There was then no possibility of regaining the lost innocence—of returning up the old road that led down from the Creation, from the Father. As we have seen, a new impulse had to begin—that of the *Son*—which would enable humanity to return once more to the Father, but this time with the power of freedom and the faculty of independent thought.

When Christ's blood flowed from Golgotha, the hereditary blood of the generations—linked with the Father Cosmos of Wisdom—gave way to the blood of Christ, which holds the full power of the recombined ethers. A possibility was then given to the human ego by the Son to transform the blood so that the spirit could now work from within to motivate the ego with the impulse of love. It was the task of esoteric Christianity to germinate and foster this impulse towards a completely new connection with the source of creation.

The rose as a symbol of esoteric Christianity displays the formation of a pentagon; the pentagram which it encloses is formed with entirely different dynamics to the hexagram/six-pointed star. To draw a five-pointed star one must repeatedly move through the centre; this activity is a reflection of the ego working from the centre, through the bodily sheaths of the human being. This then causes a reciprocal effect on the earth and gradually on the remainder of creation to reverse the effect of the Fall. Here again one sees both Parzival and the Magdalene as champions of Manichaean Christianity, emulating Christ and beginning the journey upwards again through fallen matter to the New Jerusalem.

The Templars knew that a time would come when the forces of the lily and rose would join, but as they and their brother Cathars faced torture and the fire they had to be content that this possibility must be reserved for a later date. The promise of this transformation was preserved through the centuries in the symbolism and cryptic writings of the Rosicrucians.

The cover of a certain edition of *The Chymical Wedding* shows Durer's *The Virgin on the Crescent*.[188] The Virgin stands on the crescent moon holding the Child in her arms; both figures radiate the light of the sun. The prophecy of Day Four of *The Chymical Wedding* pronounces:

> The light of the moon shall be as the light of the sun and the light of the sun shall be seven times lighter.[189]

The earth and mankind will one day be changed so that the transformed moon forces will shine out into the cosmos just as the Grail which holds the Host, the spiritual light of Christ, the one-time light of the sun now shining with a still greater brightness from the earth.

15
Alchemy Part One: The Green Stone and the Great Work

In the days when Eve was in Adam , there was no death. When she had separated from him, death arose. Again if he unite with her and receives death to himself, there shall be no death.

The Gospel of Philip

Sometime in 1994 I stood on the terrace of the Tour Magdala at Rennes-le-Château and wondered about the strange ceremony that followed the death of Berenger Saunière. The body had been robed and enthroned on the terrace, after which a procession of people had passed the body, plucking tassels from the robe. From where I stood I could look out across the great pentagram. All through my research, alchemy—that great and mysterious science of the transmutation of matter into spirit—had surfaced again and again. I had also spent much time puzzling over the motif of the Grail as the 'Green Stone'—a force connected in some very specific way with the nature forces. It was a modern-day alchemist who directed me to the solution of all these problems. Through his help I came to understand the nature of the Great Work and to see exactly where alchemy fitted within the context of the Grail quest. I found confirmation of my ideas in a mysterious Rosicrucian manuscript and in the complex verses of the recently rediscovered Gospel of Philip—two beacons of light marking the path through history of a single quest that has had many forms of historical manifestation.

The difference between our twentieth century reports of alchemy and the alchemical Great Work itself is similar to the contrast between the glass-eyed creature in the taxidermist's window and a deer running free in the cool depths of the forest. The alchemists proceeded from matter, starting with substances and working back to their cosmic causes. They knew, for instance, that there is a mysterious link between gold, the life force and the dew of morning and evening.

The origin of the name of the Rosicrucian Order has been traced to the symbol of the rose, which in turn is connected with the pentagram. Another derivation is mentioned in *The Real History of the Rosicrucians* by Arthur Edward Waite: '[Rosicrucian] is from the Latin words *Ros* (dew) and *Crux* (cross). Of all natural bodies, dew was deemed the most powerful dissolvent of gold, and the cross in chemical language was equivalent to light; because the figure of the cross exhibits at the same time the three letters of which the word *lux* or "light" is compounded.'[190]

Later in the same book Eusebius Renondot's *Conférences Publiques* is quoted: 'Dew, the most powerful dissolvent of gold which is to be found among natural and non-corrosive substances, is nothing else but light coagulated and rendered corporeal; when it is artistically concocted and digested in its own vessel during a suitable period it is the true menstruum of the Red Dragon, i.e. of gold, the true matter of the philosophers. The Society desiring to bequeath to posterity the ineffaceable sign of this secret, caused them to adopt the name Frères de la Rozée Cuite.'[191]

The Holy Grail has sometimes been referred to as 'the Green Stone which was knocked out of Lucifer's crown'. This has been described as chlorophyll, which contains the essence of the plant. The 'Green Stone' also represents potassium carbonate, known as the 'gold' of the philosophers. Potassium carbonate bears a strong affinity to life processes. If you burn any plant on a bonfire, the residue turns to ash: potash. If the potash is then put in water it is found to have a soluble and an insoluble part. The insoluble part was called 'lye' by the ancients, who used it for making soap. Having once obtained potash through burning living plant substance it becomes possible to revitalize it by bringing it into contact with the vital force which is present in the air, especially in springtime. If the dry potassium carbonate is put out on a clear May night when the moon is in the first quarter, it will reabsorb the vital force which is present in the dew.

The medieval mind still understood about the value of the dew of May and September. In the May Day revels young girls would rush out of doors to wash their faces in the dew of the early morning. Biodynamic gardeners and farmers, working with Rudolf Steiner's indications, know all about the importance of 'morning' and 'evening' forces. May and September are the morning and evening of the year.

Rosslyn Chapel near Edinburgh has been referred to by many writers in connection with the Grail. It lies at the end of the pilgrim route from Santiago de Compostella in Spain. It will be remembered that Edinburgh has been suggested as the position of a 'Third Eye' chakra in the chakra system originating in southern France. Rosslyn has also been connected with the Knights Templar via the Sinclair family. In the book *The Sword and the Grail* by Andrew Sinclair, a small tombstone is described which had '...recently been discovered with the Grail carved upon its length. Inside the communion cup was an eight-pointed cipher of the Templars, which referred to the Holy Light within Christ's blood in the shape of an "engrailed" octagon with a rose at its centre. The very name of the chapel was said to derive from the old Scottish ros-lin or rosy stream or fall.'[192] Here Andrew Sinclair adds 'again suggesting the blood of Christ', but in the light of what we have learned of the qualities of dew and the connotations of the word 'ros' we can also surmise that the name may well suggest 'dew fall'.

If one then thinks of the location of Rosslyn, which if it were situated on a main chakra point would be a major centre for the interaction of the life and chemical ethers, one can imagine that dew fall in such a place would carry maximum potency as the chemical ether rises up at sunrise and gently falls at evening.

As a result of the Fall, Lucifer's influence permeated the blood systems of the human and animal kingdoms. But the desire-free blood of the plants—the sap containing chlorophyll—which retains the full force of the four ethers, was not to be a feather in Lucifer's cap. Chlorophyll was 'struck' from his crown.

Steiner describes a Mystery centre that had been founded by Atlanteans 'north of today's Russia':[193]

What was the Mystery taught there? It was the Mystery secret that Parzival discovered and brought to its highest development: how the new budding life of nature in springtime is connected with the Mystery of the Cross. The power of reproduction in the animal and human kingdoms is also seen in the plant kingdom. In springtime the divine active power of creation shoots up out of Mother Earth. We have to recognize that a deep connection exists between the power that manifests when the earth clothes herself with her robe of green and the divine creative power.

The pupils in the initiation schools were taught as follows: 'All around you in nature you see the opening flower buds and within them the power at work which is then later concentrated in the small grains of seeds; countless seeds will come from the flower, seeds which if laid in the earth will be capable of bringing forth new plants. The process that is taking place out there in nature is the very same as that which works in the human and animal kingdoms only in nature it happens without desire or passion; it goes forward in perfect purity and chastity.' The boundless chaste innocence that sleeps in the flower bud of the plant—this is what, it was felt, must enter right into the souls of the pupils. And then they were told further: 'It is the sun that opens the blossoms. The ray of the sun calls forth the power that rests in them. Two things meet—the opening flower and the ray from the sun. Between the plant kingdom and the divine kingdom stand two other kingdoms—the animal kingdom and the human. These latter are really no more than a kind of pathway leading from the plant kingdom to the divine kingdom. In the divine kingdom we have again a kingdom of innocence and chastity as in the plant kingdom. In the animal and human kingdoms we have kingdoms of desire and passion.' But then it was told to the pupils that in the future 'all passions and desire will at length disappear. The chalice will then open, and will open from above downwards, and look down to man. And as the ray from the sun goes right down into the plant, so will man's now purified power unite itself with this divine chalice. It can actually come about that the chalice of the blossom is spiritually reversed so that it inclines downwards from heaven'...And this reversed flower-chalice which was told of in the Mysteries as an actual fact was called the Holy Grail.[194]

In the chapter on the southern Mystery stream we saw how, with the division into two sexes, the four ethers were polarized within the human organization. The reunification of the ethers at both the physically and spiritually creative poles is functionally identical with the process of purification described above, and the attainment of the Grail within the traditions of the Great Work. In line with Christ's commandment 'Be you whole', this is the essential Christian Mystery of the esoteric schools. It is the most secret sacrament of the Bridal Chamber, as depicted in the Gnostic *Gospel of Philip*.

'The mystery of marriage is great,' states the *Gospel of Philip*, 'for through it the world became numerous. For the existence of the world rests upon man. But the existence of man rests upon marriage. Understand the undefiled intercourse, for it has great power.'[195]

The mystery of marriage is not sexual intercourse, described in the *Gospel* as the 'defilement of the appearance', but the attainment of an inner condition of balanced wholeness. In his commentary on the *Gospel*, Andrew Welburn describes it as follows: 'The marriage is the union of bride and bridegroom *within*, releasing our self-creating and transforming power.'[196]

Within the cosmology of the authentic Christian Mysteries, the Fall was not a punishment but the effect of a failed initiation: 'There are two trees in the midst of Paradise. The one brings forth animals, the other brings forth men. Adam ate of the tree which brought forth animals.'[197]

With this division humanity fell prey to those evolutionary stresses originally only intended for the moulding of animal life. The power of death gains access to the human evolutionary sphere: 'If the woman had not separated from the man, she would not have died with the man. His separation became the beginning of death. Therefore Christ came that he might set right again the separation which arose from the beginning and unite the two, and give life to those who died in the separation and unite them.'[198] This central Christian sacrament of inner consummation is not a forsaking but a *redeeming* of the physical and the sensual: 'The holy man is altogether holy, including his body. For if he has received the bread, he will make it holy, or the cup, or all the rest which he receives he purifies. And how will he not purify the body also?'[199]

The work of the Bridal Chamber is then the Great Work, the quest for the Grail and the end goal of the researches of the alchemists.

The final plate in the *Codex Rosae Crucis*, reprinted with a commentary by Manly Hall, shows the highest aim of the alchemists, the Magnum Opus or Great Work, in diagrammatic form, headed with the phrase:

SUM TOTAL AND FINAL CONCLUSION[200]

This is a statement of consummation and perfection. The left side of the plate represents the divine nature, and the right side the earthly nature. These opposites are combined in a circle entitled 'By this sign thou shalt conquer'. Within this quartered circle are the symbols of the elements, the colours and the numbers which point towards the completion and the consummation of all things. The divine and earthly nature reconciled and equilibrated 'on the scales of R.C.' result in the perfected adept, a son of light, an embodiment of the Christos. The perfected man reveals the purpose of the Great Work: the achievement of conscious immortality.

The quartered circle referred to above could be interpreted as a symbol for the four ethers when they have been united at both the physical and spiritual poles. This unification may either be brought about by the overcoming of gender, as already described by Wachsmuth above, or by the overcoming of the lower nature in man through rigorous spiritual work. We are by now aware that the 'fruit of the Tree of Life' can eventually be given back to mankind as he becomes increasingly worthy to guard its potency. The figure also

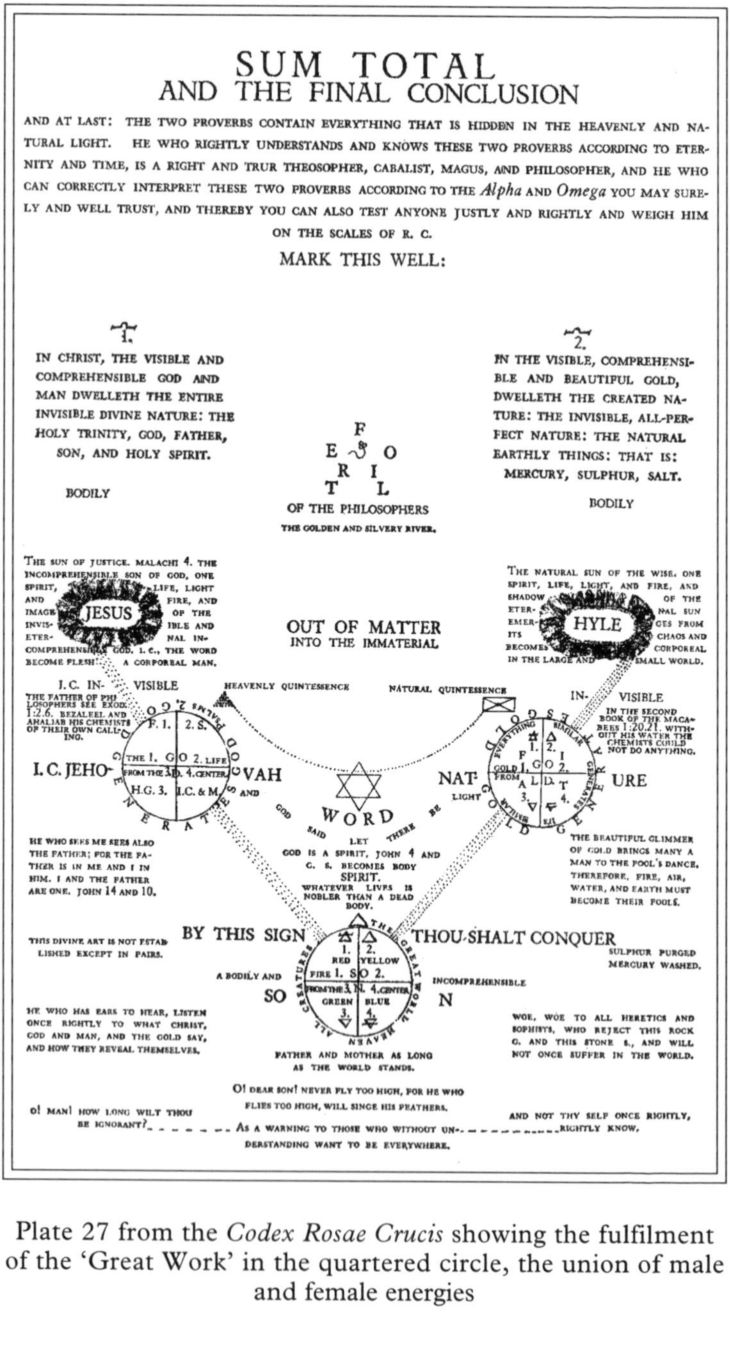
SUM TOTAL
AND THE FINAL CONCLUSION
AND AT LAST: THE TWO PROVERBS CONTAIN EVERYTHING THAT IS HIDDEN IN THE HEAVENLY AND NATURAL LIGHT. HE WHO RIGHTLY UNDERSTANDS AND KNOWS THESE TWO PROVERBS ACCORDING TO ETERNITY AND TIME, IS A RIGHT AND TRUR THEOSOPHER, CABALIST, MAGUS, AND PHILOSOPHER, AND HE WHO CAN CORRECTLY INTERPRET THESE TWO PROVERBS ACCORDING TO THE Alpha AND Omega YOU MAY SURELY AND WELL TRUST, AND THEREBY YOU CAN ALSO TEST ANYONE JUSTLY AND RIGHTLY AND WEIGH HIM ON THE SCALES OF R. C.
MARK THIS WELL:
1.
IN CHRIST, THE VISIBLE AND COMPREHENSIBLE GOD AND MAN DWELLETH THE ENTIRE INVISIBLE DIVINE NATURE: THE HOLY TRINITY, GOD, FATHER, SON, AND HOLY SPIRIT.
BODILY
2.
IN THE VISIBLE, COMPREHENSIBLE AND BEAUTIFUL GOLD, DWELLETH THE CREATED NATURE: THE INVISIBLE, ALL-PERFECT NATURE: THE NATURAL EARTHLY THINGS: THAT IS: MERCURY, SULPHUR, SALT.
BODILY
F
E O
R I
T L
OF THE PHILOSOPHERS
THE GOLDEN AND SILVERY RIVER.
THE SUN OF JUSTICE. MALACHI 4. THE INCOMPREHENSIBLE SON OF GOD, ONE SPIRIT, LIFE, LIGHT AND FIRE, AND IMAGE OF THE INVISIBLE AND ETERNAL INCOMPREHENSIBLE GOD. I. C., THE WORD BECOME FLESH: A CORPOREAL MAN.
JESUS
OUT OF MATTER
INTO THE IMMATERIAL
THE NATURAL SUN OF THE WISE. ONE SPIRIT, LIFE, LIGHT, AND FIRE, AND SHADOW OF THE ETERNAL SUN EMERGES FROM ITS CHAOS AND BECOMES CORPOREAL IN THE LARGE AND SMALL WORLD.
HYLE
I.C. IN- VISIBLE
THE FATHER OF PHILOSOPHERS SEE EXOD. 1:2.6. BEZALEEL AND AHALIAB HIS CHEMISTS OF THEIR OWN CALLING.
HEAVENLY QUINTESSENCE
NATURAL QUINTESSENCE
IN- VISIBLE
IN THE SECOND BOOK OF THE MACABEES 1:20.21. WITHOUT HIS WATER THE CHEMISTS COULD NOT DO ANYTHING.
F. 1.
2. S.
THE 1. GO 2. LIFE
FROM THE 3. D. 4. CENTER
H.G. 3.
I.C. & M.
I. C. JEHO- VAH
AND
NAT- URE
LIGHT
GOLD 1. GO 2.
FROM A L D. T
WORD
GOD SAID LET THERE BE
GOD IS A SPIRIT, JOHN 4 AND C. S. BECOMES BODY SPIRIT. WHATEVER LIVES IS NOBLER THAN A DEAD BODY.
HE WHO SEES ME SEES ALSO THE FATHER; FOR THE FATHER IS IN ME AND I IN HIM. I AND THE FATHER ARE ONE. JOHN 14 AND 10.
THE BEAUTIFUL GLIMMER OF GOLD BRINGS MANY A MAN TO THE FOOL'S DANCE. THEREFORE, FIRE, AIR, WATER, AND EARTH MUST BECOME THEIR FOOLS.
THIS DIVINE ART IS NOT ESTABLISHED EXCEPT IN PAIRS.
BY THIS SIGN
THOU SHALT CONQUER
SULPHUR PURGED MERCURY WASHED.
A BODILY AND
SO
INCOMPREHENSIBLE
N
1. 2.
RED YELLOW
FIRE 1. SO 2.
FROM THE 3. N. 4. CENTER
GREEN BLUE
3. 4.
ALL CREATURES
THE GREAT WORLD HEAVEN
HE WHO HAS EARS TO HEAR, LISTEN ONCE RIGHTLY TO WHAT CHRIST, GOD AND MAN, AND THE GOLD SAY, AND HOW THEY REVEAL THEMSELVES.
FATHER AND MOTHER AS LONG AS THE WORLD STANDS.
WOE, WOE TO ALL HERETICS AND SOPHISTS, WHO REJECT THIS ROCK C. AND THIS STONE S., AND WILL NOT ONCE SUFFER IN THE WORLD.
O! DEAR SON! NEVER FLY TOO HIGH, FOR HE WHO FLIES TOO HIGH, WILL SINGE HIS FEATHERS.
O! MAN! HOW LONG WILT THOU BE IGNORANT?
AS A WARNING TO THOSE WHO WITHOUT UNDERSTANDING WANT TO BE EVERYWHERE.
AND NOT THY SELF ONCE RIGHTLY, RIGHTLY KNOW.

Plate 27 from the *Codex Rosae Crucis* showing the fulfilment of the 'Great Work' in the quartered circle, the union of male and female energies closely resembles the 'Resurrection Flag', a symbol used in medieval and Renaissance art to represent the triumph over death. The circle is quartered; in the first quarter is inscribed 'Fire' and the colour red. The elements are not further described in the remaining three quarters but the colours yellow, green and blue are. Through the action of the etheric formative forces in the earth organism arise the different variations in the world of colour in the following fashion:

> When there is predominantly active in the illuminated world of substance of the earth organism:
> Warmth ether then appears the colour red;
> light ether then appears the colour yellow;
> chemical ether then appears the colour blue;
> life ether then appears the colour violet.
> Therefore the sea, for example, whose watery element is dominated chiefly by the chemical ether, appears blue, whereas a shining flame, which is controlled chiefly by warmth ether, appears red.[201]

We have already noted that the main goal of this 'Sum Total and Final Conclusion'—the unification of the sexes—is *conscious immortality.* This was evidently the final goal of both alchemist and Rosicrucian in the past. This goal is expressed in the diagram in bold letters, and should stand as a motto, and a high and exacting ideal for all true workers on the Path:

OUT OF MATTER,
INTO THE IMMATERIAL

16
Alchemy Part Two: The Cauldron of Ceredwin

> The theme of the regenerative Otherworld or Underworld was of great importance to the Celts, and ultimately led to the medieval heretical pagan-Christian legends of the Holy Grail. The Grail derives from an Underworld cauldron of immortality.
>
> R. J. Stewart, *Celtic God, Celtic Goddesses*

Peri Aston's story-telling again inspired the following chapter. The theme of the 'Music of the Spheres', as explored in the pages that follow, will complete our understanding of the Grail. It will be a small step from there to the resolution of the Mysteries of Rennes-le-Château.

According to the legend, the cauldron of Ceredwin 'needs stirring night and day'. This indicates the close connection between the cauldron and the life-force—with spirals and vortices, and with the rigorous stirring processes necessary for the preparation of biodynamic farming and gardening preparations.

In many Welsh and Irish tales a magical cauldron has a prominent place. The three properties of the cauldron—inexhaustibility, inspiration, regeneration—may be summed up in one word: fertility. The cauldron is associated with such goddesses as Ceredwin, Branwen, the lady from the lake. The cauldron's power of restoring life—as in the Welsh poem *The Spoils of Annwyn*—is significant since, in early belief, life is associated with what is feminine. Woman as the fruitful mother suggested that the earth, which produced and nourished, was also female. Also the cauldron symbolism would have been associated with thermal springs, as they were clear evidence of the seething, boiling energies of the underworld.

In the *Mabin of the Mabinogian* we are told that the

cauldron is 'the source or fountain of the protoplasm (Annelw) by means of which element all matter was, and is, built up into solids'.[202] Here is a very accurate description of the action of the life ether, which brings creation into the solid state—energy before matter.

Ceredwin leaves the cauldron in the charge of Gwion Bach (little Gwion) and goes to sleep for a year and a day. Again we read in the *Mabin of the Mabinogian* that Gwion is 'the personified masculine warmth descended in dew and rain, and is the father of vegetation'.[203] One also finds an account of how the warmth and chemical ethers work together to bring the cosmic Word down into vegetation on the earth's surface:

> It is represented that the earth and vegetation had been already created by the influence of the fertilising warmth descending in dew and rain from the Word of God. In the first place, in vegetation, by the cooperation of the feminine essence or sap from below ascending from the cauldron or the sacred shrine of Cariadwen; and the masculine warmth, or heat, descending from the Word of the Creator Celu (Coelus). In the second place, a new element of a material nature, described as Three Drops, descended from the masculine principle of the Word into the same essence of the cauldron...This indicates that bardic philoso-phers set forth even the fertilizing warmth, which descended from above in dew and rain, under the figure of a dramatic personality of some sort. But his transmigration, passing as life into successive animals, and finally becoming Taliesun (Sun-Son), indicates that the personality was regarded as a spirit. It is clearly taught that the Three Drops, which had descended from the Word of the Creator, were imbued in some degree with the nature of the Word, and that Word with the nature of the Creator Himself.[204]

This is further enlarged upon by Wachsmuth in *The Formative Forces of Man, Earth and Cosmos*. Having described the 'double wave' that causes 'the rhythmic change in barometric pressure', in turn caused by the rising and falling of the chemical ether, he describes the etheric activity involved in the process of reversal of temperature on and above the earth's surface:

> The action of the sun reduces to chaos the structure of the earth, bringing the warmth ether out of its own sphere, from above down below to the solid earth. The chemical ether passes out of its own sphere, from below upward. The process is completed whereby the warmth ether is gathered upon the solid earth, the chemical ether interpenetrates the atmosphere and thus the etheric basic structure of the earth is reduced to chaos: the earth wakes and lives. Climax in processes of vegetation.[205]

The Three Drops are described in the *Mabin of the Mabinogian* as 'essence derived direct from the seminal element of the Word of the Creator', and by imbibing them Gwion 'partook of the divine nature of its source' and 'was by it materially endowed with divine intelligence and foresight. The result resembled the result of Adam and Eve swallowing the sap of the fruit of the Tree of Knowledge of Good and Evil—Gwion's eyes, too, were opened like theirs were and he saw into futurity.' Here we could add that the sap of the Tree of Life would have connected him directly with the 'divine nature and its source', and that this was the pure region of 'the Music of the Spheres'. What is implied here is that the Three Drops had descended, as an emanation from the Son of God, the interpreter of the wisdom of the Creator, and, therefore, is called Menu, or the Mind of the Creator, as well as Hu Gadarn, etc. In druidic mythology the sun's divinity is called Menu, the Son of the Three Proclamations, by the Creating Word (Menu):

> This appears to be analogous to the said Three Drops as the concreted essence of the Voice uttered Three Times called Triton, or Three Tones, that is to say on March 25, June 25, and September 25, as representing the fruitful portions of the year. These three chief points include four others,

> making a total of Seven—Septentrio—referred to in Rev. 3 as the Seven Spirits of God, and the Seven Churches, the Scriptorial idea being borrowed from the seven lamps or lights of the Golden Candlesticks. Their opponents are the seven heads of the Red Dragon (Rev. 12:3), and seven she devils in Mary Magdalene.
>
> The term Seven Spirits of God is an old druidic mode of describing the sun when passing through the seven planetary spheres during the year, transmitting seven times the wisdom or emanations of the Creator, down to the earth by the agency of the Sun as Seven Notes of Music of universal harmony.[206]

This description is a beautiful picture of ancient knowledge which has once again been brought to the surface by spiritual science: the cosmic or formative forces working into the life process through the agency of the chemical ether, the tone ether, the Music of the Spheres. This process involving the action of the dew can be described in the following manner.

Form originates at the periphery of the cosmos, where it is held in the circle of the zodiac and brought into matter through the Music of the Spheres. The sun then gathers these forces from the periphery. The sun's light is reflected by the moon, which is particularly connected with the activity of the chemical ether and the fluid element.

A further possible scenario is that this formative information package is next picked up and held by the ionosphere. If we venture outside at dawn or at dusk we are all familiar with the increased moisture which hangs in the air at that time: the dew. At dawn it is caused by the belt of chemical ether rising up from within the physical earth. By midday it reaches the ionosphere. It then returns on its downward path, reaching the surface of the earth by evening.

Gardeners in the past knew that the best time to tend their plants was at dawn or dusk. They mistrusted midday for the care of their gardens, calling it 'the time of the Noontide Witch'. They knew that the upbuilding formative forces present in the moisture which were leaving the surface of the earth at dawn were no longer around to sustain the living vegetation, which was left to its own devices at midday.

In spring and summer, when the vegetation is enlivening all around us, we are particularly aware of the bird-song rising in the morning and returning at evening. In this music of the bird-song could we not be hearing part of the secret of the process whereby sound carries the formative forces needed for the qualitative differentiation of life—the shapes, scents, tastes, colours and healing qualities—from the cosmic periphery? The formative information is collected by the chemical ether, rising together with the dawn chorus of the birds, and returned at evening to bathe the vegetation with music-permeated dew.

When one considers the quality of the British countryside in spring and early summer, especially at the time around dawn and dusk, it becomes understandable that so much of the Grail legend originated in these islands. Although the progress of the chemical ether at morning and evening takes place to a greater or lesser extent all over the globe, one may observe that there is a special quality, a greeny-blueness, in the air and around all the vegetation that is characteristic of dawn and dusk in Britain. The ancient parish church nestling in depths of lush young vegetation takes on the ambience of a Grail chapel on the edge of some enchanted forest. Here science and legend meet. It will be remembered that the interpretation of the Grail that we are pursuing sees the two ethers represented by the Tree of Life as living symbols of the Grail. The daily bathing of vegetation by the chemical ether, the silent activity of the Music of the Spheres, brought earthwards in the morning and evening chorus of the birds, bear witness to the blending of fact and legend that can be uncovered in our search. It is not surprising that Shakespeare, who was familiar with the Warwickshire countryside, should have been able to describe the Music of the Spheres so eloquently when in *The Merchant of Venice* Lorenzo directs Jessica's attention to the sky:

Sit, Jessica: look, how the floor of heaven
Is thick inlaid with patines of bright gold:
There's not the smallest orb which thou behold'st
But in his motion like an angel sings,
Still quiring to the young eye'd cherubims;
Such harmony is in immortal souls;
But, whilst this muddy vesture of decay
Doth grossly close it in, we cannot hear it.[207]

In Rumo XV of the Finnish epic the *Kalevala*, the hero Lemminkainen has been slain by the death-god Tuoni and hewed into pieces. He is rescued and resuscitated by his mother. She asks the bee to fetch honey and ointment from meadow flowers, grasses and herbs. But these fail to heal him. Then she sends him 'across *nine* lakes' where there is a lovely island from which the bee fetches more honey and ointment to heal Lemminkainen. But he remains inert. His mother, realizing that earthly substance is not powerful enough to heal her son, then asks the bee to fetch more powerful ointments and honey from the charmed wood of Jumala the Creator, the cosmic origin of all the healing forces to be found on earth:

O thou bee, thou bird aërial,
Fly thou forth again the third time
Fly thou up aloft to heaven,
And through nine heavens fly thou swiftly.
There is honey in abundance,
In the wood as much as needed,
Which was charmed by the Creator,
By pure Jumala was breathed on
When his children he anointed,
Wounded by the powers of evil.

...

Thou canst rise on high with swiftness,
Fly aloft with easy effort,
O'er the moon, below the daylight,
And amid the stars of heaven,
Flying windlike on the first day

Past the borders of Orion,
On the second day thou soarest
Even to the Great Bear's shoulders,
On the third day soaring higher,
O'er the Seven Stars thou risest,
Thence the journey is a short one
Unto Jumala's bright dwelling,
And the regions of the blessed.'
From the earth the bee rose swiftly,
On his honeyed wings rose whirring,
And he soared on rapid pinions,
On his little wings flew upward
Swiftly past the moon he hurried,
Past the borders of the sunlight,
Rose upon the Great Bear's shoulders,
O'er the Seven Stars' backs rose upward,
Flew to the Creator's cellars,
To the halls of the Almighty.
There the drugs were well concocted,
And the ointment duly tempered
In the pots composed of silver,
Or within the golden kettles.
In the midst they boiled the honey,
On the sides was sweetest ointment,
To the southward there was nectar,
To the northward there was ointment.

...

Then the bee, that bird aërial,
Gathered honey in abundance,
Honey to his heart's contentment,
And but little time passed over,
Ere the bee again came buzzing,
Humming loudly on his journey,
In his lap of horns a hundred,
And a thousand other vessels,
Some of honey, some of liquid,
And the best of all the ointment.

Then did Lemminkainen's mother
Raise it to her mouth and taste it,
With her tongue the ointment tasted,
With the greatest care she proved it,
'Tis the ointment that I needed,
And the salve of the Almighty,
Used when Jumala the Highest,
The Creator heals all suffering.[208]

The saga hints at the event of the 'Fall' in these lines and also where the wood is described 'which was charmed by the Creator/ by pure Jamala was breathed on/ When his children he anointed, wounded by the powers of evil'.

The Finnish tradition points to a Fall that was not the fault of humanity, which we will see repeated in the Celtic tradition where immediately after the Three Drops spill from the cauldron it bursts in two. 'Then understanding dawns, all knowledge, all consciousness is here. He watches the remaining liquid turn into poison, hissing over the earth, destroying in its profusion.'[209] This event in the story parallels the description of the division of the four ethers as described by Steiner and Wachsmuth. Up to this point we have roughly followed the original story of the Fall: the Fall that was not the fault of man who, unlike the Sorcerer's Apprentice, does not suffer through his own pride and curiosity but through circumstances beyond his control. He is involved in a major disaster which nevertheless affords him the gift of knowledge. The devastation caused by the bursting of the cauldron is a very real picture of the result of the misuse of the Tree of Life energy which we have experienced in recent years. Chernobyl, especially, leaps to mind here.

It was especially after the event at Chernobyl in 1986 that Gernot Gräfe, a respected Austrian scientist specializing in humus research, and his colleague Maria Felsenreich, discovered that the healthy *resonance patterns* which they had monitored in water in previous years was almost non-existent. Their dowsing work with water began a few years earlier when they were driving down an *autobahn* and spied a little church in the distance. They somehow felt compelled to leave their route and visit it. The church was dedicated to Mary. Inside was a running spring. When they dowsed over its water they found it had not been affected by Chernobyl.

After this the basic principle of their work was to recognize that 'in its natural *healthy* state water could be dowsed for *nine* clearly identified resonance formations. The transformation of these resonance formations leads to the build-up of corresponding information fields, which stand in relation to specific chemical elements, vital functions and magnetic patterns.'[210]

Slightly later Gräfe and Felsenreich discovered that: 'Energy transfer has to be understood as the *basis* for life on earth. Our planet was shaped by the evolution of water which was, is and will be the media for the transport of vibrational energy...the earth-body's most characteristic feature is its *resounding quality*, which differs...from region to region and from one level of evolution to another. We may call this resounding quality of the earth-body *music*...The resounding system of the earth underwent so many changes that it is very difficult to reconstruct those parts that were completely lost long ago'.[211] 1 Here it is very interesting to compare Gräfe and Felsenreich's thoughts with those expressed by Rudolf Steiner:

> From the beginning, the earth was not only glowing and shining but was also resounding, and the tone had remained in the earth. So that when the light departed [the sun body split away from the body of the earth] the water became dark but also became drenched with tone. It was the tone that gave form to the water as one may learn from the well-known experiment in physics [Chladni Figures]. We see that tone is something formative, a shaping force, since through tone the parts are arranged in order. Tone is a shaping power, and it was this that formed the body out of the water. This was the force of tone, which had remained in the earth. It was tone, it was the sound that rang through the earth, out of which the human form, containing all of creation within itself, shaped itself.[212]

Then as a result of the Fall the original unified creation condenses. The tones no longer sound from within the planetary body. The planets are found at the periphery instead of permeating the primeval creation, and the tones which originally sounded through it now resonate through the cosmos and are thus relayed to the earth.

In a lecture given by Alan Hall of the Livewater Trust, it was suggested that the nine resonance patterns could be thought of as hieroglyphs for the notes on the musical scale. In his book *The Music of the Spheres*, Jamie Jeans points out that: 'The elder Pliny...tells us in detail exactly how Pythagoras conceived of the Music of the Spheres. Counting outward from the earth to the outermost sphere of the fixed stars, Pythagoras fixed the musical intervals as follows: from the earth to the moon was a whole step; from the moon to Mercury, a half-step; Mercury to Venus, another half-step; from Venus to the Sun was a minor third, which is equal to three half-steps; the sun to Mars, a whole step; Mars to Jupiter, a half-step; Jupiter to Saturn a half-step; and from Saturn to the sphere of the fixed stars another minor third. Thus the musical scale [of nine notes] to which Aristotle referred, the so-called Pythagorean scale, runs: C, D, E♭, E, G, A, B♭, B, D.'[213]

Plato's description of these forces demands quoting: 'These intricate traceries in the sky are, no doubt, the loveliest and most perfect of material things, but still part of the visible world, and therefore they fall far short of the true realities—the real relative velocities, in the world of pure number and all perfect geometrical figures, of the movements which carry round the bodies involved in them. These, you will agree, can be conceived by reason and thought, not seen by the eye.'[214]

At the Fall the pure tones were thrust out of the earth, to ray inwards from the periphery where the solid planets are formed as physical markers for each border between tone and tone.

In the *Kalevala* the bee first gathers substances with known healing properties from meadow flowers and grasses, but these fail to heal Lemminkainen. The bee is then told to travel across *nine* lakes to find healing *earthly* substances for Lemminkainen. When these also fail to heal the hero the bee must rise up through the *nine* heavens to the actual source of the healing forces, which, when returned to earth, will cause the miracle to happen. The dead and dismembered body of Lemminkainen is brought back to life. The number *nine* is transformed to *seven* through the *three.* The bee has to make *three* journeys so that the *nine* resonances originating from the *nine* heavenly spheres are translated into the notes of the musical scale, which completes the process gathered from the *nine* heavenly spheres.

The stirring of Ceredwin's cauldron causes the Music of the Spheres to be brought into the earth's fluid-systems by the activity of the chemical ether, which is represented in the story by the Three Drops which fly from the cauldron. This theme can perhaps best be brought to a close with a quote from one of the world's greatest authorities on the nature of water, Theodore Schwenk: 'Greatest of the secrets hidden in flowing liquids is that the harmony of the spheres resounds and vibrates within them...The phenomena in flowing liquids provide the key for man; he may see reflected in them the splendour of the harmony of the spheres.'[215]

17
Opposition to the Grail and its influence in the Modern World

> Christianity had its beginnings among the people of Galilee—a mixture of strikingly different races, thus a people who stand entirely outside all blood relationship. The Saviour is one who does not base His kingdom in the very least on blood relationships. He founds a kingdom that is quite remote from any such blood—the blood that has been sublimated, the blood that has been purified and gushes forth from the sacrificial death, for that is the cleansing process. The blood that gives rise to sensual desire has to be shed, has to be sacrificed, has to flow right away. The holy vessel with the purified blood was brought to Europe by the Templars. On Montsalvat the venerable patriarch Titurel received the Grail; he had been chosen for this beforehand. The Victory had now been won. The spiritual in the blood had overcome what was merely physical.
>
> Rudolf Steiner, from a lecture given in London on 29 July 1906

In this chapter we return to the central theme of The Holy Blood and the Holy Grail. *At this point in my research I felt that I understood the Grail stream well enough to confront its dark shadow—the anti-Grail stream that is depicted in Wolfram von Eschenbach's* Parzival *in the form of Klingsor's deadly 'Castle of Wonders'. I felt that I now knew the reason for Saunière's sudden wealth and for the mysterious ritual that took place in 1917 on the terrace of the Tour Magdala. But before I could expand on that I needed to take a longer look at the exact aims and intentions of the anti-Grail stream. In the adventures of Gawain in the Castle of Wonders I found the ideal starting-point.*

'Parzival, Gawain and Feirefis represent the original entelechy of man: the *thinking spirit, the feeling soul, and the willing body.* They are a human trinity—three in one and one in three. They exist separately on earth but they are secretly the manifestation of one organism—that is to say, they exist in the spiritual world as one indivisible unity.'[216] In his book *The Cup of Destiny*, Trevor Ravenscroft goes on to describe how: 'Parzival must so depersonalize and objectify his thinking that it becomes the vehicle of the Holy Spirit. Gawain must so purify his heart that the Christ may live within it. Feirefis must seize the powers of the will and dedicate his every deed to the service of God the Father.'[217]

With the adventures of Gawain, as described by Wolfram von Eschenbach in his *Parzival*, we move into the realm of those forces that oppose the Grail stream. It is Gawain's task to face the arduous tests of Klingsor's 'Castle of Wonders'—the anti-Grail Castle.

It is Parzival who inspires Gawain to quest for the Grail. Earlier in the poem Gawain had laid a cloth across three drops of blood that had fallen upon the snow in order to free Parzival who had become hypnotized by the sight. In this way Parzival had become dependent upon Gawain.

The Grail opposition can only flourish when there is impurity in the human heart. The impurity in Gawain is externalized in the outer shape of his personal destiny. As he

The Tour Magdala

draws ever nearer to the Castle of Wonders he arrives in a realm where there is unfaithfulness and treachery. Students turn against teachers and relatives against each other. Inspired by the words of Parzival, Gawain takes sides in a war. He chooses to fight on the side of the good forces, who are being besieged by an outer army whose cause is unjust. It turns out the Red Knight—Parzival—is fighting on the side of the outer army, on the side of evil. Ravenscroft comments: 'It is in the heart that the battle between light and darkness takes place. It is also in the heart that love dictates whether the human soul shall serve good or evil. These two armies are in conflict because, until equanimity is achieved, the conflict continues in the human heart—the confrontation between conscience and moral blindness.'[218]

In his next adventure Gawain is forced to take on the responsibility of the quest for the Grail from a knight who has been conquered by Parzival. In this way Gawain's destiny is determined by the actions of Parzival, and the situation of dependence is reversed.

In the immediate environment of the Castle of Wonders Gawain meets the lady Orgeulse. She plays with his affections, setting him tests and challenges, but balances his obvious devotion with total rejection. Despite this she will not just send him on his way but holds him in thrall, speaking scornfully to him. It is only later when Gawain has purified himself of blind desire that they can become true friends. Orgeulse is perhaps aware that until Gawain is purified his love for her is purely sensual and egotistic, having little to do with her true spiritual nature.

Gawain sights the Castle of Wonders. He questions a ferryman, whose hospitality he has accepted, about the castle. He is warned not to ask questions. Parzival is led to the Grail Castle by the Fisher King but fails to attain the Grail because he fails to ask the question. In the Grail Castle questions are welcome. In the Castle of Wonders questions are not only forbidden but are dangerous.

Entering the Castle of Wonders Gawain endures several tests that almost cost him his life. He does not bear the tests with total success but he does survive and this is what counts. He sits on a strange bed that suddenly begins to move, crashing him from wall to wall. Then he is attacked by a lion, a giant, and stones and arrows rain upon him from all directions. He uses his shield to protect himself. In this Gawain again experiences what is within as a force coming at him from the periphery. He fails in his test when he kills the lion. He should have leapt onto its back and allowed himself to flow with the process. Instead of submitting his soul in patience to a higher guidance, he resorts to violence. When he used the shield to defend himself he was safe, but when he resorts to the sword he is almost lost.

Gawain must leap across a vast chasm on horseback. At the first attempt he fails but is saved from drowning in the river below by his horse. On the second try he succeeds, a sign that he has attained to purity of heart. With this action the souls trapped within the anti-Grail Castle are liberated and the stage is set for the reunion of Parzival and Gawain, and their triumphant return to the true Grail Castle.

The story of Gawain has many profound implications, but we are here concerned only with a single aspect: that it is in his heart forces that the individual must overcome the anti-Grail stream.

In *The Holy Blood and the Holy Grail*, the authors try to establish the Order of the Prieuré de Sion as precursor to the Templars. They describe the 'cutting of the elm at Gisors' in 1188 when a formal separation occurred between the two institutions. The Ordre de Sion, which had created the Knights Templar, now washed its hands of its celebrated protégés. The 'parent', in other words, officially disowned the 'child'. This rupture is said to have been commemorated by a ritual or ceremony of some sort.

Only two years later, 1190, marks the end of the period of rulership of the Archangel Raphael. It is also the time that Rudolf Steiner has indicated as marking the eventual fading of the esoteric Grail tradition. Steiner has described how each of the Archangels rule in turn over a period of 260 years. When one studies the effect of this one can begin to see how the particular characteristics of each Archangel has influenced the period of its rulership. For example, Gabriel (according to Islam) takes Muhammad to the highest heaven, dictates the Koran, and also rules over the Victorian era. He is connected with the moon and the preservation of blood ties. The crescent moon is a symbol of Islam, and is also connected with the forces of reproduction and heredity.

Raphael is the Archangel connected with healing. His planet, Mercury, is associated with the elm tree, so that in the 'cutting of the elm' at Gisors, whatever else the significance of that ceremony might have been, we can see that it marks the end of one epoch and the start of another. The Raphaelic instinct for healing was the birthright of those living during the so-called Dark Ages. The Archangel who rules after Raphael is Samael, related to Mars, the planet that energizes the dawning age of increased independence of thought, the age that Rudolf Steiner has described as the age of the consciousness soul.

The modern Prieuré de Sion could be considered to be the continuation of an original inner group bearing the same name, dating from the time when the first Templars were sent to the Holy Land by Bernard of Clairveaux. Although the secrets of the Grail were kept hidden in the Mystery centres, there had been an outpouring of knowledge in the art and architecture of the Gothic period. This was still mostly instinctive. The involvement of Bernard of Clairveaux with the instigation of the Knights Templar has been suggested in a scenario put forward by Baigent, Leigh and Lincoln to demonstrate that the aim and purpose St Bernard had in sending out the original nine knights had been for them to rummage about for 'great quantities of bullion, sacred vessels, additional unspecified material and "treasure" of an indeterminate kind... 24 different hoards buried beneath the Temple itself'.[219] The argument is made to seem plausible when the writers state that, prior to the Templars' expedition to Palestine, the Cistercians were dangerously close to bankruptcy. Under St Bernard's guidance, they underwent a sudden change of fortune. This assumption is not, however, in keeping with the historical facts.

According to James France, a leading expert on the Cistercians and author of the book *The Cistercians in Scandinavia*, it is not accurate to say that the 'Cistercians "were close to bankruptcy". It is true that Citeaux was a small and struggling monastery when Bernard joined it with 30 members of his family and friends and that the Cistercians owed a great deal of their subsequent rapid growth to his dynamic personality. The change in their fortunes was to do with recruitment and patronage and nothing whatever to do with the Templars.'[220]

Given the connections we have explored between the Templars and the Grail wisdom in this book we can see that the motivation behind Bernard of Clairveaux's involvement with the founding of the first Templars was not crudely materialistic. Those who were familiar with the secrets which were later concealed in the Grail romances would have had no difficulty in answering many of the enigmatic questions that puzzle scholars today. In the time we have just been considering, the time of transition marked by the 'cutting of the elm', these secrets were withdrawn further into the Mysteries, their potency hidden in myth when the Grail legend began to be circulated and popularized. Wolfram von Eschenbach's *Parzival* was written some time between 1195 and 1220. Chrétien de Troyes was writing at almost the same time. Chrétien seems to have been attached to the court of the Count of Champaigne, one of the first nine knights of the Order of the Templars. The Council of Troyes first instigated an exoteric role and 'rule' for the Templars. It is fascinating that the Grail Mysteries should have been spun into myth by one proceeding from the same court. One may at this point note that there is no such thing as a Cistercian rule. 'The Cistercians followed the rule of St Benedict, and through the influence of Bernard the Templars adopted this and the degrees and uses of Citeaux.'[221]

The Archangel Michael became cosmic regent during the last third of the nineteenth century. Up to that time the progress of the consciousness-soul age had passed through the regencies of Samael and Gabriel. Their influences caused the Grail wisdom to become even more obscured as the advance of external science and materialism took an increasing hold on evolution.

There were other influences which caused the increasing pall of materialism to obscure the original vibrant stream of esoteric Christianity. Within this stream of esoteric Christianity we include Celtic Christianity, which influenced the flowering of Chartres. We learned in an earlier chapter that the Greek wisdom was permeated with the original teachings of Aristotle. With the overthrow of the Barmicides and the Persian influence, Arabism was mixed with these teachings so that Aristotelianism was increasingly intellectualized from then onwards. This event reshaped the future course of history. Through the Arabian impulse, which thus continued on to the present day in the changed nature of Aristotelianism, the conditions were created for a far steeper descent into matter than would otherwise have come about.

This materialistic impulse was not confined to the domains of science and the intellect, but infiltrated the Catholic Church via the Eighth Ecumenical Council of 869 in Constantinople. Walter Johannes Stein deals with this in his book *The Ninth Century*:

> The living spirit died when doubts of the Trinity arose. The Council of 869, through which Trichotomy was abolished—the teaching that body, soul and spirit are to be considered as distinct from one another in man—is only a completion of a long series of events. The Council merely expressed what had been accomplished in human evolution. The path to the spirit was no longer accessible in the old way. At the same time Ahriman, the Spirit of Lies, was drawing near.[222]

Pope Nicholas I had the karmic destiny of guiding Ahriman into the stream of history. He was influenced on two sides in his attempt to find a middle path between East and West. On one side was the activity of his wise counsellor Anastasius. Anastasius was witness to the Council of 869 as authenticated by Hergenrother in his work on Photius, one of the sources investigated by Johannes Stein. On the other side were the famous forgeries, the 'Isidoric-Decretals'. These documents had a profound effect upon the spiritual impulses of the times, but were carefully designed fakes strung together from many sources. Stein comments: 'It is all the same whose hand wrote the forgery. Ahriman wrote it; that Spirit of Untruth then entering humanity. But upon this fact hangs world history; for how could the modern age come about, the age of the machine, of printing, of the power of the newspaper, without the entry of this spirit? It had to enter.'[223]

The 'entry of Ahriman' is here shown to be necessary so that the independence of the human ego could be brought a stage further. Humanity has benefited, however, from its estrangement from the spiritual world. We have gained freedom and the use of the intellect which were not possible during the ages of innocence and clearer spiritual understanding. We have now passed through the Renaissance which has produced great individuals. We have all listened patiently to Galileo, Newton and Darwin. But during this period, when the light of the spirit gave way to the growing rational powers of man, other organizations became privy to the Templar secrets. As we will demonstrate, their shadow overhangs society.

Missing from the more orthodox accounts of history has been an account of the workings of the Grail family. Walter Johannes Stein was among the first historians to begin to remedy this situation. Since Stein's writings the Grail Family has been mentioned many times by various writers for different purposes. In *The Holy Blood and the Holy Grail* it was erroneously described as having descended from the union of Jesus and Mary Magdalene. It may have been connected to a Merovingian blood-line but not in the way that Baigent, Leigh and Lincoln describe it.

In *The Ninth Century in the Light of the Holy Grail*, Walter Johannes Stein relates a more plausible link between the Merovingians and the Grail Family when describing Duke Eticho of Alsace, father of St Odilie: 'He is a personality to whom all that which rests upon the individual, through the fact that his indwelling forces came by personal inheritance [i.e. by blood descent], is a grave burden of responsibility. Therefore when a child who was blind, Odilie, was born to him, he said to himself: now people will ask, "Who has sinned, the child or its parents?" He therefore wished to kill the child to escape the suggestion that it was his fault that Odilie was born lacking the sight of her eyes. Thus thought the father. Not so the mother. To rescue the child she, with the help of the child's nurse, brought her to her own family at Beaume les Dames. There the child grew up. At [her] baptism she would receive her sight. And so it befell. The cosmic power which, as light of the world, opened the eyes of him who had been born blind, gave light to the eyes of Odilie also at the touch of Bishop Erhard's baptismal water. He named the child St Odilie, Sol Dei, Sun of God. Father and daughter face each other as light and darkness.'[224]

A possibility here is that, as Rudolf Steiner has indicated, the blood of certain early European tribes remained permeated with the forces of the Tree of Life, even after its removal from the earth. This force only needed updating to carry legitimate healing power. In other words, Odilie's own hereditary healing forces were permitted to work after she was baptized. We now also know that 'holy water' will have enhanced the healing process still more because of the presence of all nine resonances.

In a letter referred to in *The Ninth Century*, Eliza von Moltke, widow of General von Moltke, commander of the German land forces during the First World War, quotes from a conversation with Rudolf Steiner:

> The Odilien cloister on the Odilienberg was originally a seat of pagan Mysteries, later Christianized by the saintly Odilie... More than once she was most wonderfully rescued, thus at one time fleeing before her father's pursuit but, under her young brother's protection, she sought refuge in the hill facing our building at Dornach [the Goetheanum] and was again rescued in a miraculous way

> on the return journey, and at that time there happened the transformation of the old Mystery centre into a Christian cloister. Thence proceeded that Christian stream which Pope Nicholas was concerned to propagate, the stream which was to be in complete opposition to the Byzantine. Later there was a continuous interchange of letters between the Odilienberg and Pope Nicholas. This stream Eticho wished to destroy; he stood in the service of the Merovingians. This cloister was a source whence the substance of Christianity spread through the West; hence Odilienberg was the centre of so many fights with Alsace.[225]

These passages seem to indicate that the Merovingians were direct opponents of the Grail stream and the true Grail family. Later in Stein's account there is a passage quoted from a biographer of Odilie, Dionysus Albrecht, who writing in 1751

> shows quite clearly that he was conscious of the mission of the line of Odilie. He writes "This ducal line became widespread as once was the line of Jacob. Viz.: from the centre of Alsace towards the evening in France, towards the morning in the Roman and Austrian realms, towards midday in Spain, and towards midnight in Saxony and Brandenburg." Just as Jacob's seed, according to the stars in their order, spread to all points of the compass, so also did the race of Odilie. And Rudolf von Habsburg is a direct descendant of Saint Odilie's brother. Maximillian boasted with pride of this descent. The House of Baden, too, derived thence, and by his marriage with Gisilbert, daughter of Lothar I, the Count of Maassgau also was united with the House of Brabant (Hessen). So, too, the House of the Dukes of Lothringen were descended through the male line from Eticho. By the marriage of Maria Theresa with Francis I, the House of Habsburg united with that of Lothringa to form what was later the Austrian Empire...Those who were connected with the history of the Grail are linked together in relationship... One sees, e.g., that Godfried of Bouillon whose companions in arms founded the Knights

> Templar stands in relationship with the family of Odile... Those who are connected with the Grail story are members of one family... As a matter of fact most of the ruling families of Europe were of the race of Odilie. And an old tradition emphasizes this. The mission of these family connections was not so much to form a powerful House, i.e. turning a family spirit into a spirit of the times; its task was to expand what was bound up with the family into what is cosmopolitan. A Gabriel blood-connection—which indeed in some of its branches bore on its coat of arms the Gabriel lily—was to become the vessel of the world-irradiating sun-impulse. Thus was the kingdom of God to arise. In the time, however, during which this should have been accomplished it was neglected.[226]

Despite all insistence on the significance of the Merovingian blood-line, we can see how it can no longer have any great significance; all hereditary blood-lines are now 'merely physical'. Supposing that Merovingian kings were to be descended from one or other of the Jesus-children, their blood would not carry any more significance than that of any other individual. Personal spiritual evolution and self-development, the full attainment of individualized ego-hood, is the modern path. Blood-ties and the power stemming from them belong to the regressive anti-Grail streams.

The task of the Grail Family was to expand to world-embracing, cosmopolitan dimensions, which once lived only in the blood of a particular group of humanity. The bearers of this blood-line were carefully married into all the royal houses of Europe so that the ego-bearing power of the Tree-of-Life imbued blood could flow to all of humanity. In his essay 'England and the Foundation of Commercial Towns: The Origin of the Lohengrin Saga Traced According to English History', W. J. Stein shows how behind the captivating legend of the Swan Knight is the hidden history of the founding of the first towns.

Stein concludes:

> Sent forth by Arthur as Knights of the Grail, fighting for

> sanctity, serving the peace-loving king, the messenger of the Holy Grail founded the cities. Just as of old, the peace-loving economic character was bestowed on the development of towns by means of valiant encounters; in like manner we of today are called upon to fight for a similar peace-loving economic significance in the evolution of the countries throughout the world. This can no longer be achieved through matrimonial alliances. It is possible today only by appropriate co-operation in concrete fields of endeavour; yet the mission still remains—to impregnate the world with the economic impulse in the light of the precious and most unselfish Blood that was shed for all humanity.'[227]

It seems that the Grail Family created the potential for what the Knights Templar, especially their inner group, could have stood for. But by their insistence on the continuation of a blood-line perpetrated in the old Gabrielic way, those who clung to their Merovingian origins betrayed the true task and original potential of the Grail Family. This may also have been an important factor in the impossibility that the inner group of Knights Templar experienced in maintaining the high ideals for which they strove.

If the central concern of the inner Grail Knights was the universality of Christ's blood, then what route did the 'failed' Grail Family take? As Walter Johannes Stein mentioned, the line of Clovis (the Merovingian line) had as its emblem the lily connected with the Archangel Gabriel. Spirituality that arises through 'heredity' has for some time brought decadent supersensible forces into the material world. Odilie's true line would have been that of esoteric Christianity, with the rose as a symbol of genuine brotherhood free of hereditary preroga-tives and privileges. The image of Templar Knights riding together on one horse demonstrates their original ideals of humility. The fact that it has recently been supposed that it was because they indulged in homosexual practices demon-strates how far off course we have wandered.

In their second book, *The Messianic Legacy*, Baigent, Leigh and Lincoln again mention the possibility of a blood-line that flows down the generations from the house of David, through Jesus to the present day. In the Epilogue, having wistfully toyed with the concept of royalty as a symbol of meaning in a world which has lost its sense of direction, they tie up the thread of their argument with the following question:

> What, for example, would be the implications for modern Israel as well as for both Judaism and Christianity if—on the basis of records and other evidence issuing from the Temple of Jerusalem—Jesus stood revealed as the Messiah expected by the people of Palestine two thousand years ago—a man, that is, who was their nation's rightful king, who married and sired children and perhaps did not die on the cross at all. Would it not at a single stroke eradicate the theological differences between Judaism and Christianity and at least some of the antipathy of Islam? In any case and quite apart from the Temple, the Prieuré de Sion can promulgate a claim which would enjoy considerable currency even in today's world. On behalf of the families it represents it can establish dynastic succession extending back to the Old Testament house of David. It can establish quite definitively and to the satisfaction of most fastidious genealogical enquiry, that the Merovingian Dynasty was of the Davidic line and was formerly recognized as being so by the Roman Church of the period. Aided by the techniques of modern public relations, modern advertising and modern political packaging, the Prieuré could thus present to the modern world a figure who by the strictest scriptural definition of the term could claim to be a biblical Messiah... A pedigree cannot be used as a stepping stone to power. Rather it is a trump card which can be played only to consolidate power once power has already been obtained. A man cannot say 'Look who I am!' and expect on that basis to be elected or promoted Pope, President, King or Emperor. But if he were already Pope, President, King or Emperor and more or less securely installed as such he could then say 'Look who I am' and expect not only to

> consolidate his position but also to invest it with a new aura, a new credibility, a new and resonant significance...a sudden coup d'état which restored monarchy in say Greece or Portugal would be counter-productive, many people would remain indifferent, regarding it simply as another change of regime to be accepted with more or less something of cynicism. If, on the other hand, a charismatic monarchical figure were swept dramatically to power by a tide of popular acclaim his mandate would be altogether different.[228]

In other words the aim of such a 'coup d'état' could be to place a modern king descended from the Merovingian line on the throne in Jerusalem. He would be acclaimed as a descendent of Jesus, supposedly of the same hereditary line as the Matthew Jesus-child. This king would then rule the world by virtue of the red dynastic blood in his veins. Such a leader, in solving some of humanity's major problems, would undoubtedly be widely hailed and accepted as a world saviour, perhaps even as Christ himself. The establishment of a European super-state, with an adjusted astrological chart, would be a massive leap forward towards completion of these anti-evolutionary designs.

This is even more clearly hinted at in the following passage from *The Holy Blood and the Holy Grail* where, according to one of the writers' informants, a M. Chaumeil, the secret society Hieron du Val d'or was planning 'a theocracy wherein nations would be no more than provinces, their leaders but proconsuls in the service of a world occult government consisting of an elite. For Europe, this regime of the Great King implied a double hegemony of the papacy and the empire, of the Vatican and of the Habsburgs, who would have been the Vatican's right arm...Such a state would have realized the centuries-old dream of a "heavenly kingdom" on earth, a terrestrial replica or mirror-image of the order, harmony and hierarchy of the cosmos. It would have actualized the ancient Hermetic promise, "As above, so below".'[229]

18
The Double

The task of evil is to promote the ascent of man.

Rudolf Steiner

The idea that evil is in some way an external force, located in other *people, or other races or nations, but never* within ourselves *or the groups* we *belong to, is a common one. This process of projecting evil onto others has been the cause of most of the suffering in human history. The most uncomfortable, and the most liberating, aspect of the Grail traditions for modern humanity is probably the Manichaean notion that evil is not only a necessary force in human evolution but that we all, each and every one of us, share in its essential nature.*

The final step towards resolving the mysteries of Rennes-le-Château is perhaps the most difficult. An understanding of the 'Double'—the evil within—is essential to the authentic Grail Mysteries. It is also the key to understanding the full import of 'Saunière's secret'—the subject of the penultimate chapter.

'It may shock you to hear of another spiritual being inhabiting the human body,' says Rudolf Steiner, concerning that entity known to spiritual science as the Double or *Doppelgänger*, 'but in biology lessons we are not shocked to learn how many other inhabitants from the animal, plant and mineral kingdoms also cohabit our physical bodies. Just as we have discovered the bacteria and fungi rather recently, so we have rediscovered the *Doppelgänger*...It is part of the physiological behaviour of these beings to move into the human body shortly before we are born and to accompany us from then on beneath the threshold of consciousness with their cleverness and their strong nature-bound will.'[230]

The fairy-tale character Rumpelstiltskin has been seen as an imaginative picture of the working of the Double. Rumpelstiltskin is found in that part of the forest where 'the fox bids the hare good-night'. The hare is a well-known symbol of the etheric. Pictures of the cat as a symbol for Lucifer and the fox as a symbol for Ahriman can be found throughout folk-tales. In bidding the hare 'good-night' Ahriman is rendering the etheric part of man unconscious in that particular part of the etheric body where the Double—Rumpelstiltskin—dwells. It is in this part of the etheric body that electrical and electromagnetic impulses have degenerated from etheric activity.

Feeding off the degenerated etheric force the Double can be monitored by standard electrical devices. Wherever currents of electricity are running in the electromagnetic phenomena of the body there is the activity of the ahrimanic beings. For this reason it will be impossible for 'New Age' science to eventually claim that electrical devices are able to detect 'finer' manifestations of the 'etheric' as these would only be 'finer' echoes of the activity of the Double. The etheric body, which is free of its influence, lies outside the range of all 'physical' investigations.

According to Rudolf Steiner:

> These *Doppelgängers* have one considerable weakness...There is one occurrence in the course of human life that they absolutely cannot bear, namely, death. Therefore they always have to leave the human body in which they have settled just before death. This phenomenon is quite well known to doctors, nurses and relations of terminally ill patients who have fought for their lives for a long time, tortured by the most horrific symptoms. Suddenly a strange and great calm sets in, everybody regains hope; the sick person is totally changed and regains his equanimity. It is hoped that the healing process has set in; a few days later the patient dies. What everybody was aware of in this process was the end of the activity of the *Doppelgänger* in the dying individual...The *Doppelgänger* cannot bear death, wants to survive death and have a human body at the disposal of its intelligence and will power, but it has to leave when the human ego is about to pass over the Threshold...[231]

It is the destiny of the human ego to die and be reborn. But the Double cannot submit to this evolutionary process. How then can the Double gain final control over human evolution? Only through tricking human beings into transferring their immortality from the spiritual realms to the physical.

In previous chapters we have seen how the ahrimanic beings have worked tirelessly in evolution, influencing the course of history. Their aim is to separate humanity from its spiritual origin by binding man to matter and material values in every possible way. One example of this is in the manner in which many inventions have come about. Some of the ideas which have inspired our mechanistically oriented science have come to the inventor when he was in a state of suppressed consciousness:

> Between 1858 and 1865, Kekulé founded modern structural chemistry, thus making a significant contribution to research in the field of the new dyes. The following incident illustrates the part destiny played here. Kekulé fell asleep while riding on the upper deck of a London bus and missed his stop. This was compensated for by a dream in which carbon atoms joined hands and danced around him in a circle. This dream inspired the creation of his structural chemistry.[232]

The overall effect of many people succumbing to the forces of the Double is the widespread subversion of human history. There is not space here to enlarge upon the many ways in which ahrimanic beings have re-routed the course of history, but one interesting connection is the history of sugar consumption. There has been a gradual descent from sweeteners derived from the flower of the plant (honey), to the stem (cane sugar), and finally to the root (beet sugar). A materialistic knowledge of diet would find no difference in the effect of sweeteners derived from these three sources. But according to spiritual science the plant is inverted in its effect upon the human body so that the 'root' affects the head forces of the human being. If the intellect is not carefully balanced with the heart, a cold, calculating 'ahrimanic' attitude will develop. It is interesting to note Napoleon's involvement with the final stage of this process:

> In 1800 the German scientist F. A. Achard, discovered the possibility of extracting sugar from beets. But 20 years passed before a commercially profitable type of beet was bred. Even so, despite all the ingenuity of German technicians and chemists, the industry would not have developed as it did if politics had not played a decisive role. Napoleon had decreed a continental blockade and thereby stopped all sugar imports. Efforts to produce a beet sugar every bit as good as cane were naturally redoubled. Napoleon himself took a personal interest in speeding the development of the beet sugar industry, with the result that quite a number of factories producing beet were in existence by 1811. After Napoleon's fall, the young industry kept going by virtue of the fact that it had made a far greater technical progress than the cane sugar industry.[233]

It is to the great advantage of ahrimanic beings to bring materialism deeper into human life and at the same time to increase their domination over the individuals they inhabit. One very effective way of doing this is by encouraging human beings to eat substances that bring the *Doppelgänger* into a place of dominance over the ego. An example of this can be seen in the case of some hyperactive children. In certain cases, chemicals in food have been shown to have a powerful role in suppressing the child's normal nature and in exchanging it for the ravings and wilful demands of a different being. Why does it take very little to lure even the most carefully trained young appetite away from foods that are beneficial to those which are full of synthetic substances and chemicals? Could it not be the *Doppelgänger* whispering to the child to take in as much as possible of a diet on which it will thrive?

What happened after Kekulé's 'inspired' dream, mentioned above? Hauschka:

> It was soon discovered that substances of this group,

> produced at intermediate stages of dye manufacture, react on the human organism. They ushered in the era of synthetic drugs...This was the start of chemical therapy, which sought to exploit the discoveries of the dye chemists. No one can dispute that this expansion of coal-tar chemistry is a triumph of the human mind. But what spiritually was behind it, and how are these substances related to the cosmic whole? Let us recall how the natural substances born of starch come into being. We saw how starchy matter is etherialized in the exhaling of the cosmic breath and changes into sugars, blossoms, colours, scents, honey, essential oils and therapeutic substances of plant origin. Downwards from the middle zone of starch there is a gradual densifying and mineralizing, via cellulose, until a biological zero is reached in carbon, or coal tar. Here human ingenuity takes hold and conjures forth a synthetic mirror-image of the natural world: synthetic colours, scents, saccharin and other sweeteners, mineral oil and therapeutic substances.
>
> Contrasting the two realms, we get the impression that the upper one is the realm of dynamic biological reality, the scene of a ceaseless harmonization of the living polarities of earth and heaven, giving rise to an endless range of metamorphosis. The underworld of coal tar chemistry, on the other hand, seems—figuratively speaking—like a ghostly reflection of the dynamic creativity of the cosmos. Here, however, the static world of atoms and calculable happenings takes the place of dynamics. Despite the calculable certainties found in this sub-earthly realm, it cannot seem more real to us than that of the greening, flowering and fruiting plants.[234]

The level of the 'synthetic mirror image' lies in the physical world with no relationship to the realm of life-forces. This synthetic world creates the 'foodstuff' for the Double, a source of nourishment that is entirely cut off from any cosmic, spiritual or living influences. Is it surprising, therefore, that a society increasingly supplied with this 'shadow food' should be unwittingly providing opportunity for those beings who are entirely without soul, who work with enormous strength and Mephistophelean cleverness to gain an increasing foothold in all the affairs of human beings. One 'way of entry' for ahrimanic beings is thus through reduced consciousness and faulty diet. Another is when cosmic forces are 'cut off' by the proximity of power cables as we saw in the 'beech-bud' experiments in Chapter 2. There is an increasing volume of data being compiled from many other sources on electromagnetic pollution to add authenticity to these pioneer experiments of Lawrence Edwards.

Our particular concern now is when this way of entry is made through the 'fallen' etheric energy of the earth, as it manifests in electromagnetism. We already know that these fallen etheric forces are inhabited by ahrimanic and luciferic powers:

> There is another characteristic of this being which has to do with the whole earth. We have to stress here that contrary to natural science the earth is not a dead mineral object in the universe but a living organism in which the mineral realm is so to speak only the bony structure. As there is differentiation in any organism so there is also within the earth. Our earth is by no means a being which radiates the same forces upwards to all her inhabitants. In the various regions of the earth different forces are radiated upwards. There are magnetic forces, electrical forces, but also forces which come up out of the earth and which influence man in different ways according to the geological formation. We have to point to a very important fact, namely, that man's *Doppelgänger* has a direct relationship to these forces which emanate from the earth in differentiated ways. Through the most intimate relationships of this being with the earth's emanations man is, according to his body, soul and spirit, indirectly in relationship with the earth...These regions where the influence on the *Doppelgänger* of what streams up from below are strongest, and where these emanations form the closest relationship with the earth, are

> where the mountain ranges stretch from north to south rather than from east to west. These forces also have to do with the magnetic North Pole; thus it is again pointed out how in this day and age particularly strong influences and effects of the *Doppelgänger* could emanate from the American continent...Rudolf Steiner points out that in the year 1413 there begins a new epoch in the evolution of man's consciousness...how already some time before this man was overcome by a certain weakness which made it impossible for him to bear knowledge of the *Doppelgänger* any more, to be protected from absorbing more than a very little which would remind him of the *Doppelgänger*. As a result the knowledge of him which existed in earlier times was lost. Certain measures were already taken before the fifteenth century so that mankind would forget all knowledge of the *Doppelgänger*...Only from the nineteenth century onwards is it supposed to be taken into man's consciousness again so that the ego can regulate its relationship with him.[235]

This can certainly be verified if we note the Double's appearance in literature at the turn of the century: Oscar Wilde's *Portrait of Dorian Grey* and *Dr Jekyll and Mr Hyde* by Robert Louis Stevenson.

Here it is necessary to point out that early sailings to America have been verified by the Vinland sagas as having taken place many hundreds of years before Columbus. By the ninth and tenth centuries it became more a matter of trade and exploration.

> America was known to be the region where these magnetic forces stream out of the earth in a particular way...Thus the American continent was marked out in that, out of its nature, the early sailings across the oceans, originally started by the Mystery centres, were aimed at studying the illnesses that arose under the influence of terrestrial magnetism...It was therefore for reasons of protection for man in western Europe when the Roman Catholic Church took care that, by means of a certain edict, contact with

> America was stopped by abolishing navigation. It was Irish monks, among them in particular Columba...who were able to convince Rome that it was necessary to cut Europe off from the West.[236]

This ban only lasted approximately between the twelfth and fifteenth centuries, but during this time there may have been secret voyages.

In the chapter on the western Mysteries we first saw how relationships to geological formations affected the intensification of the etheric at various sites on the earth's surface. Guenther Wachsmuth enlarges on this:

> If we wish to enquire further into the history of religions we shall never be able to put the geology book entirely aside...we can question geology as to whether, from that point of view, any conclusions can be drawn concerning individual points of formative force-structure on the earth, where instead of a mighty elevation above the sea-level a depression below it might be found, a place where the earth, as it were, had sucked in a portion of her surface—and had made it a portion of her inner life. Of such depression in the solid earth E. Kayser says: "Quite a number of these regions are known which, although they belong to the continents, nevertheless lie below the level of the sea. There is one in the Sahara Desert near the oasis of Jupiter Ammon." The depth of this depression amounts to 20 to 30 metres. It is interesting that in this neighbourhood also, a Mystery school was founded. And because we cannot shut out the history of religions from our memory, we are astonished when we find out what a region of the earth it is, where this depression into the interior of the earth, this antipodes to Tibet, reaches its greatest intensity. One of the deepest depressions known is that tract, 180 kilometres long, which stretches from the Sea of Galilee to the Dead Sea in the Jordan Valley. This strange Jordan Valley stretches as a narrow strip, including the Sea of Galilee, southwards from about Capurnaum until south of Jericho it reaches the Dead Sea. Within this unique region sunk deep in the earth

the Baptism of Jordan took place. It is the birthplace of Christianity.[237]

Earlier Wachsmuth had described how the etheric forces predominating on the high plateau of Tibet are predominately those of the light and warmth ethers; their 'antipodes' in the Jordan Valley would therefore be those of life and chemical ethers. This extra information makes possible an even clearer understanding of the great significance of the physical location singled out on the earth for the accomplishment of the transubstantiation and Resurrection, where the forces of the chemical and life ethers were especially involved in the transformation of Jesus Christ's physical body.

If we investigate these geological connections with the etheric earth further we begin to see a regular pattern emerging. Box Hill in Surrey has been described as one of the most powerful energy points in the South of England and there are very specific geological features there. A geological map of the Rennes-le-Château area demonstrates that there are many faults and various different rock strata in the area. As we have seen from the Siemonze quotation above, the American continent is particularly affected by geological conditions in relation to the Double. Wachsmuth also describes this: 'Now if we go further, across the Atlantic Ocean, and come to the great mountain-chain which lies on the west coast of the American continent, we shall find that these mountains have been formed by forces moving partly from west to east.'[238]

We have seen how the Knights Templar situated themselves over sites of intensified etheric activity. One therefore wonders if the Knights of Malta, developed from the Knights of St John, emulated the Templars by basing themselves on an island in the Mediterranean which is situated at an intersection of tectonic-plates creating a fault stretching across the Mediterranean through Sicily to Cyprus. We know very well that Cyprus has been the home of Templars and other related orders for centuries; also legend has it that there is a huge rock in Cyprus which is kept in the air by some unaccountable energy.

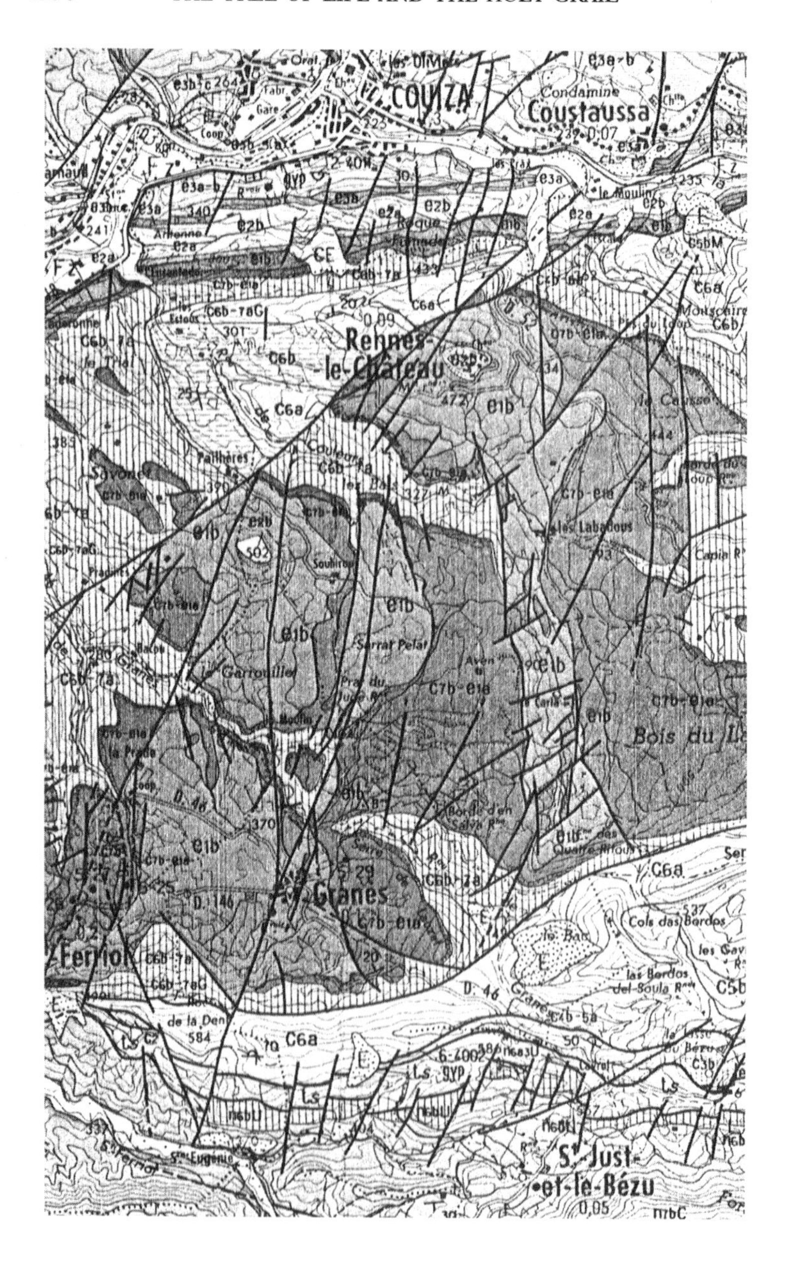

A geological map of Rennes-le-Château and surrounding area, showing fault lines and other geological features

Because of its location in relation to the tectonic plates, the terrain of Sicily also includes two volcanoes: Mount Etna near the east coast, and Stromboli on an island between the north coast and the Italian mainland. In a series of eight lectures given in Paris between 25 May and 14 June 1906, Rudolf Steiner spoke of volcanic activity in relationship to the human will:

> Underneath the solid earth there are a large number of subterranean spaces which communicate to the sixth layer, that of fire. [Steiner was speaking of nine concentric layers within the earth.] This element of the fire-earth is intimately connected with the human will. It is this element which produced the tremendous eruptions that brought the Lemurian epoch to an end. At that time the forces which nourish the human will went through a trial which unleashed the fire catastrophe that destroyed the Lemurian continent. In the course of evolution this sixth layer receded more and more towards the centre and as a result volcanic eruptions became less frequent. And yet they are still produced as a result of the human will which, when it is evil and chaotic, magnetically acts on this layer and disrupts it. Nevertheless, when the human will is devoid of egoism, it is able to appease this fire. Materialistic periods are mostly accompanied and followed by natural cataclysms, earthquakes, etc. Growing powers of evolution are the only alchemy capable of transforming, little by little, the organism and the soul of the earth.
>
> The following is an example of the relationship between the human will and telluric cataclysms: in human beings who perish as a result of earthquakes or volcanic eruptions one notices during their next incarnation inner qualities which are quite different. They bring from birth great spiritual predispositions because, through their death, they were brought in touch with forces which showed them the true nature of reality and the illusion of material life.
>
> One has also noticed a relationship between certain births and seismic and volcanic catastrophes. During such

> catastrophes materialistic souls incarnate, drawn sympathetically by volcanic phenomena—by the convulsions of the evil soul of the earth. And these births can in their turn bring about new cataclysms because reciprocally the evil souls exert an exciting influence on the terrestrial fire. The evolution of our planet is intimately connected with the forces of humanity and civilizations.[239]

The deepest layer of all is described earlier:

> This last layer is composed of a substance endowed with moral action. But this morality is the opposite of the one that is to be elaborated on the earth. Its essence, its inherent force, is one of separation, of discord, and of hate. It is here in the hell of Dante that we find Cain the fratricide. This substance is the opposite of everything which among human beings is good and worthy. The activity of humanity in order to establish brotherhood on the earth diminishes the power of this sphere. It is the power of Love which will transform it inasmuch as it will spiritualize the very body of the earth. This ninth layer represents the substantial origin of what here appears on earth as black magic, that is, a magic founded on egoism.[240]

In a series of four lectures given in Berlin from 3 to 7 February 1913, Rudolf Steiner speaks of how the powerful etheric forces emanating in Sicily were misused in the past, causing 'Double' activity to flow in the opposite direction—from man to earth. In the light of the above quotation one can understand how access to the interior of the earth caused by the geological conditions in Sicily also gave rise to these activities:

> Whereas it has been said that the Castle of the Grail is situated in the west of Europe, the stronghold of hostility to the Grail must be located in another place, a place where, on account of certain spiritual forces there, a person can have just as great and powerful and good an impression as he can have also of its opposite, through other forces which have remained there to this present time like an Akashic

after-effect from those opponents of the Grail of whom we have been speaking. For at that place one can speak of the very worst forces, and they are still perceptible in their after-effects. At one time evil arts were practised in that place, arts which penetrated right into physical life and thence launched their assaults on the part of the human soul that had become unconscious and on the portion of the human organism that had become dead [in other words the 'Double']. All this is closely connected with a figure who glimmers across from the Middle Ages as a legendary being, but is well known to anyone acquainted with the nature of the Mysteries: a personality who was quite real in the middle of the Middle Ages, Klingsor, the Duke of Terra de Labur, a district we have to look for in what is now southern Calabria. From there were carried out the incursions of the enemy of the Grail, especially over to Sicily. Even as today—if we tread Sicilian soil and have occult sight—we are aware of the Akashic after-effects of the great Empedocles still present in the atmosphere, so we can still perceive there the evil after-effects of Klingsor, who allied himself from his Duchy of Terra de Labur, across the Straits of Messina, with those enemies of the Grail who occupied the fortress known in occultism and legend as Kalot Bobot [Kalta Bellota; and similar variations].

In the middle of the Middle Ages, Kalot Bobot in Sicily was the seat of the goddess called Iblis, the daughter of Eblis; and among all evil unions which have taken place within the earth's evolution between beings in whose souls there were occult forces the one known to occultists as the worst of all was between Klingsor and Iblis, the daughter of Eblis. Iblis by her very name is characterized as being related to Eblis, and, in Mohammedan tradition, Eblis is the figure we call Lucifer. Iblis is a kind of feminine aspect of Eblis, the Mohammedan Lucifer, and with her Klingsor united his own evil arts, through which in the Middle Ages he worked against the Grail. These things must needs find expression in pictures, but in pictures that correspond to realities; they cannot be expressed in abstract ideas. And the whole of the hostility to the Grail was enacted in that fortress of Iblis, 'Kalot Bobot'...[241]

Walter Johannes Stein informs us:

> When I once asked Dr Steiner whether Klingsor was a real person or merely a figure in the legend he told me that Klingsor was an actual personality; he could not tell me with certainty whether he could be proved to be so from documentary evidence. From spiritual investigation, however, it can be established that Klingsor was the Count of Capua. Thence Klingsor sought alliance with the Sicilian Arabians at the castle of Kalot Bobot. It is the place which, on the map, for example the atlas of Andrees, is designated Kalta Bellota, which is to be found in south-west Sicily not very far from where on the coast the name Sciacca stands. Here in Kalta Bellota was the centre to which Klingsor attached himself. Kalath al-Bellut, referred to by Wenrich...as the Castle of the Oaks. Here African Mohammedanism was established. In 840 Kalta Bellota was conquered by the allies of Abu-l'kal-Aghlab ibn Ibrahim who were at the same time the lords of Palermo. Then came the conditions described in the Grail Legend.

Stein goes on to stress that 'The description of Klingsor's character given by Wolfram von Eschenbach has its historic archetype in Landulf II, Duke of Capua.'[242]

In his biography of Cardinal Newman, *The Pillar of Cloud*, Meriol Trevor describes how on a tour of Italy Newman was suddenly compelled to return to Sicily after an initial visit there. His fellow travellers decided to journey home, but Newman organized servants to accompany him there alone, and then suffered experiences which affected him so dramatically that he fell seriously ill and nearly died:

> He himself had set his heart on Sicily; his earlier glimpse of its wild beauties had only whetted his appetite for more. The Froudes [his fellow travellers] did not actively advise against it, but it was plain they would have liked him to

return with them, and thought his expedition 'over-venturesome'. In spite of this, and of his knowledge, from their trip to Egesta, of the discomforts of travel there, he was determined to go back. Bugs, bandits, foreign food, foreign talk, loneliness, nothing put him off...One of his secret reasons for going was to see what it was like 'to be solitary and a wanderer'. He *wanted* [author's italics] to rough it alone. *At least part of him wanted it* [our italics]; at moments he dreaded it...What was more, it was to be no easy tourist's visit. He would take a servant and mules and his own provisions and walk and ride round the island, visiting all the most famous ancient sites. This was really an extraordinary plan for an Oxford don who had never been out of England before, and was worthy of the toughest professional travellers of the time.

Newman knew this was a strange episode in his life from start to finish, but this aspect never seems to have struck him. Either he took his own courage for granted, or it did not occur to him that he needed courage to undertake an expedition so unlike anything he was accustomed to do. But he knew that Sicily was a wild place and that people quite frequently got murdered there. Yet the only thing that worried him before going seems to have been the inevitable discomforts.

Much stranger was the complete break with the whole habit of his mind. For years all his acts had been ruled by duty and determined by circumstance, which he had accepted as God's will. But no duty called him to Sicily. Circumstances rather suggested a return with the Froudes to the duties at home. It was perhaps the only time in his life he acted upon an urgent wish of his own, and yet he hardly knew himself why he was so determined on it. In the event the whole adventure perfectly realized in action the psychological and spiritual crisis within, resolved the uncertainties and renewed the life in him, so he went back to England charged with a new power. Perhaps that obscure intuition of his drove him back to the beautiful terrible island he called man's tomb.[243]

As he lay ill in Sicily Newman wrote: 'I felt God was fighting against me—and felt at last I knew *why*—it was for self-will. I felt I had been very self-willed...'[244] Earlier the biographer describes Newman descending to the crater of Vesuvius on the mainland, then comments: 'It was a suitable beginning to his classical expedition to make a descent into the underworld, especially as he was about to make a similar descent into the underworld. The depths of the earth have always been associated with the depths of the human soul and with the loss of light and vital power.'[245] Later the biographer comments: 'Having the fever and going through a crisis were all part of the same experience; it deeply affected the whole of his being and his life.'[246]

Prompted into an encounter with the Double, Newman was able to use the experience to deepen and intensify his personal evolution. The secret of this is contained within *The Gospel of Philip*: 'The archons [the fallen Powers] thought that they do what they do by their power and will. But the Holy Spirit secretly brought about everything through them as He wished.'[247]

There were those who worked from very early times to purify and raise the energy of these powerful areas. Long before the Knights Templar the ancient peoples of north-western Europe built dolmens and stone circles over the energy points, thus directly connecting them with the approaching Christ, the Sun Being who was descending to bring back the higher vibration, the pure life and chemical ethers to the earth. In these areas, thus transformed by ancient peoples and more recently by the Templars, one can feel that one is walking into the etheric world. Powerful areas, however, still manifest both ends of the spectrum. The Virgin Mary and Christ have been experienced in many places: Mejegure and Lourdes, but at Mallory Grotto in Ireland the devil also appeared. Box Hill in Surrey is said to be a very powerful energy-point, and has a reputation as a 'trouble spot'. It is interesting to note that the village which lies below Box Hill was named Mickelham, possibly at a time when there was still a feeling: 'where lies the dragon so there also Michael is needed to help human beings to overcome him'. It is also useful to record that there is a Dragon's Green close to the tiny hamlet Shipley in Sussex. The Templars had a settlement there and there is powerful dowsable energy both in and around the church, which is dedicated to Mary as is usually the case with Templar churches.

Where the powerful life ether of the earth has been linked with the approaching Christ in ancient times a healthy relationship between the activity of the life ether and the qualifying influence of the Logos has become an ongoing dynamic; these places have therefore been recognized as centres of healing by subsequent civilizations.

There is an abundance of mistletoe clinging to the branches of the trees which fringe the foot of Box Hill. Further west, at Shere, where the Harry Edwards Healing Centre is situated, mistletoe-laden trees dominate the skyline. There is mistletoe to be found at Rennes-le-Château and also on the slopes of the Goetheanum hill (Dornach) in Switzerland; both places have been referred to as powerful energy points. It is possible that in some way these powerful earth-energies create the right environment for mistletoe to flourish. Is it also because these particular areas have been 'worked on' by the ancient peoples? We saw earlier that there was a possible 'geological' connection with earth energies. Could this also apply to the siting of mistletoe?

According to the 1994 Weleda Calendar: 'The plant grows mostly in western and central Europe, but spreads as far as Scandinavia to the north, Sicily to the south and the Caucasus to the east. Temperature and moisture are the main limiting factors. Mistletoe is more common in some regions than others, and there are in fact some areas where it is quite unknown. This suggests the influence of micro-climates and geology.'[248]

Rudolf Steiner has described how mistletoe is a unique and ancient plant which is connected with Ancient Moon evolution. The special quality of mistletoe may be due to the possibility that in passing over from Ancient Moon to the present Earth evolution it has brought with it a 'plant-like' astrality which has not been subject to the Fall. Thus in present Earth evolution we have a plant that in some way retains the innocent astrality of Ancient Moon evolution. We then begin to realize that the 'astrality' of the mistletoe might still be permeated with all of the cosmic attributes that would have pertained to the human and animal astral body during present Earth evolution *if the Fall had not happened.* Is this why Steiner said that mistletoe is a plant that has healing properties for the combating of cancer?

Cancer is an illness caused when the life ether works too strongly in the cells without sufficient formative forces. The particular activity of the life ether causes the 'coming into being of matter' which, without the qualifying influence of the formative forces, results in proliferation of unqualified growth. In short, the 'form' principle has been thwarted.

In a lecture given at the 1984 Conference of the Anthroposophical Society at Michael Hall School in Sussex, Lawrence Edwards described how he had taken thousands of photographs of the leaf buds of beech trees, whose buds for the new year are already formed in September, where they hang on the branches until they open in the spring. Lawrence's photographs show that the buds were changing all through the winter, turning in their sleep in accordance with the great celestial movements of the moon and Saturn—that whenever the moon drew into a straight line with Saturn, the sleeping bud gave a little 'wave' as if to acknowledge Saturn, the ruling plant of the tree. Buds of all trees ruled by Saturn can be measured as to a related movement. When he continued these experiments the following year choosing a different tree to observe, Lawrence was disappointed to find that the graph no longer demonstrated the regular influence of the tree's ruling planet. In Lawrence's own words, 'The tree was no longer playing the game!' On close observation Lawrence noted that the buds on this second tree were misshaped and that *there was an electrical generator* situated near the tree with an electrical cable passing over it. In other words it appeared that the generator and overhead cable had effectively screened out the effect of the chemical ether so that only *unqualified* growth could take place. These experiments of Lawrence's have thrown further light on our knowledge of the effect of electromagnetic pollution on the healthy growth of plant, animal and human. The screening out of the formative principle is the main cause of cancer: the proliferation of 'growth' without 'form'.

In interpreting the story of the Fall and its relationship with cancer it is very important to understand that at some time in history the story of the Fall was distorted so that suffering individuals were led to believe that the cause of their suffering was original sin. Because of this there is a danger that an element of individual guilt can creep into our minds when a connection is made between cancer and the Fall into matter. When this took place humanity was innocent and unable to 'choose', but has also benefited from the results of 'eating of the Tree of Knowledge'.

In Druid times the 'sacred grove' would have been composed of several varieties of trees, shrubs and herbaceous plants, each of them corresponding to a different planet. The grove itself would have been imbued with 'the harmony of the spheres' which were merged with the upward rising earth-energy over which the grove was positioned.

Much later the sacred geometry of the religious buildings covering these same holy places brought in the cosmic word in another way. The soaring arches and fan vaulting of the sublime Gothic cathedrals subtly echoed a distant memory of the sacred grove. Colin Dudley remarks how sacred geometry was 'so easy for these architects that they had no need of complicated mathematical head work'.[249] Why? Because the divine proportions were playing through their very being. The cosmic word is easy to recreate when you listen for it, it is sounding through your every limb!

In the eighth century, St Boniface was passing through a forest when he came across pagan priests about to sacrifice a small boy under an oak tree. The saint took an axe and hewed the oak. Where the tree had fallen, a little fir tree was found growing in its roots. From this legend arose the significance of the fir tree as a symbol of the Christian Christmas festival. The oak tree was sacred to the Druids; Mistletoe growing on an oak tree was especially revered, and when it was culled a silk sheet was held underneath so that the mistletoe would not fall on the earth. This practice illustrates the wisdom with which the Druids venerated a plant that had originated from a time when the Fall into matter—literally onto earth—had not yet taken place. They knew the mysterious connection between this plant and the time before Earth evolution had even begun, long before a rift had occurred between the astral and etheric bodies. The attainment of the Grail will signify the progressive overcoming of the Double. The true alchemy of creation will require the membering of the human being back into the mighty Pleroma, the cosmic Word. Rudolf Steiner has defined the Christmas tree as the 'Second Tree of Life'. Here symbolism points to the forces of the Tree of Life returned to the earth by Christ:

> When the candles are lit on the Christmas tree, the human soul feels as though the symbol of an eternal reality were standing there and that this must always have been the symbol of the Christmas festival, even in a far distant past. For in the autumn, when outer nature fades, when the sun's creations fall as it were into slumber and man's organs of outer perception must turn away from the phenomena of the physical world, the soul has the opportunity—not only the opportunity but the urge—to withdraw into its innermost depths, in order to feel and experience: Now, when the light of the outer sun is faintest and its warmth feeblest, now is the time when the soul withdraws into the darkness but can find within itself the inner, spiritual light that is kindled in the outer darkness. And because what we feel to be the spirit light of the soul shining into the darkness of nature seems to be an eternal reality, we imagine that the lighted fir tree shining out to us on Christmas Night must have been shining ever since our earthly incarnations began.[250]

19
Saunière's Secret

TO DAGOBERT II, KING, AND TO SION BELONGS THIS TREASURE AND IT IS DEATH.

Readers who have accompanied the book this far will have long since realized that the term 'Holy Grail' refers to a reality of great complexity. We have had to look at our various themes from many perspectives. For instance, in the four Mystery chapters, the question of the relationship between good and evil was looked at from several very different, perhaps even seemingly contradictory, perspectives. Different aspects of these investigations will have resonated with different readers. This is true to the nature of the Grail, the path to which is always unique and individual. The object of the quest is never simple; it is always subtle and complex. Yet to the willing soul the secrets of the Grail are never hidden and the steps upon the path are guided by divine law.

The perspective from the anti-Grail is more basic. There is a trend that seeks to bind the human race together as a simple unity, under a rulership that only pretends to the divine. With this chapter on 'Saunière's secret' we have arrived in the very depths of the Castle of Wonders. In the original manuscript of this book this chapter occupied little more than a paragraph. However, during a recent visit to Turkey, I was able to take some time out from a busy schedule to retrace the path I had gone in the writing of this book. In the process I uncovered vast tracts of material that had been sitting 'under my nose' all the time, and that allowed me to back up my thesis with fascinating confirmation from the works of Rudolf Steiner and other sources. This chapter presents my final conclusions on the mystery of Rennes-le-Château. However, we will not dally for long in the illusory flower gardens of Klingsor. Beyond Rennes-le-Château and beyond Saunière and the mysterious Priory rise the mighty turrets of our true destination: the Grail Castle.

Baigent, Leigh and Lincoln begin to sum up their conclusions concerning the nature of the treasure found by Saunière at

Rennes-le-Château in the following words:

> We did not discount the argument that Saunière discovered treasure. At the same time it seemed clear to us that, whatever else he discovered, he also discovered a secret—an historical secret of immense import to his own time and perhaps to our own as well. Mere money, gold or jewels would not, in themselves, explain a number of facets to his story. They would not account for his introduction to Hoffet's circle, for instance, his association with Debussy and his liaison with Emma Calve. They would not explain a priest's refusal to administer the last rites to a dying man, or the visit of a Habsburg archduke to a remote little village in the Pyrenees...On these grounds we grew increasingly convinced that Saunière's story involved more than riches, and that it involved a secret of some kind, one that was almost certainly controversial.[251]

Our research suggests a different, but no less challenging, scenario: not worldly treasure, but a treasure which none the less gives its owner great power; an enigmatic secret that conferred power on those who guarded it. This secret is openly displayed in the mysterious parchment supposedly found by Saunière:

TO DAGOBERT II, KING, AND TO SION BELONGS
THIS TREASURE AND IT IS DEATH.

What greater power than to wield sovereignty over death itself? A sovereignty which would bestow 'advantages which even kings would have great pains to draw from him'.[252] According to a recent authoritative Prieuré publication:

> Saunière himself was little more than a pawn and his role in the mystery of Rennes-le-Château has been much exaggerated. The real force behind the events at the mountain village is said to have been Saunière's friend, the Abbé Henri Boudet, curé of the adjacent village of Rennes-les-Bains. Boudet is said to have provided Saunière with all his money—a total of 13 million francs between 1887 and

> 1915. And Boudet is said to have guided Saunière on his various projects—the public works, the construction of the Villa Bethania and the Tour Magdala. He is also said to have supervised the restoration of the church at Rennes-le-Château, and to have designed Saunière's perplexing Stations of the Cross—as a kind of illustrated version, or visual equivalent, of a cryptic book of his own [*The True Celtic Tongue* published in 1886].[253]

According to Henry Lincoln in his book *The Holy Place—The Mystery of Rennes-le-Château*: 'Boudet's thesis is that all languages derive from one universal tongue, spoken by the sons of Noah before Babel...and that language was English! Or rather, Anglo-Saxon, as spoken by the race of Celts. According to Boudet, a group of Druids rushed about the world giving names to everything in sight. These Druids were known as the Neimheid which (in English) reveals their task: They were the Name (*Neim*) Head (*heid*).'[254] Later Lincoln refers to David Wood in demonstrating a corollary between Boudet's work and the English measure: 'The Rennes-le-Château discovery [the discovery of the Pentagram] will unquestionably confirm the sophisticated ability of its designers. Its corollary—the measure which they used—will demonstrate that those designers were using a unit which survives in the English measure.'[255]

Later in this chapter a relationship is indicated between the Bardic (Celtic) tradition of which Boudet was so knowledgeable and Pythagorean and Cabbalistic schemes. Here we are looking at a mechanism where, through the Music of the Spheres, the information of the formative forces can be turned into a working pattern: language which can be turned into number. This also reveals that the cosmic Word may best be represented in a language that relates to English measurement. Bearing all this in mind we shall turn our attention from the Languedoc to Westminster Abbey in London where in front of the high altar is an enigmatic inscription dating back to the thirteenth century, which is also influenced by bardic tradition.

Berenger Saunière, the enigmatic priest of Rennes-le-Château

In February of 1989 the great Westminster pavement was briefly exposed to public view for the first time in many years. In *Patterns of Thought,* Richard Foster describes how the carpet that had concealed the great marble pavement was rolled back and, for the first time in more than a generation, its interweaving circles and squares were revealed.[256]

Richard Foster's fascinating book ably demonstrates that the pavement was constructed by craftsmen towards the end of the thirteenth century under the direction of individuals who were still influenced by the Grail wisdom. In a later chapter, Foster continues:

> The earliest record of the complete wording of the inscription appears in Flete's *History of Westminster Abbey* compiled in 1443. The Westminster manuscript of Flete's history gives the inscription as follows:
>
> *Si lector posita prudent – cu – cta revoltat?*
> *hic fine – primi mobilis inveniet*
> *Sepes trina canes et equos ho – nesque subaddas,*
> *cervos & corvos aquilas immania cete*
> *mundu – qdque sequens preuntis triplicat Annos*
> *Spericus Archetipu – globus hic monstrat macrocosmu –*
> *Cristi milleno bis centeno duodeno*
> *cum sexageno subductis quatuor uno*
> *Tertius Henricus Rex urbis Odoric – & Abbas*
> *hos compigere porphyreos lapidesa*
>
> (– indicates a contraction sign in the manuscript hand)
>
> In classical Latin *finem ponere* meant to fix boundaries or limits, both in space and time, and an echo of this expression is caught in the second line of this verse:
>
> *hic fine – primi mobilis inveniet*
>
> 'Here,' the inscription tells the reader, 'he will discover (*inveniet*) the end (*finem*) of the *primum mobile*. The *primum mobile*, literally the 'first moved', provided the motive power of the universe.[257]
>
> Foster continues by outlining the medieval model of the

universe, which was a series of concentric spheres with the earth at its centre. The sun, moon and the five known planets each had its own heavenly sphere which carried it on its course around the earth. These were enclosed by an eighth sphere for the fixed stars. Beyond this was a ninth and invisible heavenly sphere, the *primum mobile*—the Unmoved Mover, or primal cause. What would '*the end*' of the *primum mobile* have signified to the thirteenth-century reader? *Finis* can mean the limit or the completion of a sequence of events, the destruction of something, or even the goal to which an action may be directed.[258]

There are many layers of meaning in the symbolism of the pavement. In commenting on the medieval mind Richard Foster observes: 'There was no single or absolute interpretation, and it is this ability to shift and shimmer through layers of meaning that endowed medieval symbolism with its rich vitality. In his annotation of Flete's text, Richard Sporley explains that the central roundel represented the archetype mentioned in the inscription ("Here is the perfectly rounded sphere which reveals the eternal pattern of the universe") because it contains within itself the colours of the four elements.'[259]

The phrase 'colours of the four elements' reminds us of the quartered circle in the final plate of the *Codex Rosae Crucie*. The philosopher Calcidius suggests that the comment in Genesis that the earth was 'without form, and void' shows that 'earth' must refer to corporeal matter, the primary substance of the world before it assumed various forms shaped by the skill of the divine Maker. During this phase it was still without colour or quality, and hence invisible and shapeless. It is a recipient of all qualities, it possesses no quality of itself and so is described as being empty and void. Calcidius calls this undifferentiated stage of matter *silva*. Bernardus Silvestris opens his *Cosmographia* with the personification of Silva 'yearning to emerge from her ancient confusion' and demanding 'the shaping influence of number and the bonds of harmony...'[260] The Logos is the biblical equivalent of this shaping influence. Its intervention causes the random movement of the silva to become directed to the formation of the forms of the four elements—in their ideal archetypal form.

In dealing with the phrase '*Spericus Archetipu – globus hic monstrat macrocosmu*' – Richard Foster comments that the inscription's Platonic undercurrent is made explicit by the use of Latin transliterations of three Greek words: *sphericus*, *macrocosmum* and *archetipum*. The last is the Platonic term given to the ideal Forms which were believed to exist in the Divine Mind—the universal spiritual 'moulds' from which the imperfect copies of material creation were cast.

Here is a description which is very close to all that we have so far been learning of the connection between the ethers and the formative forces as described by Rudolf Steiner and Guenther Wachsmuth. As we have seen from the above inscription, the secret Grail knowledge is implicit in its message. Bearing in mind that much of the Grail story stems from Celtic sources it is very interesting that, although the 'Platonic undercurrent' provides much of the background to the pavement, its original influence can be traced back to Bardic tradition. We are also reminded that Henri Boudet closely studied Celtic traditions, sharing his knowledge with Saunière when he took up his position at Rennes. Richard Foster points to the remarkable similarity between the form of the Westminster calculation of the world's duration and a traditional Irish poem, said to date from the ninth century, in a fifteenth-century compilation known as *The Book of Lismore*, edited and translated by Whitley Stokes in 1890.[261]

After the 'Cutting of the elm', the Grail wisdom was handed down through secret neo- Templar and other groups to the present time. One prominent member of such a group in the last century was the Third Marquess of Bute who was responsible for the reconstruction of Cardiff Castle with the help of his great friend and fellow occultist, the well-known Victorian architect William Burgess. A Latin inscription on the floor of the summer smoking room at Cardiff Castle is described in Andrew Collins's book *The Seventh Sword*:

The prime moving barrier will reveal three each of dogs and horses and men. You will add to this stags and crows, eagles, sea monsters. If the reader by carefully placing his sound, turns around, here is the end of the world that is waning.

[This was written in the black tiles of the outside black ring and the bar which cut horizontally across the whole circle. There was a further inscription wrapped around a world map in the centre:] *'This globe shows a microcosm.'* [On an opposite arm:] *'It trebles the passing years.'* [262]

'Trebles the passing years' seems to be similar to the treatment of time in triple aspect used in the above quoted passage from Bardic tradition. While the entire inscription bears a similarity to the translation of the text of the Westminster pavement:

If the reader wittingly reflects upon all that is laid down,
he will discover here the measure of the primum mobile
the hedge stands for three years,
add in turn dogs, and horses and men,
stags and ravens, eagles, huge sea monsters, the world:
each that follows triples the years of the one before

Here is the perfectly rounded sphere which reveals
the eternal pattern of the universe.

The striking similarity between these two inscriptions, written eight centuries apart, seems to add additional weight to the possibility that the secret Grail knowledge was preserved and handed down through the various 'neo-Templar' organizations to the last century and possibly further. What have these organizations been doing with it and where can we find evidence of its misuse in the past? In his recent book about the ancient Scottish Sinclair family and Rosslyn Chapel, *The Sword and the Grail*, Andrew Sinclair describes how the Apprentice Pillar at Rosslyn Chapel near Edinburgh was supposedly designed and constructed by 'the legendary Apprentice who carved the pillar and was killed by his Master Mason. In fact, he represented Hiram, the martyred builder of the Temple of Solomon...It was the secret of the Shamir that the martyr Hiram, the architect of the Temple, refused to surrender in Masonic tradition, and that remained one of the grand secrets [for Freemasons] in higher degrees. Furthermore, eight worms or serpents were grouped in a rough octagon round the base of the Apprentice Pillar.'[263] The pillar has been compared to 'Yggdrasil, the tree of Norse myth that held up the heavens from the earth, which itself was kept together by a serpent or dragon twining its body nine times round the circumference of the world. It also referred to the Tree of Knowledge of Good and Evil in the Garden of Eden, for the Serpent with its tail in its mouth was not only Lucifer but also part of the secret wisdom of the Cathars and Templars.'[264]

What was the 'secret wisdom' of the Cathars and Templars—the secret of the Shamir that the martyr Hiram, the architect of the temple, refused to surrender? From our previous investigation it begins to seem possible that it may well have been knowledge of the manipulation of 'incarnation' and 'excarnation'—tampering with the 'coming into being' and the dissolving of matter. The serpent is a symbol for the forces of the etheric which were invaded and subsequently severed as a direct result of the Fall.

One might also connect the Shamir's ability as a 'stone-cutting' creature with the fallen ethers. The Shamir is described as being able to 'slit and shape stone'. The power of the fallen ethers—electricity, magnetism and the Third Force—might be indicated in this description. The possibility that knowledge of the events of the Fall were an important feature of the 'secret wisdom of the Cathars and Templars' which was later held by the Rosicrucians and absorbed by the higher degrees of Freemasonry is further born out in *The Sword and the Grail* when Andrew Sinclair describes how:

> The eight serpents on the base of the Apprentice Pillar are further evidence of Gnostic teaching. As the early Christian author of *Testament of Truth* wrote, 'For the serpent was wiser than any of the animals that were in Paradise...but the Creator cursed the serpent and called him devil.' For

> He had given to Adam and Eve the knowledge of good and evil, as if they were divine. They had to be cast from Paradise in case they ate from the Tree of Life and lived for ever, or so the Gnostics taught. The Apprentice Pillar with its serpents and a complementary ornate pillar on the south of the lady chapel represented the two trees of the Garden of Eden, those of Life and of the knowledge of Good and Evil. They symbolized the hermetic knowledge, the secret understanding of the cosmos, given by the serpent to mankind.[265]

As we saw in the previous quotation from *The Sword and the Grail*, and as one also reads in the Genesis account, the serpent is a very real symbol of the life force which we have described as the etheric principle, subdividing into separate ethers symbolized in turn by the Tree of Knowledge and the Tree of Life. The casting out of Adam and Eve from Paradise gives a very accurate illustration of the envisaged dangers caused by misuse of the forces of the Tree of Life.

Alexander Horne's *King Solomon's Temple in the Masonic Tradition* is referenced by Andrew Sinclair: 'There is mention of the stone-splitting worm Thamir as early as the fourteenth century in the Polychronicon of Ranulf Higden, manuscript in Huntingdon Library, Pasadena, California: "In the Orphic Gnostic tradition, naked members of the cult worshipped a sacred winged serpent. A bowl depicting the rite is recorded in Emma Jung, *The Grail Legend*" (Boston, 1968). As Hippolytus says in his Elenchos: "Now no one can be saved and rise up again without the Son, who is the serpent." Through Arabic sources, Gnostic cult objects reached Spain and the South of France. *Coffrets gnostiques*, boxes portraying naked initiates, were prevalent in Provence in the twelfth and thirteenth centuries, when the *Cathari*, the pure ones, preached their faith.'[266]

Here, maybe, is an example of a Gnostic cult attempting to gain control over the forbidden 'Tree' of chemical and life ethers through sexual practices. The chemical ether would be accessible in this way through its fallen counterpart magnetism, which manifests to a certain extent in sexuality. Deeper magical knowledge would presumably render the illicit evocation of the life ether. Could this point in the direction of the Rennes-le-Château mystery? How might it be related to Saunière's secret?

Rennes-le-Château has already been connected with the earth goddess in all her varied forms, among them Isis and the Magdalene. As we know, the earth goddess can be seen as a very fitting symbol for earth-energy, energy before matter, which is what the Tree of Life represents. The serpent, dragon or Shamir, as we have already seen, also represents this energy. Ophiuchus, the Serpent Bearer, may also relate to the Shamir. There has been a Cathar and Templar presence at Rennes-le-Château throughout most of the history of both these groups; the Freemasons have also continually shown an interest in the area. Might Saunière's secret not have had something to do with a revival of the Cathar rites which involved the nature of the Shamir, in addition to a revival of more distant Merovingian ceremonies?

In Chapter 8, the area around Rennes-le-Château was linked with activities possibly performed during Atlantean times. It was conjectured that this western region of Europe manifested a powerful ancient Atlantean chakra system which had been prevented from sinking with the rest of the continent by the miscreant Atlanteans themselves. These initiates had possibly 'siphoned out' the energy of the 'sacral chakra' situated at Rennes to create bodies for themselves using the 'maverick' zodiacal sign 'Ophiucus', the 'Serpent Bearer'. Recent corroboration for this was found in a very old theosophical booklet which commented that the traditional date for the beginning of Noah's Flood—the Biblical account of the destruction of Atlantis—was 22 November. If 22 November was the date for the 'maverick' incarnation, what of its correlative, 17 January?

On 17 January 1917, Saunière, then in his sixty-fifth year, suffered a sudden stroke. The date of 17 January is perhaps suspicious. The same date appears on the tombstone of the

Marquise d'Hautpole de Blanchefort—the tombstone Saunière had eradicated...But what makes Saunière's stroke on 17 January most suspicious is the fact that five days before, on 12 January, his parishioners declared that he had seemed to be in enviable health for a man of his age. Yet on 12 January, according to a receipt in our possessions, Marie Denardaud had ordered a coffin for her master.

As Saunière lay on his deathbed, a priest was called from a neighbouring parish to hear his final confession and administer the last rites. The priest duly arrived and retired into the sick-room. According to eyewitness testimony, he emerged shortly thereafter, visibly shaken. In the words of one account he 'never smiled again'. In the words of another he lapsed into an acute depression that lasted for several months. Whether these accounts are exaggerated or not, the priest, presumably on the basis of Saunière's confession, refused to administer extreme unction.

On 22 January Saunière died unshriven. The following morning his body was placed upright in an armchair on the terrace of the Tour Magdala, clad in an ornate robe adorned with scarlet tassels. One by one certain unidentified mourners filed past, many of them plucking tassels of remembrance from the dead man's garment. There has never been any explanation of this ceremony.[267]

If we turn to *The Holy Blood and the Holy Grail* once more we find very interesting information concerning the Merovingian kings' healing powers: 'By virtue of some miraculous property in their blood they could allegedly heal by laying on of hands: and according to one account the tassels of the fringes of their robes were deemed to possess miraculous curative powers.'[268]

Thin red silk cords have been connected with Masonic and Templar ritual, where they symbolize the blood. Possibly the Red Snake referred to in yet another enigmatic document connected with the Rennes mystery, 'The Serpent Rouge', which is described as 'uncoiling across the centuries', is a reference to the Merovingian blood-line which held the transformative power of the four ethers working together in concert. In other enigmatic documents known as the Dossiers Secret were found maps of the Rennes area in Merovingian times. Both the terrestrial forces and the forces of the Merovingian blood-line combining enabled 'materialization and dematerialization', 'incarnation and excarnation' at will! 'The Serpent Rouge' includes a list of strange entries for each zodiacal sign, including the thirteenth. Under Leo one is reminded of not only the Magdalene and Isis, but also of the Lady Venus lying in her deep sepulchre: 'From she whom I desire to liberate, there wafts towards me the fragrance of the perfume which impregnates the sepulchre.'[269]

Is she the figure to whom the shepherds turn in Poussin's painting *Les Bergères d'Arcady* which Saunière went to see at the Louvre during his mysterious visit to Paris. Is she 'liberated' by the manipulation of ancient blood-lines, terrestrial energy and magic power? The Lady Venus of *The Chymical Wedding* waits to be redeemed by the transformation of the fallen chemical and life ethers.

It will be remembered by those who have read *The Holy Blood and the Holy Grail* that much of the mysterious fortune Saunière received was spent on the construction of the impressive terrace and the Tour Magdala. From this vantage point it is possible to see some of the points of the landscape-pentagram first mentioned in the last *Chronicle* programme on BBC2. It only surfaced again in Lincoln's much later lone effort, *The Holy Place*. We have already learned of the significance of the pentagram correlated to the movement of Venus in relation to the sun. It is interesting to note what Willi Sucher, pioneer of Astrosophy, has to say about it in relation to an earthly ground-pattern:

> Let us first speak of Tintagel, the legendary birthplace of Arthur. This is an island in the spiritual sense, for its very shape is remarkable, as you will see from its ground plan. This can be obtained from the official guide. Myths describe spiritual facts in a form palatable to a certain age and we must penetrate the legendary form of this spiritual truth.

> The island is roughly this shape: you will see therefore that it is a pentagon, which is the foundation of the pentagram star. This is a cosmic pattern, for the ground plan is cosmology, a picture of the gestures of the planet which is called Venus. I shall refer to this in future as Mercury; for it is known as the Occult Mercury for reasons I will not go into now. It has the qualities of Mercury, which are true healing...Does this seem far fetched? We have many ancient monuments in Britain which deliberately reflect such cosmic facts. Stonehenge was used in ancient times as a celestial calender, whilst the isle of Avalon at Glastonbury reveals the features of the zodiac according to recent survey (aerial). These are imprinted into the land by hedges, ancient roads, rivers, brooks, etc.[270]

We have seen how the interaction of Venus (Occult Mercury) with the sun facilitates the introduction of 'form' into matter. The pentagram bears within it a beautiful form-principle: the Golden Section or the Golden Mean, which demonstrates a proportion found in nature, in the human being and in traditional art. The mathematician Filius Bonacci (called Fibonacci) wrote a treatise on the number series related to the Golden Mean. Pythagoras claimed that its proportions were musical, and it is true that the harmonious blending of musical intervals is governed by the series.

This ratio can be repeated *ad infinitum*; which brings 'as above so below' into its true relationship—cosmic patterns being brought into earthly creation down a ladder of ever-decreasing pentagrams and pentagons. There is here a slight correlation with the properties of the substance mercury which were mentioned in Chapter 16. This indicated that when the substance mercury divides it separates into ever smaller versions of the original form. It will be remembered that we considered it possible that the *metals* of the planets Venus and Mercury, copper and mercury respectively, might be interchangeable.

The pentagram at Rennes mirrors the greater pentagram caused as Venus relates to the sun, bringing form into matter.

'As above, so below'. A ladder of ever-decreasing pentagrams and pentagons

This in turn translates itself into the forms of nature, offering either the possibility of healing or of extending the formative influence after the legitimate moment of death. According to the recent Prieuré publication, 'Saunière remained essentially ignorant of the real secret for which he acted as custodian—until Boudet, in the throes of approaching death, confided it to him in March 1915...Marie Denarnaud, Saunière's housekeeper, was in fact Boudet's agent. It was through her that Boudet supposedly transmitted instructions to Saunière. And it was to her that all the money was made payable.'[271]

It has been suggested that the enigmatic Prieuré had possibly been behind the suppression of the 50 texts from the Dead Sea Scrolls which have only recently been publicly accessible. One of the main reasons given for their concern in suppressing these documents was that they include references which change the day of the month when Noah's Ark was said to have come to rest, so drawing attention to the significance of their 'special day': 'For instance, the full year, 364-day cycle is completed at the bottom of column 1 and the beginning of column 2 with the notice that the earth was completely dry on the seventeenth day of the first month, not the twenty-seventh as in biblical tradition.'[272]

This quotation highlights 17 January although one realizes that the date as it is mentioned in the Dead Sea Scrolls can only be symbolic. The date, 22 November, given in the theosophical booklet mentioned earlier, is also symbolic. It is interesting to note that: 'On 22 November Clement V promulgated the bull *Pastoralis Preeminentae*, in which he praised King Philippe, stating the official papal position that the charges against the Templars appeared to be true and calling upon all the monarchs of Christendom to arrest and torture all of the Templars in their domains. From that day forward, the Pope pursued the Templars with enthusiasm.'[273]

John F. Kennedy was assassinated on 22 November 1963. November 22 also marks the end of Margaret Thatcher's years in power as Prime Minister of Britain. In both of these cases 22 November marks a decisive turning-point in history caused by the overthrow of great power. While Margaret Thatcher's political policies were on the whole in line with the anti-Grail impulse, her opposition to developments in Europe resulted in her fall from grace.

How could all of these dates point back to a group of people who had mastered the earth's life force and caused the end of Atlantis? Could the flood itself in this case symbolize the course of the life force which maintains a human being in incarnation from birth to death? We have already seen how the 'illicit incarnation' process on Atlantis *caused* the flood. January 17 in this context could logically represent the opposite pole: an illicit death, the Ark coming to rest at the end of its voyage. Did Saunière 'excarnate' at will possibly using 17 January as an 'exit' date? Were the group of people who filed past his body to touch the red silk tassels on his robe fellow members of the Prieuré de Sion, taking part in a mysterious ceremony connected with Saunière's unorthodox demise?

Anthroposophical researcher Margaret Jonas provides further clues:

> There is also an astronomical connection. On 17 January, approximately (it may vary slightly from year to year), the sun enters the sidereal constellation (i.e. the actual stars) of Capricorn. In earlier times this constellation was known as the Gate of Death. Capricorn was also associated with an inverted pentagram—note the pentagram stands for the etheric body. Also Eliphas Levi connects the Goat (Capricorn) and the inverted pentagram with Baphomet! Gérard de Sedé thinks that Saunière was linked with an occult society of a neo-Rosicrucian type such as one following Levi or Papus. Is it a coincidence that the sun enters *tropical* Capricorn on 23 December (i.e. according to the ordinary zodiac)—the death day of Dagobert II? Could this be connected with what Steiner refers to as 'an ahrimanic transposition of time'? Another such curiosity is Hallowe'en, the ancient Celtic festival of Samhain, festival of the Dead. The sun in the ordinary tropical zodiac reaches 7 degrees Scorpio on this date. If we look to see when the sun would reach 7 degrees of Scorpio in the *sidereal* zodiac, now, in the 1990s, the date would be approximately 24 November. However, between 1700 and 1800 the date would have been 22 November! And the church of St Sulpice—feast day 17 January—was built in 1746.
>
> One more point of interest. November 22 in the tropical zodiac corresponds to the sun 'between Scorpio and Sagittarius', passing through Ophiucus, serpent handler. What would the date be to correspond with this in the sidereal zodiac? December 17—feast day of St Bega. Gérard de Sedé also stresses the Rosicrucian mythology surrounding Saunière, opening tombs and other similar activities. Was he seeking 'Rosicrucian immortality' and ending up with 'ahrimanic' immortality?[274]

Dagobert was educated in Ireland and married a Celtic princess. He was stabbed through the eye with a lance supposedly while sleeping at Stenay on 23 December 679, which became his feast day. He was cannonized 200 years later. In the mid-nineteenth century, a curious document came to light. It was a poem, a 21-verse litany, entitled *De Sancta Dagoberto martre prose*—implying that Dagobert was martyred 'to, or for something'. An epigraph in an account of his life, a quotation from the Fourth Gospel, affirms: 'He is among you and you do not know him.'[275] Dagobert was in his prime in the year 666. The old name for Stenay, capital of the Merovingian dynasty, was 'Satanicum'. Through Dagobert's veins coursed much of the original force of the Tree of Life energy manifesting before and after the creation of matter. We have seen how many of the early European tribes retained this peculiarity, which probably accounted for the Merovingians' purported healing powers. Was Saunière picked for the job because he was a native of this area which had once been the habitat of these tribes? Were both he and Dagobert in possession of innate abilities which were able to overcome the barriers set by the disintegration of the human body at death? Was Saunière prepared to repeat 'martyrdom to or for something', choosing an already well tried date, 17 January, when the sun entered the sidereal sign of Capricorn. Might his predecessor Dagobert have carried out a similar 'martyrdom' on 23 December when the sun entered tropical Capricorn? The enigmatic message on the parchment found in the church at Rennes could relate to the activities of both individuals: TO DAGOBERT II, KING, AND TO SION BELONGS THIS TREASURE AND IT IS DEATH.

Certainly this hints at an advantage 'which even kings would have great pains to draw from' one who kept the secret. Even kings are subject to the limitations of human death. It is mentioned in *The Holy Blood and the Holy Grail* that 'two other locations have been stressed repeatedly, assuming a status now apparently commensurate with Rennes-le-Château. One of these is Gisors, a fortress in Normandy... the other is Stenay, once called Satanicum, on the fringe of the Ardennes—the old capital of the Merovingian dynasty, near where Dagobert was assassinated in 679.'[276] It is described how at Gisors 'on the land adjacent to the fortress there was a meadow called the Champs Sacre, the "Sacred Field". According to medieval chronicles the site had been deemed sacred since pre-Christian times.'[277]

Knowing of the significant energy at Rennes-le-Château, one might therefore complete the equation by presuming that Stenay is also a sacred site with similar special qualities—qualities which encouraged both Dagobert and Saunière to achieve 'martyrdoms'.

Referring back again to the inscription in the tiles of the summer smoking room at Cardiff Castle we read: 'If the reader by carefully planning his sound turns around, here is the end of the world that is waning.' This last sentence seems to take the *hic fine – primi mobile inveniet* of the Westminster text and transform it through one of its possible interpretations: 'The completion of a series of events, the destruction of something; even the goal to which an action may be directed'. It could refer to a cancelling out of the legitimate course through which the formative forces proceed from the cosmos through divine authority. By prefixing it with 'If the reader by carefully planning his sound turns around' it hints at the possibility of implementing an illicit direction in creation. Could this last phrase refer to manipulation of the sound or chemical ether? The whole passage hints at an unlawful use of the ordered Music of the Spheres.

The possibility that Boudet may have both designed the new church decorations at Rennes-le-Château, only confiding the final secret on his deathbed, leads one to wonder if Saunière's colleague had not been planning some amazing undertaking for years. He may have been instructing Saunière in the preparations for a plan that he, Boudet, was unable to complete. The possibility that he knew that this would be so in advance is confirmed by the fact that Madame Denarnaud worked together with Saunière from the beginning while supposedly acting as Boudet's agent. What was Madame Denarnaud's function in the plan? We have seen how the Great Work was the ultimate goal of alchemists and Rosicrucians. We also know that in order to carry out the Great Work the alchemist needed the co-operation of a female assistant. Not a physical union, but the working together of two devoted individuals, combining the function of both separated groups of ethers at the spiritual pole. The plan contained in Boudet's cryptic book was, as we have already been told, transferred to the church in the form of the strange Stations of the Cross, which, in this case, may have represented the stages of the actual operation itself, ending with the individual concerned leaving the tomb in which he had been laid. At this point the significance of the name 'Villa Bethania' sharpens into focus when one remembers what happened at Bethany, namely, the raising of Lazarus.

In *The Holy Place*, Lincoln finds connections between the Stations of the Cross in the church and the great pentagram inscribed into the landscape outside. Earlier we found a correlation between the quartered circle in the Rosicrucian diagram and Wachsmuth's arrangement of the four ethers in the same colours. It is therefore of great interest to note that Henry Lincoln describes the positioning of the same inscription above the statue of the devil in the church at Rennes-le-Château:

> Between the angels who make the sign of the Cross and the devil is written the phrase 'By this sign ye shall conquer'... Between the holy water and the angels are two curious and unreal little beasts. These beasts are salamanders, who were supposed to be born out of fire, to be elemental spirits of Fire. Now at last the imagery sharpens into focus. The angels are creatures of pure spirit, or Air; the devil is *Rex Mundi*, Lord of the Earth. The group is composed of symbolic elements. The devil (earth) supports the Water, which in turn supports the salamanders (creatures of Fire), and crowning all are the angels (creatures of Air). Earth, Water, Fire, Air. The four elements of all Hermetic thought—of astrology, of alchemy.[278]

We have already noted that final main goal of the alchemists and Rosicrucians had been unification of the sexes, *conscious immortality*. However, as the centuries progressed the original high ideals of alchemy disintegrated. We have

The 'alchemical' statues designed by Saunière, and found within the entrance to the parish church of Rennes-le-Château

already noted that other aims took the place of the original ideals of the Grail quest. In examining the phenomenon of the 'Double' we have learned that the human etheric body carries, alongside its subtler constitution, a denser, fallen aspect vibrating with electromagnetic energy. This part of the etheric has been indicated by Steiner as the region where the ahrimanic Double dwells in the individual to whom it is attached. As a direct result of Christ's deed on Golgotha, this Double is unable to pass through death and is left behind in the material world while its human host continues on to the spiritual world. It might, therefore, be possible to strike a 'Faustian' pact with one's Double, should one wish to continue to 'live' on in a shadowy half-life rather like the nine Ring-wraiths in J. R. R. Tolkein's *Lord of the Rings*. The Double itself would also benefit from such an arrangement as this would enable it to continue to live on with its 'host' who would still be 'existing' on the material plane.

In his book *Rennes-Le-Château, le Dossiers, les Impostures, les Phantasomes et les Hypothèses*, Gérard de Sède mentions a certain Georges Monti. Monti was secretary to Josephin Peleden, who founded the Order of the Temple and Rose Cross, being keen to refound the Templar Order, to also revive the OTO, and to bring about a reconciliation with the Church. Peleden founded the Order of Alpha Galet and may have been a German secret agent. Monti was reported by de Sedé to have kept a surveillance on the anthroposophists in Paris, gaining their confidence by translating Assyrian and Chaldean texts for them. Monti was active among the various occult orders in Paris between 1900 and the year he died, 1935. Therefore it is very likely that he knew Saunière. It is also very interesting to note that Rudolf Steiner, who was giving a course of 12 lectures, *The Karma of Untruthfulness*, between 1 and 30 January 1917, had an interview with a prominent French anthroposophist after a break in the lectures on 15 January and then continued to lecture on 20 January. In the lecture he gave on that date, three days after Saunière's apparent stroke, he made the following statement:

> Those who enter the circle of certain societies practising ceremonial magic are securing for themselves a power that reaches beyond death, a kind of ahrimanic immortality.

For these people this is their main concern. For them, the society they enter provides a kind of guarantee that certain forces—which should by rights only live in them until the moment of death—will continue to live, even beyond death. More people than you might think are nowadays filled with this idea of guaranteeing for themselves an ahrimanic immortality, which consists in exercising influence not only as an individual human being, but also through the instrument of a society of this kind. Such societies exist in the most varied forms, and individuals who have attained certain degrees of advancement in these societies know: As a member of this society I shall become to some degree immortal because forces which would otherwise come to an end at my death will continue to work beyond death.

What these people then experience through this ceremonial magic makes them quite oblivious to a thought which would concern someone who takes such things seriously and in a genuinely dignified way. This is that the more the person gains by way of materialistic immortality, or rather ahrimanic immortality, the more he loses the consciousness of true, genuine immortality. Yet materialism has taken such a hold on many souls today that they remain unconcerned about this and are tricked into striving for ahrimanic immortality. It could indeed be said that societies exist today which, from a spiritual or occult point of view, could be called 'insurance companies for ahrimanic immortality'!

It is only a small number of people in each case who understand all these things. For as a rule these societies are organized in such a way that the ceremonial magic they practise influences only those who are unaware of the implications, merely desiring to make contact with the spiritual world by means of symbolic ceremonies. There are many such people. And those who have this desire are by no means necessarily the worst. They are accepted as members of the circle of ceremonial magic among whom there are then a few who simply use the rest of the members

> as instruments. Therefore one should beware of all secret societies administered by so-called higher grades. These administrative grades usually comprise those who have been initiated to a stage at which they only have a vague idea of what I have just been explaining to you. They comprise those who are to work positively in connection with certain goals and aims which are then realized by the wider group of those who have been merely inveigled into the circle of ceremonial magic. Everything these people do is done in such a way that it leads in the direction required by the higher grades but is strengthened by the forces which come from ceremonial magic.[279]

It was in keeping with Rudolf Steiner's method of dealing with anything that he felt needed a counterbalance to throw light on the event in question as it took place. Sometimes, as in the above lecture, which was in fact on the subject of the causes of the First World War, he felt it necessary to interrupt the subject in hand in order to make this comment. In *The Bodhisattva Question* by T. H. Meyer it is pointed out that on the day that the initiation of Krishnamurti as the vehicle for a supposed twentieth-century incarnation of the Christ took place...

> On *the same day*, 12 January 1910, in far off Stockholm, he [Rudolf Steiner] speaks *for the first time* to members of the Theosophical Society about the reappearance of Christ *in the etheric spiritual realm*, as an event which was to take place in the course of the twentieth century. The contemporaneity of these two events must be regarded as one of the factors which makes this first announcement of the Etheric Christ so significant! That it was not by accident or, more irrelevantly, for the want of a more 'appropriate' theme, that Steiner spoke thus to his theosophical audience is attested to by the following fact: the German General Secretary [Steiner] 'insisted that this lecture was to take place at what was, for the custom in Stockholm at that particular time, a quite unusual hour, namely, at 5.30 p.m.' Steiner must have chosen this theme quite deliberately and for a special

reason. Its cause must be looked for in the details of this parallel spiritual event taking place on the Indian sub-continent. Parallel with this in time we can observe how Rudolf Steiner discloses his knowledge of the reappearance of Christ in the etheric realm, first of all on 12 January 1910 in Stockholm, then in different German towns, and in Rome and in Palermo at the southern tip of Europe in April. So while the Adyar version of the Christ-event of Besant and Leadbeater was spreading from its centre in the East, from India towards the English-speaking West, Rudolf Steiner's compensatory words were travelling simultaneously from Scandinavia in the North to the Sicilian South of Europe.[280]

In the previous chapter we learned that the forces of the 'Double' are especially active in Sicily, which may also have contributed to Rudolf Steiner's choice of location to speak on the subject of the 'Etheric Christ'. He may well have considered Sicily as a site of extreme urgency for encouragement of the burgeoning Christ-forces in the etheric earth at this crucial time. Also when Halley's Comet appeared in 1910 Rudolf Steiner pointed out that the comet did not have a positive effect, and he sought to offset the comet's negative influence by launching into an intensive lecture tour, travelling as extensively as he could to counterbalance the wide arc made by the comet's progress over the earth.

Throughout all of his work Steiner constantly drew attention to the dangers of applying materialistic ideas to the realms of the spirit. The 'I' is already immortal though it must at the present time pass through incarnation within perishable vehicles. The yearning for immortality is one of the deepest and most profound aspects of human nature. In the anti-Grail Castle of Klingsor it is an immortality gained through union with the material plane, and involves the loss of true I-consciousness. But for the Grail Knights immortality must include both heaven and earth if the divine spark in the human soul is to attain the goal of conscious immortality.

20
Healing the Grail King

> We have come to the culminating point—or the centre. The Teachers who now follow have to preserve what has come into being and put it into application again on the physical plane. Thus the Christian tradition is preserved in the Brotherhood of the Holy Grail. Christianity is involved in a process of continual degeneration. New impulses have therefore continually to be given from what is known as Montsalvat, the Grail.
>
> Rudolf Steiner, *On the Migrations of the Races*

On the Fifth Day of The Chymical Wedding, *the guests reach a tower which is situated on a square island. Inside the tower is a laboratory where they are set to work. They 'had to beat and wash plants and precious stones and all sorts of things, and extract their juice and essence, and put up the same in glasses and deliver them to be laid up. And truly, our Virgin was so busy with us and so full of her directions, that she knew not how to give each of us employment enough, so that on this Island we were fain to be mere drudges, till we had achieved all that was necessary for the restoring of the beheaded bodies.' Here is a vision of a humanity that has realized its great responsibility towards the earth and is actively working to heal Amfortas—the wounded Grail King. In this way our long journey has led us not to a finishing point but to a beginning. For the fulfilment of the quest for the Grail lies ahead of us still.*

'Brother, what ails thee?'

With these words Parzival heals the wounded Amfortas and attains to the Grail. When human beings begin to realize that all of creation is suffering like the Grail King then responsibility for the healing process can begin to be entrusted to them. The Tree of Life can be handed back for the first time since the Fall. Once the question has been asked a new journey begins: to study the science of the Grail. The range of practical activities founded by Rudolf Steiner can provide this new direction. Anthroposophical medicine, biodynamic agriculture, the movement for a Threefold Commonwealth, the Camphill Movement, Waldorf schools, and curative eurythmy, to name just a few. A detailed description of some other applications of the Grail science can be found in Appendix I.

The Tree of Life and the Tree of Knowledge begin to grow side by side once more, their roots entwined, and a new science is required that can integrate their two perspectives. In his intellectual, brain-centred Tree-of-Knowledge-consciousness, the human being dies into lifeless isolation. This is the 'place of the skull', the meaning of the word 'Golgotha', where the Christ is crucified. The new Tree of Life faculties will be centred on the organ that is especially adapted for understanding the activity of the etheric world—the organ which is linked to the sun, the human heart. In a lecture Ehrenfried Pfeiffer outlines this development:

> In our time there are certain changes taking place in the heart, by which a fifth chamber will develop. In this fifth chamber man will have a new organ which will allow him to control life forces in a different way than is possible at the moment...the heart is not a pressure pump, but an organ in which etheric space is created so that the blood is sucked[281] to the heart rather than pumped. With every pulse of the heart a certain amount of substance is absorbed, is taken away as physical pressure and added to the etheric substance. This then begins to radiate outward. The radiation from this etheric organ of the heart is actually developing into a spiritual sense organ.[282]

Rudolf Steiner's insistence that 'hearts must begin to think' was elaborated on by Walter Johannes Stein:

> Whenever we are thinking we forget ourselves, the thinker, altogether. We live in utterly selfless devotion to the object of which we are thinking at the given moment. This devotion does not rise into our consciousness, but it is

> there. All that comes into our consciousness is the result of our thinking, namely, the resulting act of knowledge. We can bring into consciousness the love and devotion which live as a rule unnoticed in the act of knowledge. When we do so we discover that all knowledge really rests on love, and moreover that all truly selfless love is knowledge.[283]

We have now almost reached the end of our Grail quest. It began with a quiet and ancient village nestling in the foothills of the Pyrenees. Somehow, interest in that village has stirred many of us into undreamed of adventures. The key to all this seems to have been the fact that Rennes-le-Château is a significant centre of etheric activity. We have learned that a time is developing when enormous qualitative changes are taking place between the physical and the etheric world. These changes will gather momentum as individual human beings work on themselves and gradually step into the etheric world—the Grail Castle—as a result of their own effort. The list of recent therapies and new applications of Grail science listed in Appendix I bears witness to the fact that:

> As at the end of a solar year of 365 days the Sun shines forth from the same group of stars as 12 months earlier, so meetings of earth and Venus, having passed round almost an entire zodiac since the ninth century are now approaching the places they had during Parzival's life. The star rhythms are expressions of divine thoughts. The Venus rhythm indicates that the end of a cycle is near and that seeds can now put forth their shoots.[284]

We are now fast approaching a time when life on this planet will become impossible unless a new form of energy is discovered, an energy which will enhance life instead of destroying it. Steiner often indicated that the earth is now crumbling and that new strides must be taken by humanity to enter the etheric world like a form of cosmic air-raid shelter before the physical world crashes around our ears.

If the wise guardians of evolution will not allow this secret energy in its pure state to be wielded by those who are unworthy, there must be a process whereby the *sheep* are separated from the *goats*. It seems that only the truly 'alive' and alert individuals stumble over its secret. Their main hallmark is that they have no wish to utilize it in a greedy or egotistical way, but for improving the conditions of mankind on earth, and for furthering the goals of creation. In a book recently published within the fortress of the scientific establishment the following comment can be found:

> Along the main stream of scientific knowledge there are isolated pools of what (to choose a neutral term) I would call would-be sciences...What possible physical signal from our brains could move distant objects and yet have no effect on scientific instruments? Defenders of astrology sometimes point to the undoubted effects of the moon and the sun in producing tides, but the effects of gravitational fields of the other planets are much too small to have detectable effects on the earth's oceans, much less on anything as small as a person...At any one moment one is presented with a wide variety of innovative ideas that might be followed up; not only astrology and such, but many ideas closer to the mainstream of science, and others that are squarely within the scope of modern scientific research. It does no good to say that all these ideas must be thoroughly tested; there is simply no time. I receive in the mail every week about 50 preprints of articles on elementary particle physics and astrophysics, along with a few articles on all sorts of would-be science. Even if I dropped everything else in my life, I could not begin to give all of these ideas a fair hearing. So what am I to do?[285]

This attitude automatically allocates its adherents to the goat pen, while those who strive to understand and foster the knowledge of the Tree of Life for the benefit of evolution inherit the responsibility of the true Templar Knights. Awareness will gradually dawn that knowledge of this new energy demands as a prerequisite a life-style of selflessness and dedication. The Grail King Amfortas was wounded by its misuse. It carries its own built-in protection.

But what of Feirefis? Wolfram von Eschenbach has told us that Feirefis, our 'Black and White Brother', who represents the entire human race, may not be left behind. Parzival is only allowed to enter the Grail Castle when he approaches it in Feirefis's company. There are many billions 'out there' who fall between the sheep or goat category. Maybe the Templar Knights among us must 'buy more time' until Feirefis is ready, for are we confident that the gates of the Grail Castle will open to us if we arrive on the doorstep alone?

The old Grail King is suffering from an affliction caused by his immersion in matter. Parzival will become the new Grail King if he fathoms the problem of the old King's affliction. When we begin to see through the veil cast over fallen nature by Ahriman, when the spiritual origins of creation are again revealed, the healing process can begin.

When Trevrizent first counselled Parzival no one had yet been able to follow Christ's footsteps to those depths where the deepest powers lie, guarded by the fallen or backward angels of dark Saturn. Because of this Trevrizent later admits that before Parzival set out to the Grail Castle he had lied to him about the fallen angels being redeemable. At that time it was still not known whether humanity would ever be able to follow Christ and continue the process of the 'harrowing of hell'. This seems to be implicit when Trevrizent says to Parzival: 'But I am very sorry you had such a hard time. It was never the custom that any should battle his way to the Grail; I wished to divert you from it.'

The Knights Templar worked for a high ideal, but they were as yet only able to *guard* the Grail. No one knew whether it could be won or not. For *Parzival* is a myth of the future and the great event described within it has not yet happened. It still MUST happen, but can only do so if we admit that Parzival has yet to rise from the ranks of humanity if the Grail is to be won.

Epilogue

I have my place.
I know my number,
And seven are the heads that slumber.
Five are the gates to the ruined wood
And two more gates to be understood.

I carry in my head and heart
Two pure seeds to be kept apart.
Song and dance will make the round
Fire will spring from the holy ground.
Kings will dance to the beat of the tune
Living thoughts from the rock be hewn.
Knights will sing and minstrels battle
Snakes will walk and the sistrum rattle,
Night and day will be confounded.
When this mystery is expounded.
Set will flee across the plain,
The Son of Man will come again.

Richard Carlyon

Appendix I

This is a brief list of modern practitioners whose work we have encountered during the research for this book. The individuals listed below have rediscovered Tree of Life energies using Tree of Knowledge faculties. We feel that they belong to the stream of Grail Knights pioneering a new science for the future, but we must stress that their work is their own achievement, independent of any spiritual or scientific orthodoxy.

The Music of the Spheres and Healing

In Chapter 15, 'The Cauldron of Ceredwin', it was described how the bee was only able to bring back healing substances for the wounded hero when he travelled to the region of the Music of the Spheres, the region which we have learned was closed to man after the Fall. By utilizing Tree of Life energy we are once again entering this domain from which all healing proceeds. In Chapter 2 we saw how the negative space forces bring the forms, scents and colours into matter via the astral and etheric bodies. When this process is interrupted illness occurs. The aim of all true healing and therapy is to restore the full effect of these forces. For example, the aromatherapist is working backwards by applying a scented oil directly to the physical body, enabling its effects to reach the cosmic source of its origin—either from the sphere of a particular planet or from a specific position in the zodiac. A direct contact is then established between the physical body and the specific area in the spiritual cosmos from which healing is required for the particular problem.

Gernot Grafer and Maria Felsenreich—Nine Resonance Patterns in Water

There is an intimate relationship between water and the etheric negative space forces. Water in its natural healthy state has been shown in the work of Genot Grafer and Maria Felsenreich to be capable of nine clearly identified and dowsable resonance formations. The transformation of these resonance formations leads to the build-up of corresponding information fields, which stand in relation to specific chemical elements, vital functions and magnetic patterns. These fields are required by living bodies in the process of building their tissues. The whole of life on earth, together with the water which is its chief constituent and carrying element, is a transformation matrix for the energy radiations originating from the cosmos and the earth itself.

Alan Hall of the Livewater Trust in Gloucestershire has worked closely with the Felsenreichs and is carrying out very exciting experiments which are conscientiously scientific in their approach.

Sharry Edwards—Signature Sounds

The resonances could be a manifestation of the Music of the Spheres. The most consistent body of practical, therapeutic and scientific evidence for this position can be found in the work of Sharry Edwards. Sharry is a housewife from Ohio, USA, and a former university instructor in the field of parapsychology. Sharry has unusual hearing abilities. She first became aware of her unique hearing when reading about tinnitus, a disease involving ringing in the ears. Tests revealed that she had extremely acute hearing—well beyond the normal human range of 20 to 20,000 cycles per second. When asked to demonstrate what she was hearing, it was discovered that she could produce pure tones (sine waves) with her voice. She was told that this was impossible for a human voice, and agreed to do a research study that would substantiate what she was hearing.

The results of the study concluded that she could not only produce pure tones but could duplicate pure tones within her vocal range with exacting precision. It was then discovered that these tones were found to be able to affect blood pressure.

The questions left unanswered by that first project prompted Edwards to probe further. Two decades of investigation have led to some startling conclusions. In 1982 Edwards discovered that the sounds she was hearing and duplicating could be related to musical notes missing from a person's speaking voice. Working with an emphysema patient in critical condition, Edwards discovered that, much like vitamin therapy, essential sounds could be replaced with astounding results. Preliminary studies completed by Edwards show that when a person's missing sounds are returned to the environment, the body begins to rebuild itself—even from previously incurable diseases.

Very early on, Edwards saw that her work could provide a necessary paradigm for a unifying field theory for subtle energy medicine. According to Edwards each individual has what she has defined as a *signature sound* that is distinctive. A signature sound is a specific individual frequency or series of frequencies thought to emanate from living systems which may indicate physical, spiritual and emotional status. These individualized frequencies are apparently created from a combination of genetic coding, geographic locale, brain and neural functions, biochemistry, emotions, physical structure and environment. Signature sounds correspond to physiological and psychological status. Vocally missing tones also correspond to physiological and psychological status. Signature sounds and vocally missing tones have been found to correspond to notes traditionally assigned to individual astrological signs. Forty per cent of the time a person's sound has been found to correspond to the musical note assigned to that person's sign by traditional astrology. Forty per cent of the time the sound matches the musical note assigned to the sign opposite. Twenty per cent of the time there is no correspondence. The diatonic musical scale was designed using the ratios of the planets at their farthest distance from the sun. The harmonics of the diatonic tempered musical scale, in frequencies below normal hearing range, correspond to brain-wave cluster patterns. Brain dominance plays an important part in determining what tone formulation to use in support of signature sound techniques.

Indicators of physical distress and emotional states can be categorized according to missing vocal notes and octaves. A musical scale designed from the atomic weights of elements found in the human body closely correlates to the already established diatonic scale designed by Kepler. A musical scale using the atomic weights of elements as a foundation emulates brain-wave clusters at lower octaves. To date, frequency formulas based on signature sounds have been able to assist in such conditions as emphysema, high blood pressure, epilepsy, multiple sclerosis, traumatic pain, eye disorders, depression, drug dependency and biochemical disorders.

Man-made electricity and electromagnetic energies seem to be the most influential factors in causing a signature sound to change its originating boundaries. Polluted food and water, negative emotions and environments all have about equal effect, depending on the body's vulnerable characteristics. Geographic incompatibility, partner unsuitability and unhealthy habits, such as drugs and alcohol, are also effecting factors.

Edwards states that she does not know all of the implications of her work nor does she understand the complexity of the techniques involved. 'I'm not a medical practitioner, a physicist, a musician or an engineer. What I do is backwards science. Normally you construct a theory and attempt to prove its merit. In my case, I have an auditory and vocal talent that seems to affect people psychologically and physiologically. My work is an attempt to create an avenue for others to duplicate, by mechanical means, what I first began to do vocally.' (Quoted from publicity literature.)

A. A. Tomatis

A similar discovery in this area has been arrived at via a very different route by the French electronics engineer A. A. Tomatis who developed an 'audiometer' through which he established that there seemed to exist a phenomenon of listening 'assimilation' which conditioned vocal or musical expression. That, for example, great singers like Caruso and Gigli had an amazing vocal range because their 'hearing' was of the highest quality.

These discoveries of Tomatis and Edwards have led to therapies which work on the individual to bring 'lost' resonance, the Music of the Spheres, back to resound through the individual human being as it once did at the very beginning of Earth evolution before the Fall.

New anthroposophical work is being done in an exciting venture called Tonalis, which has started a three-year course at Emerson College, Forest Row, Sussex. Tonalis aims to remind people of the deeper powers in music: '...what we are reminded of is not something from our personal past at all, but something from our Platonic childhood—the awareness of the world of archetypal forms and images, the *mundus imaginalis*.

Brown's Gas

Yull Brown, an Australian citizen, was born in Bulgaria on the stroke of midnight on Easter Eve. Brown, who is featured in a series of articles by Christopher Bird, has discovered how water, 'cracked back into its two fundamental components, can be returned once again to a gaseous state', and its 'constituent gases', hydrogen and oxygen, ignited and burned safely without risk of explosion—a result widely if not almost universally held to be impossible. (All quotes in this section are from *The American Raum & Zeit*, Vol. 3, Nos 2, 3 and 6, 1992.)

Properly mixed in stoichiometric proportion, the gases were non-explosive and therefore as safe as any conventional fuel in current use. The word stoichiometric is almost impossible to find in ordinary dictionaries, but it concerns the proportions of the component atoms, molecules and ions of chemical substances. Brown's gas, as it is now familiarly called, is stable because the ratio between the hydrogen and oxygen is very nearly the same, 2:1, as in the fluid that is chemically represented as H_2O, from which it is derived.

None among the many novel uses for Brown's discoveries is more remarkable than the one which can harness the 'free' power of atmospheric pressure. This, in turn, is directly related to the *implosive* nature of Brown's gas. 'In a length of pipe 18.6 inches long filled with gas, and sealed and sparked as described, the imploded gas would leave behind only enough water to fill a tenth of an inch in the pipe the remaining volume of which, taking up 18.59 inches of its length, would be filled with a vacuum...' With the instant creation of a high vacuum, as so easily effected by simply igniting Brown's gas, the door is opened to 'triggering atmospheric pressure as a source of energy'.

The spin-offs from this are mind-boggling. One is a flame that alters its temperature depending upon the material with which it comes into contact. 'The most unusual property of this flame is that it is not formed as a set of explosions, as are ordinary flames, but as a set of implosions. Consequently, all classical theory about combustion products, highest temperature regions, and other specifics are up for revision.' If the description of the sun given in Blattman's book, quoted on page 122 of this book, is accurate, then one could perhaps theorize that the flame generated by Brown's gas may be close in nature to the flame on the surface of the sun.

It is interesting to read the comments of two Japanese scientists—one a professor of physics, the other a professor of chemistry—enthusiastically writing to Brown from the International Christian University, Mitaka, Tokyo: 'We suspect,' they wrote to him in 1986,' that you may have found some way to keep the originally formed hydrogen atoms and the oxygen atoms at their atomic state (H and O) so that the energy loss in the molecular formation (H_2 and O_2) could be avoided and, at the same time, you have solved the problem of storing a large amount of highly explosive gas in a molecular form. Are we right?'

In this present Earth evolution, at the 'atomic state', before the atoms have combined to form the molecules of gases, the life ether predominates which is why the Tree of Life energy rushes in to the tube when the two gases hydrogen and oxygen are separated. This is also why the flame they produce when ignited has properties so different from the usual Tree of Knowledge form of energy.

BioCeramica

Nearly three thousand years ago Japanese villagers used to keep drinking water in vases made from a very special clay. No one knew why, but the water in these vases stayed fresh much longer than water kept in vases made of ordinary clay. Some time in the late twentieth century a Japanese natural science specialist, looking for some way to use his wealth and expertise for the benefit of the whole of humanity, discovered segments of this seemingly miraculous ceramic in the Japanese Natural History Museum. The ceramic was known to Japanese archaeologists as *Jyomon-Doki*, and Mr Mori decided to see if he could reproduce this ceramic. The ceramic is made from a clay that is found on the Japanese mainland, and it took him 20 years to perfect the firing process. He gave the end result a simple but elegant name—BioCeramica.

The ministry of agriculture and fisheries in Japan carried out intensive experiments which showed that fields of rice irrigated with BioCeramica will grow stronger plants that are also more resistant to disease and damage. It was also shown that fish that are bred and reared in water treated with BioCeramica grow larger and are exceptionally healthy. Elsewhere it was discovered that when introduced into cooking oils BioCeramica causes the cooking oil to remain fresher longer, and to be cooked more thoroughly.

One of the most exciting discoveries occurred when BioCeramica was introduced into a public swimming bath in Japan. Observers noticed that strange vortices were appearing in the water. Films were made and studied revealing what has been called 'the embryo of water'. The vortices of 'empty space' appeared to be the process of 'matter in creation' made visible—the activity of the etheric as 'negative existence' working creatively into the manifest world.

Experimentation and research have shown that the effects of BioCeramica are not related to atomic radiation and are impossible to evaluate within the context of materialist science. The ceramic is a powerful, qualitative tool that has nothing but positive effects. The creators of this ceramic, in searching for an explanation as to how their product works, have recently looked to etheric science as the one place where an understanding of the ceramic can be attained.

Individuals such as Mr Mori can be seen as modern day Grail Knights, using their expertise and resources to begin the healing of the earth.

Appendix II

Reich, Orgone and the Etheric

The details that follow were originally intended to be part of Chapter 2 of this book. But the exact relationship between Reich's Orgone energy and the ethers remains controversial. The researches of Wilhelm Reich were carried out independently from that of Steiner and Wachsmuth. However, that there is a deep connection between their respective findings is confirmed by a passage from the biography of Reich, *The Man who Dreamed of Tomorrow* by W. Edward Mann and Edward Hoffman:

> Although Reich apparently had no knowledge of Steiner, his latter-day excursions into religion and science suggest that he was moving inexorably towards a similar philosophical standpoint...It may be that the Orgone corresponds to one of [the] four 'etheric' forces, although at this stage of our understanding it is difficult to say precisely which one. However, Trevor James Constable, a prominent student of Reich and a leading practitioner of Reichian cloud busting, feels that the Orgone is equivalent to the chemical ether. On the other hand, there also seem to be suggestions that Orgone is akin to the life etheric forces [the life ether] since this force comes from the sun, as Reich once posited Orgone does, and is responsible for the rhythms of day and night and of the seasons, variations that Reich also ascribed to the Orgone energy envelope (the atmospheric Orgone ring surrounding the planet).

Perhaps the Orgone is best seen as the working in tandem of *both* the Tree of Life energies. New discoveries in this area must wait for a future publication.

Appendix III

Iscador from Mistletoe: Rudolf Steiner's Treatment for Cancer

Iscador is a preparation derived from mistletoe specifically for the treatment of cancer. It was developed by anthroposophical medical practitioners following the indications of Rudolf Steiner. We mentioned in Chapter 2 that the ethers are destructive forces when working on their own. Into the ethers must be mixed a formative force coming from the stars and planets. Steiner has indicated that mistletoe resists the action of the ethers when they work in an uncontrolled and proliferative manner—much like the Sorcerer's Apprentice working without the authority of his master. Anthroposophical medical research has demonstrated that mistletoe repulses the 'terrestrial forces' (i.e., the forces of the Fall), and thus behaves in a manner which is the opposite of that of a tumour which *opens* itself to them.

The following speculations of our own build upon these insights. We have pointed out that mistletoe has often been found growing in places where powerful—fallen and pure—etheric energies predominate. Rudolf Steiner has described how mistletoe is a unique and ancient plant which is still at the stage of Ancient Moon evolution. In *Occult Science* he describes how during a certain stage of Ancient Moon evolution there was an 'animal-plant kingdom'. Below this was another composite 'plant-mineral' kingdom. We know from our study of the Fall, which happened during our present Earth evolution, that the human and animal astral bodies were invaded by luciferic beings. We also know that the plant kingdom was exempt from this attack.

The astral principle was bestowed on humanity during Ancient Moon evolution and was at that time also in a still 'pure' condition. Humanity at the stage of Ancient Moon was at the stage of 'animal man'. One therefore wonders if the special quality of mistletoe may not be due to the possibility that in passing over from Ancient Moon to the present Earth evolution it has brought with it a 'plantlike' astrality, so that in present Earth evolution we have a plant that in some way retains the innocent astrality of that earlier time. The 'astrality' of the mistletoe may still be permeated with all of the cosmic attributes that would have pertained to the human and animal astral body during present Earth evolution *if the Fall had not happened.* Is this why Steiner has indicated that mistletoe is a plant which has healing properties for the combating of Cancer?

Cancer is an illness caused when the life ether works too strongly in the cells without sufficient formative, cosmic forces. The particular activity of the life ether causes the 'coming into being of matter' which, without the qualifying influence of the formative forces, results in proliferation of unqualified growth where the 'form' principle has been thwarted.

As we have already seen, the formative forces come down to us from the spiritual regions of the planets and zodiacal stars. Mistletoe has a special relationship with the planets Mercury, Venus and the moon. The influence of these on mistletoe was consistently studied for several decades. However, the influence of Uranus has proven to be even more marked and consistent in capillary dynamic images produced from mistletoe extracts. Uranus is the planet of the future and of radical change. It is considered the planet of our time. Baron von Tubeuf wrote a monograph that gave mistletoe its place in modern botany, and almost at the same time Rudolf Steiner began to make mistletoe part of a renewed medical discipline designed to meet the needs of the present age.

Uranus lies outside the boundary circumscribed by Saturn which is the remnant of Ancient Saturn evolution, that period when the laws of matter were first laid down. In combating cancer we are beginning to reverse these laws in a first attempt to take the whole of evolution, dating back to Ancient Saturn, towards regaining the original blueprint for creation.

In short, mistletoe heals the breach between the etheric and astral which had been brought about through the impact of the Fall. Iscador can now, in certain cases, be obtained on the (British) National Health Service.

Notes

1. Taking up the Challenge

1. All the books mentioned in this chapter are fully referenced in the Bibliography.

2. Investigations into a New Science of Life

2. Steiner, R., *The Temple Legend*, p. 167.
3. Ibid.
4. *Weekend Telegraph*, August 1990.
5. The case of Wilhelm Reich is one example of this, though there are many more. Reich believed himself to have discovered a primal life force that he called 'Orgone'. He evolved techniques to work with this energy and had considerable, and well-documented success treating illnesses and revitalizing arid desert areas around Oregon in Maine, USA. See Appendix II. Reich was a forceful and bold thinker who has been criticized for his cross-disciplinary approach.

   Reich's work was suppressed and his research papers, books and notes thrown into into an incinerator by court injunction. In their book *The Man Who Dreamed of Tomorrow* (J.P. Tarcher, 1980), Edward Mann and Edward Hoffman give a balanced account of Reich's battles with the Food-and-Drug Administration in America. According to them: 'The FDA spent years gathering evidence against Reich. In 1954 an FDA-initiated federal court injunction ordered his hardcover books banned from circulation and his softcover books, including all his English language scientific periodicals, burned.'

   After a protracted legal battle Reich was sent to jail. Hoffman and Mann continue: 'In what is clearly one of the most ignoble acts in the history of American civil liberties, all of Reich's softcover books that even mentioned the Orgone theory were burned on order of the United States Government. Appeals by the American Civil Liberties Union proved fruitless.'
6. For an excellent account of the forbidden 'vitalist' tradition

see *The Magical Staff—The Vitalist Tradition in Western Medicine* by Matthew Wood, North Atlantic Books, 1992.

7. See Steiner, R., *Goethean Science.*
8. Goethe, *The Metamorphosis of Plants.*
9. Adams, G., and Whicher, O., *The Plant Between Sun and Earth*, p. 35.
10. Ibid.
11. Schwenk, T., *The Basis for Potentization Research*, p. 6.
12. Ibid, p.6.
13. Ibid, p.7.
14. These phenomena are now lost for ever due to the spread of industrial cities and the wholesale destruction of the natural landscape. One of the reasons for the success of materialistic theory has been the eradication of those areas in which the etheric forces worked with the greatest vitality.
15. For more on Schauberger see Alexandersson, O., *Living Water—Viktor Schauberger and the Secrets of Natural Energy.*
16. This research is elaborated upon in Lawrence Edward's *The Vortex of Life.*
17. Steiner, R., and Wegman, I., *Fundamentals of Therapy—An Extension of the Art of Healing through Spiritual Knowledge*, p. 17.

3. Rudolf Steiner and the Foundation of a New Etheric Science

18. Largely dictated by Steiner from his deathbed, this book together with the two listed in Note 19 are excellent introductions to Steiner's inner spiritual development.
19. See Shepherd, A. P., *Rudolf Steiner—Scientist of the Invisible* and Easton, S., *Rudolf Steiner—Herald of a New Epoch* for excellent introductions to Steiner's life and work.
20. Steiner, R., *The Philosophy of Freedom*, p. 32.
21. Ibid, p. 32.
22. Ben-Aharon, J., *The New Experience of the Supersensible.*

4. The Four Ethers

23. Rudolf Steiner often refers to the etheric body as a 'time organism'. It also has to do with the preservation of memory. In reports of near-death experiences a common content is the

experience of the individual's life laid out before them in the form of a tableau, embracing past, present and future. This is an experience that takes place within the etheric realm, into which we pass immediately after death. See Ritchie, G., *Return from Tomorrow* for a classic example of this.

24. Steiner, R., *Occult Science—An Outline*, p. 121.
25. Steiner, R., *Man as a Symphony of the Cosmic Word*, p. 59.
26. Steiner, R., *Occult Signs and Symbols*, p. 28.
27. Steiner, R., *Genesis*, p. 65.
28. Lehrs, E., *Man or Matter*, p. 323.
29. Steiner, R., *The Gospel of John in Relation to the Other Gospels*, p. 38.
30. Steiner, R., *The Temple Legend*, p. 299.

5. The Fall

31. Lehrs, E., *Man or Matter*, p. 472.
32. Steiner, R., *The Spiritual Beings in the Heavenly Bodies and in the Kingdoms of Nature*, p. 92.
33. Wachsmuth, G., *The Etheric World in Science, Art and Religion*, Chapter 12.
34. Steiner, R., *Genesis*, p. 111.
35. Steiner, R., *Occult Science*, p. 166.
36. Steiner, R., *The Gospel of St John*, p. 52.

6. The Significance of the Incarnation

37. Acts, 2: 1–4.
38. Gospel of St John, Kalmia Bittleston translation, Floris books.
39. Wachsmuth, G., *The Etheric World in Science, Art and Religion*.
40. Steiner, R., *From Jesus to Christ*, p. 57.
41. Gospel of St Luke, 1: 78–79.
42. Gospel of St Luke, 2: 46–47.
43. This is from an unpublished translation in typescript at the Library, Rudolf Steiner House, London.

7. Resurrection and Transubstantiation

44. The Jews followed a lunar calendar, and were bound by the

principle of blood ties.

45. 'And I saw a new heaven and a new earth...And I, John, saw the Holy City, New Jerusalem, coming down from God out of heaven, prepared as a bride adorned for her husband.' (Revelation 21: 1–2.)
46. A more detailed account of the Temptation is given in Steiner, R., *The Fifth Gospel.*
47. Sergei O. Prokofieff, *The Cycle of the Year as a Path of Initiation Leading to an Experience of the Christ Being—An Esoteric Study of the Festivals*, p. 96.
48. Salt is connected with the life ether, therefore 'the salt-processes' would describe the dismantling of matter of Christ's physical body through the activity of the life ether.
49. Heidenreich, A., *The Etheric Christ and the Risen Christ,* p. 21.
50. Steiner, R., *The Temple Legend*, p. 26.
51. Steiner, R., *The Fifth Gospel*, p. 33.
52. Lecture given by Rudolf Steiner at Munich, October 1911.
53. Steiner, R., T*he Gospel of St John in its Relation to the Other Gospels*, p. 149.
54. 1 Corinthians 13: 4–12. Many of Paul's texts seem to have suffered from additions made by a later editor. Also, as Emil Bock demonstrates in his book *Saint Paul*, Luther's translation of Paul's writings often *reverses* the meaning of the original text. The view of Paul as a sort of paranoid schizophrenic with manic depressive tendencies hardly fits with the emphasis in Paul's writings on love as the authentic dimension of inner moral freedom.

8. The Western Mystery Stream

55. Seddon, R., *The Mystery of Arthur at Tintagel*, p. 175.
56. Ibid, p. 176.
57. Published in *The Death of Merlin*, p. 114.
58. Ibid, p.115.
59. Seddon, R., *The Mystery of Arthur at Tintagel*, p. 170.
60. Steiner, R., C*osmic Christianity*, Lecture 6.
61. Ibid, p. 38.
62. Quoted in Tautz, J., *W. J. Stein—A Biography.*
63. Quoted in Stein, W. J., *The Ninth Century*, p. 91.
64. Ibid, p. 91.
65. Ibid, p. 6.

66. The Spear symbolizes the power of Saturn, the slow-moving planet that governs inflexible fate and bestows the power of steadfastness.
67. The union of the two streams marked the eclipse of the Arthurian stream. This is one of the esoteric backgrounds to the legend that Arthur sleeps, waiting for the time when he will be awakened.
68. From an article by 'E' in the December 1904 issue of *Theosophical Review*. Quoted from Steiner, R., *The Temple Legend*, Note 15 to Lecture 9.
69. Wood, D., *Genisis*, p. 198.
70. Jonas, M., unpublished essay.
71. See Lincoln, H., *The Messianic Legacy*.
72. Jeans, J., *The Music of the Spheres*, p. 64.
73. Steiner, R., 'The Tree of Knowledge and the Tree of Life', lecture given at Dornach, 24 July 1915, in *The Golden Blade*, 1965.
74. Baigent, M., Leigh, R., and Lincoln, H., *The Holy Blood and the Holy Grail*, p. 203.
75. Morizot, P., *The School at Chartres*, pp. 5–6.
76. Pfeiffer, E., *The Heart Lectures*, p. 14.
77. Morizot, P., *The Templars*, p. 10.

9. The Eastern Mystery Stream

78. Stein, W. J., *The Ninth Century*, p. 80.
79. Ibid, p. 88.
80. Steiner, R., *The Temple Legend*, Lecture 6.
81. Quoted in Stein, W. J., *The Ninth Century*, pp. 81–83.
82. Steiner, R., *The Mission of the Archangel Michael.*
83. Stein, W. J., *The Ninth Century*, p. 84.
84. Ibid, p. 85.
85. Steiner, R., *The Mission of the Archangel Michael.*
86. Stein, W. J., *The Ninth Century*, p. 68.
87. Published in Stein, W. J., *The Death of Merlin*, p. 138.
88. Ibid, p. 140.
89. Stein, W. J., *The Ninth Century.*
90. Ibid, pp. 86–87.
91. Rudolf Steiner indicated on many occasions that the majority of those individuals who laid the foundations for materialistic science had previously been incarnated in the Arab world.

See Steiner's *Karmic Relationships*, published by Rudolf Steiner Press, for more details.

92. Steiner, R., *Cosmic Christianity*, Lecture 2.
93. Stein, W. J., *The Ninth Century*, p. 277.
94. Ibid, p. 89.
95. Ibid, p. 78.
96. Ibid, p. 79.
97. Gospel of St Luke, 23: 39–42 (New International Version).
98. Eschenbach, W., *Parzival*, quoted in *The Ninth Century*, p. 166.
99. Ibid, p. 182.
100. Ibid, p. 194.
101. Ibid, p. 194.
102. Ibid, p. 95.
103. Eschenbach, W., *Parzival*, quoted in *The Ninth Century*, p. 204.

10. The Southern Mystery Stream

104. Lievegoed, B., *Mystery Streams in Europe and the New Mysteries*, p. 49.
105. Welburn, A., *The Beginnings of Christianity*, p. 19.
106. Lievegoed, B., *The Battle for the Soul.*
107. Steiner, R., *The Temple Legend*, p. 150.
108. Gospel of St John.
109. See Steiner, R., *The Temple Legend.*
110. Wachsmuth, G., *The Etheric World in Science, Art and Religion*—quoting from Chapter 4 of an early edition of *Occult Science.*
111. Ibid, Chapter 7.
112. Ibid, Chapter 7.
113. Lievegoed, B., *Mystery Streams in Europe and the New Mysteries*, p. 49.
114. Lievegoed, B., *Battle for the Soul.*
115. Steiner, R., 'Christmas as a Time of Grievous Destiny', lecture given at Basel on 21 December 1916.
116. Steiner, R., *The Temple Legend*, p. 143.
117. Oakley, I. C., *Masonry and Medieval Mysticism*, p. 37.
118. Charpentier, L., *The Mysteries of Chartres Cathedral*, p. 57.
119. Ibid, p. 57–59.
120. Oakley, I. C., *Masonry and Medieval Mysticism.*

11. The Northern Mystery Stream

121. Ravenscroft, T., *The Spear of Destiny*, p. 287.
122. Lievegoed, B., *Mystery Streams in Europe and the New Mysteries*, p. 28.
123. See Heyer, K., *The Middle Ages.*
124. Steiner, R., *The Riddle of Man.*
125. Ibid, p. 24.
126. Quoted in ibid.
127. Eschenbach, W., *Parzival*, quoted in *The Ninth Century*, p. 257.
128. Ibid, p. 257.
129. The 'clouds of heaven' is a reference to the etheric realm.
130. See Prokofieff, S., *The Cycle of the Year.*
131. Steiner, R., 'The Whitsun Mystery and its Connection with the Ascension', lecture given at Dornach on 7 May 1923, in *The Festivals and their Meaning.*
132. Heidenreich, A., *The Risen Christ and the Etheric World*, lecture given at New York on 22 April.
133. Ibid.
134. Steiner to Countess Keyserlingk, Skene, 'Twelve Days with Rudolf Steiner', typescript, Rudolf Steiner House Library, London.
135. Personal correspondence from Jehanne Mehta.
136. Zeylmans van Emmichoven, F. W., *The Foundation Stone*, p. 36.

12. The Grail Chalice

137. Falk-Yitter, H., *Aurora*, p. 82.
138. Ibid, p. 99.
139. Wachsmuth, G., *The Formative Forces in Earth, Man and Cosmos*, Chapter 4.
140. Falk-Yitter, H., *Aurora*, p. 99.
141. Wachsmuth, G., *The Formative Forces in Earth, Man and Cosmos*, p. 81.
142. Falk-Yitter, H., *Aurora*, p. 79.
143. Ibid, p. 112.
144. Blattmann, G., *The Sun*, p. 216.
145. Ibid, p. 71.
146. Falk-Yitter, H., *Aurora*, p. 36.

147. Wachsmuth, G., *The Formative Forces in Earth, Man and Cosmos*, Chapter 3.
148. Steiner, R., *The Temple Legend*, p. 301.
149. Steiner, R., 'Parzival', lecture given at London on 29 July 1906.
150. Steiner, R., *Christ and the Spiritual World and The Search for the Holy Grail*, p. 114.
151. Ibid, p. 118.
152. Steiner, R., *The Spiritual Individualities of the Planets.*
153. Steiner, R., *Christ and the Spiritual World and The Search for the Holy Grail*, pp. 99–100.

13. Changing Face of the Goddess

154. Peri Aston. The original idea for this chapter came from Peri's Triple Image which depicts the triple Goddess in mime and story-telling.
155. Cotterel, M., 'The Undiscovered Third Force', *Anthroposophical Quarterly*, Autumn 1961.
156. Ibid.
157. Steiner, R., *Faust and the Mothers.*
158. Hutton, R., *The Pagan Religions of the Ancient British Isles*, p. 153.
159. McCulloch, J. A., *The Religion of the Ancient Celts*, p. 67.
160. Wyatt, I., 'Black Virgin of Chartres', *Anthroposophical Quarterly*, Vol. 17, No. 4, Winter 1972.
161. Baring, A., and Cashford, C., *The Myth of the Goddess*, p. 587.
162. Anderson, W., and Hicks, C., *The Green Man*, p. 68.
163. Graves, R., *The White Goddess*, p. 371.
164. See Nichols, R., *The Book of Druidry.*
165. Graves, R., *The White Goddess*, p. 179.
166. Godwin, J., *Arktos*, p. 146.
167. Kirby, W. F., *Kalevala.*
168. Wachsmuth, G., *The Formative Forces in Earth, Man and Cosmos*, p. 80.
169. Wachsmuth quoted in Falk-Yitter, H., p. 107.
170. Baring, A., and Cashford, J., *The Myth of the Goddess*, p. 591.
171. Ibid, p. 522.
172. Schindler, M., *Europe—A Cosmic Picture*, p. 39.
173. Mann, E., *Sacred Architecture*, p. 22.
174. Schindler, M., *Europe—A Cosmic Picture*, p. 33.

175. Emmichoven, Zeylmans van, *The Foundation Stone*, p. 61.
176. Ibid, p. 56.
177. Foxcroft, E., *The Chymical Wedding*, Minerva Books edition, p. 54—explained in notes on p. 84.
178. Ibid.
179. Wachsmuth, G., *Formative Forces in Earth, Man and Cosmos*, footnote on p. 144.

14. Knights Templar—Guardians of the Grail

180. Quoted in Stein, W. J., *The Ninth Century*, p. 75 (our italics).
181. Steiner, R., 'The Templars', lecture given at Dornach, 2 October 1916, unpublished.
182. Steiner, R., *Manifestations of Karma*, Lecture 10.
183. Wachsmuth, G., 'The Face of the Earth and the Destiny of Mankind', lecture given at Dornach on 27 December 1923. This was later published in *Gaia-Sophia*, the first yearbook issued by the Section for Natural Science at the Goetheanum.
184. Morizot, P., *The Templars*, pp. 22–23.
185. Pietzner, C., 'The Templar Impulse in our Time', lecture given in Copake, New York, on 31 December 1966, typescript.
186. Lecture given by Rudolf Steiner at Dornach on 27 March 1921.
187. See Steiner, R., *The Fall of the Spirits of Darkness*, Lecture 12.
188. Foxcroft, E., *The Chymical Wedding*.
189. Ibid, Day Four, p. 43.

15. Alchemy—Part One

190. Waite, A. E., *The Real History of the Rosicrucians*, p. 9.
191. Ibid.
192. Sinclair, A., *The Sword and the Stone*, p. 2.
193. See Chapter 6.
194. Steiner, R., 'Parzival', lecture given at London, on 29 July 1906, typescript.
195. Quoted from Welburn, A., *Gnosis*.
196. Ibid.
197. Ibid.
198. Ibid.
199. Ibid.
200. Hall, M., *Codex Rosae Crucis*, Plate 27.

201. Wachsmuth, G., *The Formative Forces in Cosmos, Earth and Man*, Chapter 8.

16. Alchemy—Part Two

202. Morgan, M. O., *The Mabin of the Mabinogian*, p. 8.
203. Ibid, p. 9.
204. Ibid, p. 9.
205. Wachsmuth, G., *The Formative Forces in Cosmos, Earth and Man*, Chapter 3, p. 63.
206. Morgan, M. O., *The Mabin of the Mabinogian*, p. 7.
207. Shakespeare, W., *The Merchant of Venice*, Act V, Scene 1.
208. Kirby, W. F., *Kalavala*, Rumo XV: p. 161, lines 473–82; 493–542.
209. Morgan, M. O., *The Mabin of the Mabinogian.*
210. Felsenreich, M., information from the Forschungsstelle für Bienergie.
211. Ibid.
212. Steiner, R., *Egyptian Myths and Mysteries*, p. 55.
213. Jeans, J., *Music of the Spheres*, p. 40.
214. Quoted in ibid, p. 52.
215. Schwenk, T., *Sensitive Chaos.*

17. Opposition to the Grail

216. Ravenscroft, T., *The Cup of Destiny*, p. 120.
217. Ibid, p. 120.
218. Ibid, p. 132.
219. Baigent, H., Richard, L., and Lincoln, H., *The Holy Blood and the Holy Grail.*
220. Personal correspondence from James France.
221. Ibid.
222. Stein, W. J., *The Ninth Century*, p. 277.
223. Ibid, p. 277.
224. Ibid, p. 282.
225. Ibid, p. 290.
226. Ibid, p. 291.
227. Quoted in Stein, W. J., *The Death of Merlin.*
228. Baigent, M., Leigh, R., and Henry, L., *The Messianic Legacy*, p. 322.

229. Baigent, M., Leigh, R., and Lincoln, H., *The Holy Blood and the Holy Grail*, p. 208.

18. The Double

230. Quoted in Simonze, C., *The Doppelgänger in Man.*
231. Ibid.
232. Hauschka, R., *Nutrition.*
233. Ibid.
234. Ibid.
235. Simonze, C., *The Doppelgänger in Man.*
236. Ibid.
237. Wachsmuth, G., *The Etheric World in Science, Art and Religion*, Chapter 5.
238. Ibid.
239. Steiner, R., *An Esoteric Cosmology.*
240. Ibid.
241. Steiner, R., *Mysteries of the East and of Christianity*, p. 65.
242. Stein, W. J., *The Ninth Century*, p. 278.
243. Trevor, M., *Newman—The Pillar of the Cloud*, p. 120.
244. Quoted in ibid, p. 121.
245. Ibid, p. 123.
246. Ibid, p. 139.
247. Quoted from Welburn, A., *Gnosis.*
248. Article in the 1994 Weleda Calendar by Harmutt Ramm.
249. Dudley, C., *The Sacred Geometry of Canterbury Cathedral*, RILKO lecture.
250. Steiner, R., 'The Birth of the Sun as the Spirit of the Earth, The Thirteen Holy Nights', lecture given at Hanover on 26 December 1911 in *The Festivals and their Meaning.*

19. Saunière's Secret

251. Baigent, M., Leigh, R., and Lincoln, H., *The Holy Blood and the Holy Grail*, pp. 35–36.
252. Ibid, p. 38, Abbé Louis Fouquet to his brother Nicholas describing a meeting with the painter Poussin in 1656.
253. Ibid, p. 204.
254. Lincoln, H., *The Holy Place*, p. 79.
255. Ibid, Chapter 9.

256. See Foster, R., *Patterns of Thought*, p. 1.
257. Ibid, p. 86.
258. Ibid, Chapter 5, p. 96.
259. Ibid, p. 104.
260. Ibid, p. 154.
261. Ibid, p. 101.
262. Collins, A., T*he Seventh Sword*, p. 292.
263. Sinclair, A., *The Sword and the Grail*, p. 83.
264. Ibid, p. 5.
265. Ibid, p. 83.
266. Ibid, p. 209 (Notes).
267. Baigent, M., Leigh, R., and Lincoln, H., *The Holy Blood and the Holy Grail*, p. 30.
268. Ibid, Chapter 9.
269. Ibid, p. 101.
270. Sucher, W., 'The Return of King Arthur'—notes from an unpublished lecture.
271. Baigent, M., Leigh, R., and Lincoln, H., *The Holy Blood and the Holy Grail*, p. 204.
272. Eisenman, R., and Wise, M., *The Dead Sea Scrolls Uncovered*, p. 78.
273. Robinson, J., *Born in Blood*, p. 133.
274. Jonas, M., unpublished essay.
275. Baigent, M., Leigh, R., and Lincoln, H., *The Holy Blood and the Holy Grail*, p. 482.
276. Ibid, p. 105.
277. Ibid, p. 121.
278. Lincoln, H., *The Holy Place*, Chapter 3.
279. Steiner, R., *The Karma of Untruthfulness*, Vol. 2, p. 148.
280. Meyer, T., *The Bodhisattva Question*, p. 47.

20. Healing the Grail King

281. It should be noted here that the etheric is *suctional*, this being an aspect of its nature as negative-space.
282. Pfeiffer, E., *The Heart Lectures*, Lecture 1.
283. Quoted in Tautz, J., *W. J. Stein—A Biography*.
284. Schindler, M., *Europe—A Cosmic Picture*, p. 220.
285. Weinberg, S., *Dreams of a Final Theory*, p. 37.

Bibliography

Abbreviations:

RSP = Rudolf Steiner Press (London)
AP = Anthroposophic Press (New York)
MER = Mercury Press (Spring Valley, New York)
SGP = St George Publications (Spring Valley, New York)
SBC = Steiner Book Centre (Canada)

Rudolf Steiner

Christ and the Spiritual World and the Search for the Holy Grail, RSP, 1963.
Cosmic Christianity and the Impulse of Michael, RSP, 1953.
Esoteric Christianity and the Mission of Christian Rosenkreutz, RSP, 1984.
An Esoteric Cosmology, SGP, 1978.
Esoteric Development, AP, 1982.
The Fall of the Spirits of Darkness, RSP, 1993.
The Festivals and their Meaning, RSP, 1955.
The Fifth Gospel, RSP, 1968.
From Jesus to Christ, RSP, 1973.
Fundamentals of Therapy [with Ita Wegman], RSP, 1983.
Genesis—Secrets of the Bible Story of Creation, RSP, 1982.
Goethean Science, MER, 1988.
Gospel of St John, AP, 1948.
Gospel of St Luke, RSP, 1988.
Inner Impulses of Evolution—The Mexican Mysteries: The Knights Templar, AP, 1984.
The Karma of Untruthfulness, Vol. 2, RSP, 1992.
Knowledge of the Higher Worlds, RSP, 1969.
Manifestations of Karma, RSP, 1969.
The Mission of the Archangel Michael, AP, 1961.
The Mission of the Trinity and the Mission of the Spirit, AP, 1991.
The Mysteries of the East and of Christianity, RSP, 1989.
Occult Science—An Outline, RSP, 1972.
The Philosophy of Freedom, RSP, 1979.
The Riddle of Man, MER, 1990.
Rosicrucianism and Modern Initiation, RSP, 1982.

Rosicrucian Esotericism, AP, 1978.
The Search for the New Isis, the Divine Sophia, MER, 1983.
The Spiritual Beings in the Heavenly Bodies and in the Kingdoms of Nature, SBC, 1981.
The Story of My Life, AP, 1928.
The Temple Legend—Freemasonry and Related Occult Movements, RSP, 1985.
Three Streams in Evolution, RSP, 1985.
World Ether—Elemental Beings—Kingdoms of Nature (texts from Rudolf Steiner compiled and with commentary by Ernst Hagemann), MER, 1993.

General Bibliography

Adams, George, *Physical and Ethereal Spaces*, London, Rudolf Steiner Press, 1978.
Adams, George, and Whicher, Olive, *The Plant Between Sun and Earth*, London, Rudolf Steiner Press, 1980.
Alder, *The Battle of the Trees—The Final Conclusion to the Holy Grail*, Greece, Freedom House, 1995.
Alexandersson, O., *Living Water—Viktor Schauberger and the Secrets of Natural Energy*, 1995.
Anderson, William, *Green Man—The Archetype of Our Oneness with the Earth*, London, Harper Collins, 1990.
Ashe, Geoffrey, *Mythology of the British Isles*, London, Guild Publishing, 1990.
Baigent, Michael, and Leigh, Richard, *The Temple and the Lodge*, London, Jonathan Cape, 1989.
Baigent, Michael, and Leigh, Richard, *The Dead Sea Scrolls Deception*, London, Jonathan Cape, 1991.
Baigent, Michael, Leigh, Richard, and Lincoln, Henry, *The Holy Blood and the Holy Grail*, London, Corgi, 1983.
Baigent, Michael, Leigh, Richard, and Lincoln, Henry, *The Messianic Legacy*, London, Jonathan Cape, 1986.
Baring, Anne, and Cashford, Jules, *The Myth of the Goddess*, London, BCA, 1991.
Begg, Ean, and Begg, Duke, *In Search of the Holy Grail and the Precious Blood*, London, Harper Collins, 1995.
Bittleston, Adam, *Our Spiritual Companions*, Edinburgh, Floris Books, 1980.

Blattmann, Georg, *The Sun—The Ancient Mysteries and a New Physics*, Edinburgh, Floris Books, 1985.
Bock, Emil, *The Childhood and Youth of Jesus*, unpublished typescript, Rudolf Steiner House Library, London.
Boehme, Jacob, *The Signature of All Things*, Cambridge, James Clarke, 1981.
Charpentier, Louis, *The Mysteries of Chartres Cathedral*, RILKO Publications.
Churton, Tobias, *The Gnostics*, London, Weidenfeld and Nicolson, 1987.
Collins, Andrew, *The Seventh Sword*, London, Century, 1991.
Corbu, Claire, and Captier, Antoine, *L'Heritage de l'Abbé Saunière*, Nice, Belisane, 1985.
Coveney, Peter, and Highfield, Roger, *The Arrow of Time*, London, W. H. Allen, 1991.
Eastern, Stewart, *Rudolf Steiner—Herald of a New Epoch*, New York, Anthroposophic Press, 1980..
Eisenman, R., and Wise, M., *The Dead Sea Scrolls Uncovered*, Dorset, Element, 1992.
Eschenbach, Wolfram von, *Parzival*, London, Penguin Books, 1980.
Emmichoven, F. W. Zeylmans van, *The Foundation Stone*, London, Rudolf Steiner Press, 1983.
Falck-Yitter, Harald, *Aurora—The Northern Lights in Mythology, History and Science*, Edinburgh, Floris Books, 1985.
Foster, Richard, *Patterns of Thought*, London, Jonathan Cape, 1991.
Foxcroft, Edward, *The Chymical Wedding*, London, Rudolf Steiner Press.
France, James, *The Cistercians in Scandinavia*, Michigan, Cistercian Publications.
Godwin, Joscelyn, *Arktos—The Polar Myth*, London, Thames and Hudson, 1993.
Godwin, Malcolm, *The Holy Grail—Its Origins, Secrets, and Meaning Revealed*, London, BCA, 1994.
Goethe, Wolfgang von, *The Metamorphosis of Plants*, Biodynamic Farmers and Gardeners Association, 1974.
Graves, Robert, *The White Goddess*, London, Faber & Faber, 1984.
Hall, Manly, *Codex Rosae Crucis*, The Philosophical Research Society, 1971.
Hauschka, Rudolf, *Nutrition*, London, Stuart & Watkins, 1967.

Heidenreich, *The Etheric Christ and the Risen Christ*, London, Rudolf Steiner Press, 1969.

Heyer, Karl, *The Middle Ages*, Steiner Schools Fellowship, 1994.

Hutton, Ronald, *The Pagan Religions of the Ancient British Isles*, London, Blackwell, 1991.

James, Jamie, *The Music of the Spheres*, London, Little Brown, 1994.

Kirby, W. F., *Kalevala*, London, Dent, 1970.

Lehrs, Ernst, *Man or Matter*, Faber & Faber, 1958.

Lincoln, Henry, *The Holy Place*, London, Jonathan Cape, 1991.

Lievegoed, Bernard, *The Battle for the Soul*, Stroud, Hawthorn Press, 1994.

Lievegoed, Bernard, *Mystery Streams in Europe and the New Mysteries*, New York, Anthroposophic Press, 1982.

Lievegoed, Bernard, *Man on the Threshold*, Stroud, Hawthorn Press, 1985.

Loomis, Roger Sherman, *The Grail—From Celtic Myth to Christian Symbol*, Suffolk, Constable and Constable, 1992.

MacCulloch, J. A., *The Religion of the Ancient Celts*, London, Constable and Constable, 1991.

Mann, A. T., *Sacred Architecture*, Dorset, Element Books, 1993.

Mann, W. Edward, and Hoffmann, Edward, *The Man who Dreamed of Tomorrow*, Los Angeles, J. P. Tarcher, 1980.

Matthews, Caitlin, *Sophia—Goddess of Wisdom*, London, Aquarian Press, Harper Collins, 1992.

Meyer, T. H., *The Bodhisattva Question*, London, Temple Lodge, 1993.

Morizot, P., *The School at Chartres*, New York, St George Publications, 1987.

Morizot, P., *The Templars*, New York, Anthroposophic Press, 1960.

Morgan, Morien O., *The Mabin of the Mabinogion*, London, RILKO Trust, 1984.

Nichols, Ross, *The Book of Druidry*, London, Aquarian Press, Harper Collins, 1990.

Oakley, I. C., *Masonry and Medieval Mysticism*, London, Theosophical Publishing House,1900.

Pfeiffer, Ehrenfried, *The Heart Lectures*, New York, Mercury Press, 1989.

Prokofieff, Sergei O., *The Cycle of the Year as a Path of Initiation*, London, Temple Lodge, 1991.

Prokofieff, Sergei O., *The Spiritual Origins of Eastern Europe and the Future Mysteries of the Holy Grail*, London, Temple Lodge, 1994.

Querido, René, *The Golden Age of Chartres*, Edinburgh, Floris Books, 1987.
Ravenscroft, Trevor, *The Cup of Destiny*, London, Rider and Co., 1981.
Ravenscroft, Trevor, *The Spear of Destiny*, London, Neville Spearman, 1972.
Robinson, John J., *Born in Blood—The Lost Secrets of Freemasonry*, London, Guild Publishing, 1989.
Schindler, Maria, *Europe—A Cosmic Picture*, Sussex, New Knowledge Books, 1975.
Schwenk, Theodor, *The Basis of Potentization Research*, New York, Mercury Press, 1988.
Seddon, Richard, *The Mystery of Arthur at Tintagel*, London, Rudolf Steiner Press, 1990.
Sède, Gérard de, *Rennes-le-Château, les Dossiers, les Impostures, les Phantasomes et les Hypothèses*, Editions Péladon Robert Laffont, Paris, 1988.
Shepherd, A. P., *Rudolf Steiner—Scientist of the Invisible*, Edinburgh, Floris Books, 1983.
Simonze, C., *The Doppelgänger in Man*, unpublished translation.
Sinclair, Andrew, *The Sword and the Grail*, London, Century, 1993.
Stein, Walter Johannes, *The Ninth Century*, London, Temple Lodge, 1991.
Stein, Walter Johannes, *The Death of Merlin*, Edinburgh, Floris Books, 1989.
Strachan, Gordon, *Christ and the Cosmos*, Scotland, Labarum Publications, 1985.
Tautz, J., *W. J. Stein—A Biography*, London, Temple Lodge, 1990.
Trevor, Meriol, Newman, *The Pillar and the Cloud*, London, Macmillan, 1962.
Wachsmuth, Guenther, *The Formative Forces in Earth, Man, and Cosmos*, unpublished translation.
Wachsmuth, Guenther, *The Formative Forces in Art, Science, and Religion*, New York, Anthroposophic Press, 1932.
Waite, Arthur Edward, *The Real History of the Rosicrucians*, London 1887. Republished 1960 by Health Research, Mokelumne Hill, California.
Weinberg, Steven, *Dreams of a Final Theory*, London, Random House, 1993
Welburn, Andrew, *The Beginnings of Christianity*, Edinburgh, Floris Books, 1991.

Welburn, Andrew, *Gnosis*, Edinburgh, Floris Books.
Wood, David, *Genisis—The First Book of Revelations*, Kent, The Baton Press, 1985.
Wood, David, and Campbell, Ian, *Geneset—Target Earth*, Middlesex, Bellevue Books, 1994.
Wyatt, Isabel, *From Round Table to Grail Castle*, Sussex, The Lanthorn Press, 1979.

Selective Index